Rambles *of a* Runaway *from* Southern Slavery

Carter G. Woodson Institute Series
Deborah E. McDowell, Editor

Rambles

of a

Runaway

from

Southern Slavery

Henry Goings

Edited by Calvin Schermerhorn,
Michael Plunkett, *and*
Edward Gaynor

University of Virginia Press   *Charlottesville and London*

University of Virginia Press
© 2012 by the Rector and Visitors of the University of Virginia
All rights reserved
Printed in the United States of America on acid-free paper

First published 2012

1 3 5 7 9 8 6 4 2

LIBRARY OF CONGRESS CATALOGING-IN-PUBLICATION DATA
Goings, Henry, b. ca. 1810.
Rambles of a runaway from southern slavery / Henry Goings ; edited by Calvin
Schermerhorn, Michael Plunkett, and Edward Gaynor.
p.   cm. — (Carter G. Woodson Institute series)
Includes bibliographical references and index.
ISBN 978-0-8139-3238-5 (cloth : alk. paper) — ISBN 978-0-8139-3240-8 (e-book)
1. Goings, Henry, b. ca. 1810. 2. Slaves—United States—Biography.
3. Freedmen—United States—Biography. 4. African Americans—Canada—
Biography. 5. Slave narratives—United States. 6. Slaves—United States—Social
conditions—19th century. 7. African Americans—Social conditions—
19th century. I. Schermerhorn, Calvin, 1975– II. Plunkett, Michael, 1942–
III. Gaynor, Edward, 1959– IV. Title.
E450.G65 2012
306.3′62092—dc23
[B]   2011036683

Contents

Preface   vii

Acknowledgments   xi

Introduction   xiii

Chronology   xxxv

Rambles of a Runaway
from Southern Slavery

CHAPTER 1   3

My birth and birth place in Virginia.—My name, Elijah Turner.
—Changes from one master to another,—In North Carolina,—Tennessee,
—Alabama,—Georgia,—Mississippi,—New Orleans,—Emigrating from
plantation to plantation,—My marriage,—Death of my last master

CHAPTER 2   38

My Change of Name and Escape from Slavery,—Through Tennessee,
—Kentucky,—Illinois,—Indiana,—Ohio to Michigan,—Employed at various places, and at Perryburg, (Ohio)

CHAPTER 3   48

Landed in Canada,—Nearly victimized into slavery again,—Returns after
his wife,—Trial at Perrysburg,—Escape to Canada,—Marriage of second
wife

CHAPTER 4   56

Observations on Slavery,—The present War,—The Church,—The Irish
Orator, Shiells

CHAPTER 5   67

Remarks on some of the Southern States, and Emigration to them

APPENDIX   79

EDITORS' APPENDICES

A. *Maps* 123

B. *Interviews with "Henry Gowens" and
"Mrs. Henry Gowens"* 127

C. *Letter to the Editor, by Henry Goins* 131

D. *"Farm for Sale" Notice Showing Henry Goings
as Sales Agent* 133

Bibliography 135

Index 151

Preface

EDWARD GAYNOR *and* MICHAEL PLUNKETT

In 1855 the Boston journalist Benjamin Drew traveled to Canada, where he interviewed dozens of fugitive slaves from the United States. Among the interviews he published the following year in *A North-Side View of Slavery* is one given by a Henry Gowens of Galt (now Cambridge), Ontario (see appendix B). In the interview, Gowens talked primarily about his life as a slave in Lauderdale County, Alabama, but then added, "I shall give the particulars more in detail when I publish the whole history of my life to the people of the United States and Canada."[1] One hundred and thirty years later, in 1985, C. Peter Ripley reprinted a "Circular by Henry Gouins, 22 December 1843" in volume 2 of *The Black Abolitionist Papers*, noting that Gouins had planned to publish a narrative of his life but the project apparently was never completed.[2]

The University of Virginia Library's Special Collections has long been committed to acquiring African American materials, and slave narratives are a particular area of interest. In August 2006, Tom Congalton, an antiquarian book dealer and the owner of Between the Covers Rare Books, offered for sale to us a published slave narrative entitled *Rambles of a Runaway from Southern Slavery*, authored by one Henry Goings. With some research, we located the Gowens interview in *A North-Side View of Slavery*. The close correspondence between details in Henry Gowens's interview with Drew and those in Henry Goings's book made us virtually certain that they were same the man. We realized we were in possession of the narrative promised by Gowens in 1855 and deemed uncompleted by C. Peter Ripley in 1985. After an exhaustive search through bibliographic databases, bibliographies, reference works, and library catalogs in both the United States and Canada, we were unable to locate any other copies of the published narrative, a finding that excited us more. Especially sig-

---

1. Drew, *A North-Side View of Slavery*.
2. Ripley, Herrle, and Cimbala, *The Black Abolitionist Papers*, vol. 2, *Canada, 1830–1865*.

nificant to our collecting priorities was the fact that Goings was a Virginian. According to his published narrative, Goings was the son of enslaved parents, Abraham and Catharine Turner, born in Virginia on the estate of James Walker, "within three miles of a place called Window Shades"—possibly Windsor Shades Plantation in New Kent County. His birth name was Elijah Turner. We eagerly agreed to purchase the book.

It has thus far proved impossible to establish a complete chain of provenance for the book before its entry into the antiquarian book trade a few years ago. Tom Congalton purchased the book from Jim Roberts, the owner of Books End in Syracuse, New York, who had acquired the narrative a few years earlier at a library book sale, most likely in Cazenovia, New York. The back flyleaf of the volume contains a penciled inscription by Nellie Mackyes of Onondaga, near Syracuse, whom we have identified as the daughter of Edwin L. Mackyes, a lifelong resident of Onondaga. As is well known, Syracuse was a major center of abolitionist activity, including support of antislavery societies in Canada.

The book's publisher is given as J. M. Robb. We located a census record for John Monteith Robb, which listed him as a publisher, age thirty-nine years, living in Stratford, Ontario, in 1871. The record states that Robb was a native of Ireland; his wife, Elizabeth (age twenty-six years) was a native of the United States; and that his three children, Elizabeth Sarah Robb, John Monteith Robb, and Samuel Robert Robb, were natives of Ontario. Ontario marriage records show that John and Elizabeth were married on May 2, 1860, in Perth County, Ontario, and that John's parents were Samuel and Margaret Robb, and Elizabeth's parents were Robert and Sarah Monteith. In William Johnston's *History of the County of Perth from 1825 to 1902* there is an entry about local newspapers. *The Perth County News* was first published in 1863 by Vivian and Maddocks, and was shortly afterwards, in June of that year, issued as the *Herald*. John M. Robb bought it out in 1867 and published it until 1872, after which it was published until 1874 by Alex. Williamson and H. T. Butler. The newspaper was then purchased by James Robb.[3] The same book lists an entry for a John M. Robb, who was an auditor for the town of Stratford in 1858.

We were not able to locate any evidence that the book was advertised in the *Herald*. As noted in Canadian book history, presses capable of large print runs were found throughout Canada, and since the printing of a

---

3. Johnston, *History of the County of Perth from 1825 to 1902*.

newspaper did not fill an entire workday, many shops also produced books and engaged in job printing.[4]

From the moment we decided to purchase Goings's narrative, we hoped to republish it. As we prepared the text, we have largely maintained Goings's original spelling and orthography throughout the manuscript. We eliminated end-of-line hyphens and did not note when Goings used British (as opposed to American) spellings. The maps locate place names in a contemporary, not historical, setting.

Narratives such as Goings's are a fundamental resource for the study of eighteenth- and nineteenth-century American history and literature. The need for and the power of these narratives did not diminish with the conclusion of the Civil War. Former slaves documented their experiences of enslavement both to remind Americans what had precipitated the Civil War and to continue the struggle for full inclusion in American society. We are pleased and proud to have had a small part in bringing Henry Goings's story to light.

4. Fleming, Lamonde, and Bruce, *History of the Book in Canada*, 2:215–16.

Acknowledgments

For their contributions to this volume, we thank the following people at the University of Virginia: Christina Deane, Christian Dupont, Jason Eldred, Chris Gist, Richard K. Holway, Kelly Johnston, Ervin L. Jordan Jr., Bethany Nowviskie, and George Riser. We would also like to thank Sandra Alston and Christina Tooulias-Santolin of the University of Toronto, Tom Congalton of Between the Covers Rare Books, William LaMoy of Syracuse University, Catherine O'Donnell and James Rush of Arizona State University, Jim Quantrell of the Archives, City of Cambridge, Ontario, and E. Lee Shepard of the Virginia Historical Society.

The maps in this volume were prepared by Chris Gist and Kelly Johnston of the Scholars' Lab, Geospatial Information and Data Services, at the University of Virginia Library and by Edward Gaynor and Michael Plunkett.

Introduction

CALVIN SCHERMERHORN

I have had a wide experience of the evils of slavery, in my own person, and have an extensive knowledge of the horrors of slavery, in all their length and breadth, having witnessed them in Old Virginia, North Carolina, New Virginia, Tennessee, Alabama, and Mississippi. I belonged in the State of Virginia, and am, I suppose, about forty years old. Were I to write out all my experiences and what I have observed, (and I intend to do this, having commenced already) it would make quite a large volume.

—HENRY GOWENS [Goings], Galt, Canada West, 1855

With those words, the barber and steamboat steward known as Henry Goings revealed how he was giving voice to his experiences as a slave and a free man. He had been a fugitive for eighteen years, and a resident of Ontario, or Canada West as it was then called, for thirteen. Although it never became a large volume, *Rambles of a Runaway from Southern Slavery* would take fourteen more years to reach publication. In it, the author would detail his "wide experience of the evils of slavery," presenting himself as an articulate witness to American slavery and as an eloquent essayist. Goings's is an exceptional autobiography because it contains within its covers both the author's account of his own life and also essays on the momentous times in which he lived, including commentary on the American Civil War, the destruction of the slave South from which he escaped, and the beginnings of Reconstruction. The resulting book is a hybrid of genres, spanning both a time of upheavals in American civilization and the author's own intellectual transformation. It was also one of the few ex-slave autobiographies to be published in Canada.[1]

Goings was a keen observer and an economical writer. He noticed places and people, memorized names, remembered small details many years later, and shrewdly assessed those whom he encountered, especially whites who held his fortune in their hands. His compact yet detailed nar-

---

1. Henson, *An Autobiography of Rev. Josiah Henson ("Uncle Tom") from 1789–1881;* Mallory, *Old Plantation Days;* Robertson, *Book of the Bible against Slavery;* Smallwood, *A Narrative of Thomas Smallwood, Coloured Man.*

rative illustrates many of the major themes scholars have struggled to understand about the antebellum South, including forced migration, family separation, and the expansion of the cotton kingdom. Goings gives illuminating accounts of planter and slave mobility, labor practices, slaves' communications networks, and enslaved family life.

Goings was an appropriate name for the author. While in bondage, he traveled extensively in the Old South and witnessed the emergence of the most robust and dynamic slave society in the Americas at the time. Born Elijah Turner about 1810, Goings's rambles took him from his home in the Tidewater region of Virginia, one of the oldest sites of English settlement in North America, to the Middle Tennessee frontier, by way of Halifax and Raleigh, North Carolina. He participated in a great involuntary movement of African Americans to the Deep South, arriving in the boomtown of Florence, Alabama, in the early 1820s. Like more than a million other African Americans in the early republic, Goings was moved about the landscape of a rapidly expanding political nation according to the designs of slaveholders and slave traders. His rambles as a slave owed much to the restless ambition of planter Joseph Lawrence Dawson Smith, who owned him for the better part of two decades. From Florence, Goings traveled as Smith's groom and personal servant, to Milledgeville, Georgia, Pontotoc, Mississippi, and down that mighty river to Vicksburg and New Orleans while Smith transacted business and sought out new plantations. In those travels in the 1820s and 1830s, Goings saw cotton become king as slaveholders drove African Americans to grow the snowy lint on lands Native Americans were forced to vacate. After Smith died and Goings's separation from his wife Maria White seemed eminent, he struck out for the North. His peripatetic escape shows how perilous a fugitive slave's life was, yet he risked his freedom—and nearly lost it—to attempt to rescue his first wife from slavery.[2]

Goings's voice was that of a fugitive and an African American expatriate whose career was otherwise seemingly unremarkable. In freedom, he lived by the sweat of his face, working in service jobs to help support a family that included his second wife Martha Bentley and their five children by 1851. From that vantage point, Goings witnessed some remarkable events,

---

2. Johnson, *Soul by Soul*; Deyle, *Carry Me Back*; Gudmestad, *A Troublesome Commerce*; Berlin, *Generations of Captivity*, chap. 4; Tadman, *Speculators and Slaves*; Miller, *South by Southwest*; Rothman, *Slave Country*; Perdue and Green, *The Cherokee Nation and the Trail of Tears*.

glimpsing larger developments within the nation he had left and the African diaspora of which he was a part. The author begins his narrative with three chapters that describe his life in slavery, his escape on the Underground Railroad, his furtive travels around the western Lake Erie region, and his tragic attempt to rescue his first wife, whom he was forced to leave behind. These chapters were completed by 1859 or 1860. Later, he added his reflections on his new life in Canada. These final two chapters, plus a lengthy appendix, amount to a political manifesto. In them, Goings shifts his attention to the broader cause of African American freedom and citizenship. Written between 1863 and 1869, they unfold the author's evolving understandings of the Civil War, Emancipation, African American national destiny, civil rights, and the course of Reconstruction.[3]

Unlike so many ex-slave autobiographers, Goings wrote without the sponsorship of abolitionists. He likely penned his own story, rather than dictating it to an amanuensis, which was the case for many former slaves who lacked the ability to write. *Rambles* seems to have been composed in Goings's own voice, without editorial assistance; Goings probably paid for its printing as well. Goings's composition suggests that he possibly learned how to read and even to write before escaping to Canada. If he did not, he learned quickly soon after. In an 1849 letter to the editor of the *Chatham Chronicle,* for instance, Goings protests racist responses to the Elgin Association's efforts to help relocate freed and fugitive slaves in Canada (see appendix C). In it he claims to "have written this merely to show that, although we have received injuries without number, we yet have some sensibility left, and can perceive, and deeply feel a home thrust, like that aimed at us and our children." He wrote with art and feeling, at a level that it would take many years to attain. Beyond emphasizing his authorship, Goings's commitment to African American civil rights in Canada and elsewhere reflects the life of his community, even if he remained on the periphery of organized civil rights struggles.[4]

Goings was an everyman. He spoke as an independent observer and someone who made his living from the quotidian activities of barbering, waiting, stewarding, and selling, real estate and his own labor. The con-

3. 1851 Personal Census of Canada West, Enumeration District 2, Town of Chatham, Kent County, Ontario, p. 8.

4. Andrews, *To Tell a Free Story,* chap. 1; *Courier and Western District Advertiser,* November 3, 1849; Hepburn, *Crossing the Border,* 22–23; Walton, "Blacks in Buxton and Chatham, Ontario, 1830–1890," 50.

trast between his life and writings and those of three of his peers is strik-
ing. On the Underground Railroad, in his adopted home of Kent County,
or while working on steamboats plying the River Thames and Lake Erie,
he could have crossed paths with Henry Bibb, William Wells Brown, or
Josiah Henson. Before the Civil War, Bibb, Brown, and Henson became
three of the most renowned American ex-slaves who became expatriates in
Canada. All lived or worked near to where Goings did, but these three had
careers as abolitionist speakers and agents connected to a broader network
of activism. Bibb escaped slavery for good in 1837, settled in Detroit and
later Ontario, and published the first Afro-Canadian newspaper, *Voice of
the Fugitive*, which Goings read and in which he placed an advertisement
in 1852. Bibb lectured on the abolitionist circuit with Brown and collabo-
rated with Henson to found the Refugees' Home Colony in 1851. Brown
had escaped slavery in 1834 and became active on the Underground Railroad. He ferried fugitive slaves to Canada on Lake Erie steamers, arriving
at destinations where Goings worked in 1842 and 1843. That was Brown's
entrée into an abolitionist speaking career that took him to Europe and
segued into a successful career as a playwright, novelist, and historian.
Henson, a generation older than Bibb, Brown, or Goings, had escaped
slavery in 1830 and was instrumental in founding the Dawn Settlement
for fugitives. He traveled to England, and was even received by Queen Victoria. Goings shared with all three the experience of having been sold and
separated from loved ones and then moved about the antebellum American landscape by slave owners. All four published their autobiographies
during their lifetimes.[5]

Goings found his voice in the trials of life as a fugitive. Unlike Bibb,
Brown, and Henson, he labored in relative obscurity. Goings pitched his
voice and addressed his message to African Americans like himself, namely,
those who may have been involved in hemisphere-wide freedom struggles
but focused their time and energies, as he did, on raising families and earning a living. After arriving in Ontario, Goings sought to build a reputation
as a diligent and honorable private citizen, showing that virtue and probity

---

5. *Voice of the Fugitive*, December 16, 1852; Bibb, *Narrative of the Life and Adven-
tures of Henry Bibb, an American Slave, Written by Himself*; Brown, *Narrative of
William W. Brown, a Fugitive Slave. Written by Himself*; Henson, *The Life of Josiah
Henson, Formerly a Slave, Now an Inhabitant of Canada, as Narrated by Himself*;
Henson, *An Autobiography of Rev. Josiah Henson ("Uncle Tom") from 1789–1881*; Mull,
The Underground Railroad in Michigan, chaps. 4, 8; Bordewich, *Bound for Canaan*,
264–67, 377–95.

were regular components of the souls of black folk. "Every thinking, every candid man that knows me," he told an interviewer in 1855, "knows that I would not utter any thing that is not true." His career and writings reflect that sense of honor. In Canada, he participated in the uplift of other African Americans as a member of the rank and file. In his earliest known writing, he blew the whistle on a fellow African American who, by promising to bring his wife to Ohio, deceived Goings into crossing the border back into the United States, where he was arrested and nearly returned to slavery. After this ordeal, Goings appealed to the "sympathy" of fellow Chatham, Ontario, residents, asking for "such assistance" as would "enable me to honorably and honestly redeem my promise to those, my benefactors, thereby showing to the world, that though we were once slaves, that now we are free we will be honest." He had lawyers' bills to pay and needed his fellow citizens' financial support to do so. In a desperate attempt to preserve his family, he had risked his freedom, and he was now compelled to sell his property and rely on the charity of others to pay his debts.[6]

As if to highlight his career in service occupations, the narrative Goings wrote is largely a story about others. In the autobiographical chapters of *Rambles*, the author avoids revealing his innermost thoughts, his writing muting the pain of family separations as well as the violence he witnessed in slavery. Rather, he relates details matter-of-factly, even when he is recalling the scenes of families being torn apart when owners decide to move west with their slaves. "Not only is the child separated from the parent, but not unfrequently the husband is separated from the wife," or "This is one of many of the dark sides of the picture, which cannot be treated with too much severity." In these descriptions, Goings chose not to elaborate further.

In the autobiographical chapters of *Rambles*, Goings focuses primarily on whites, while revealing little about his own personal affiliations and commitments. That is partly the result of his having been a groom and manservant while a slave, a position that made him a spy within the world of the planter's household, a world inaccessible to most agricultural workers. He spent a considerable amount of time in the company of one roving planter, listening to his owner's conversations and looking over his own

---

6. *Chatham Journal*, December 23, 1843, cited in Ripley, Herrle, and Cimbala, *The Black Abolitionist Papers*, vol. 2, *Canada, 1830–1865*, 99–100; Drew, *A North-Side View of Slavery*, 143; Abdi, "Reflections on the Long Struggle for Inclusion"; Hembree, "The Question of 'Begging'."

shoulders. From that viewpoint, Goings was able to articulate a world that few enslaved Americans knew firsthand. Yet this portrait, written by an African American, says comparatively little about slaves' concerns. For example, Goings's portrait of the execrable overseer he endured in Alabama is far more detailed than anything we learn from Goings about the woman he married in slavery, Maria White, or the woman he married in freedom, Martha Bentley.

Goings represents himself as an articulate witness to slavery rather than as the hero of his own narrative. That narrative strategy was partly the result of his independence. Because he did not incorporate the by then standard tropes of abolitionist rhetoric into his writings, Goings's *Rambles* resembles the compositions of an earlier generation of slave narrators, writers such as Solomon Bayley and Charles Ball. Their narratives were more memoirs of events than literary performances rehearsed on the public stage or crafted for a white antislavery readership. Bayley and Ball wrote before Bibb and Brown's generation of ex-slave autobiographers wove personal heroism into the texts of their autobiographies. In contrast to his contemporaries, Goings refused to sensationalize his adventures or to dwell on the heroic or tragic aspects of his struggles. Even during a thrilling escape from a sheriff determined to re-enslave him, for instance, Goings credits sympathetic townspeople and a conductor on the Underground Railroad, rather than his own gifts or guile, for his escape.[7]

Goings's intended audience of African Americans, many of whom were formerly enslaved, already knew the hardships and heartaches that characterized slave life. There was no need to dramatize those aspects. Goings had been largely exempted from the fieldwork and the lash that punished the bodies and distressed the souls of most of the enslaved. Representing such violence and humiliation—a standard trope in abolitionist literature aimed at a white readership—was not a priority or something for which his readers would thirst. That stands in contrast to scenes depicting the violence done to black bodies that by turns horrified and electrified the white middle-class readers of slave autobiographies, those who flocked to hear abolitionist orators like Brown and Bibb and who hastened to buy copies of their narratives. (Goings's 1855 interview with the white abolitionist Benjamin Drew, appended below, contains more-intense depictions of

---

7. Ball, *Slavery in the United States;* Bayley, *Narrative of Some Remarkable Incidents in the Life of Solomon Bayley;* Andrews, *To Tell a Free Story,* 62–66, 78–85; Roth, "'How a Slave was Made a Man.'"

violence than any of the passages from his autobiography.) Goings's imagined audience was far different from white readers who read Henson's own popular narrative, first published in 1849.[8]

Goings's narrative strategy was to present a portrait of slave life that supplied detail enough for readers to form judgments about slavery and life in the American South, without a sentimental overlay. Every autobiography is artifice, and each autobiographer omits some details and emphasizes others. But Goings does not use the conventions of African American autobiography, including pathos, to the extent of his contemporaries. In contrast to Bibb's *Narrative of the Life and Adventures of Henry Bibb, an American Slave, Written by Himself* (1849), which in places drips with emotion, Goings presents himself as an unsentimental witness to events, sparing much editorial commentary. He often leaves it to his readers to supply the moral, such as in a passage in which his mother "begged" her son's new master not to sell Goings from his sister, because brother and sister "were so much attached to each other." Ignoring that plea, the bankrupt owner sells Goings's sister Maria to a slave trader. "The feelings or desires of the slave, however, are of little account to his merciless owner," Goings remarks, adding that, "even where humanity would sometimes yield, the stern necessities of bankruptcy forbid its beneficent exercise." The subject is then dropped, and Goings does not mourn the loss of his sister for readers.[9]

Goings's details are vivid, despite spare descriptions, but he does not employ such literary devices as extended reconstructed discourses. Those are a hallmark of what William L. Andrews calls the "culmination of a century" of African American autobiography, exemplified by Frederick Douglass's *My Bondage and My Freedom* (1855), Jacob D. Green's *Narrative of the Life of J. D. Green, a Runaway Slave, from Kentucky, Containing an Account of His Three Escapes, in 1839, 1846, and 1848* (1864), and Harriet Jacobs's *Incidents in the Life of a Slave Girl* (1861). Goings refused to reconstruct dialogue for the sake of dramatizing his memories. He also reins in his emotions, suppressing his resentments and deep sense of dis-

---

8. Henson, *The Life of Josiah Henson, Formerly a Slave, Now an Inhabitant of Canada, as Narrated by Himself;* Drew, *A North-Side View of Slavery,* 138–46; Heglar, *Rethinking the Slave Narrative,* chap. 2; Roth, "'How a Slave was Made a Man'"; Rohrbach, *Truth Stranger than Fiction,* chap. 2.

9. Bibb, *Narrative of Some Remarkable Incidents in the Life of Solomon Bayley,* 147; Heglar, *Rethinking the Slave Narrative,* chap. 3; Andrews, *To Tell a Free Story,* 143–66.

appointment, such as at the end of chapter 3, when he recalls, "The last information that I have been able to gain of my first wife, was, that she had been married to another slave of the family with whom she resided. I married a second wife in Canada, and have a family." No further comment is offered.

Still, in the final chapters of *Rambles,* Goings did have his say.[10] Written during and after the Civil War, they exhibit a significant shift in attitude and subject matter from the earlier, autobiographical chapters. Almost without pause from that spare description of the fate of his family, which ends chapter 3, chapter 4 begins with Goings's report of the "death knell of slavery," which was "now being rung" amid the storms of civil war. "The slaveholders themselves have long trembled for the fate of their despotic institution," Goings thunders, glossing: "Jefferson forewarned the people of its downfall, and the sword is now dealing its foretold destruction." That is a jarring shift of frame from Goings's descriptions of his sojourn in the North as a fugitive slave. Though he has been unflappable when narrating his personal life, in his essays Goings's righteous indignation pours out.

Goings's essays reveal the author as one of the thousands of former slaves with meager resources who nevertheless were able to create neighborhood ties that became community bonds, that in turn blossomed into African American political consciousness. Goings's views on the subjects of African American citizenship and civil rights transcend a merely national focus. He wrote as part of a hemisphere-wide struggle for African Americans' freedom, political equality, and the right to rise as far in any society as talent would take them. He addresses his audience as "my colored brethren" of the United States and Canada. The book, which begins with concise descriptions, mainly of whites, closes with earnest appeals to black Americans to seize citizenship along with their freedom or else seek their civil rights beyond the boundaries of the United States. The transition in tone can be accounted for by the fact that, by 1863 and 1864, the author viewed the stakes on African American freedom as having risen dramatically. His autobiographical chapters were complete before the war began, and they carried personal interest. The epochal events Goings witnessed unfolding during the U.S. Civil War carried a great deal more significance, which

10. Andrews, *To Tell a Free Story,* chap. 6; Douglass, *My Bondage and My Freedom;* Green, *Narrative of the Life of J. D. Green, a Runaway Slave . . . ;* Jacobs, *Incidents in the Life of a Slave Girl. Written by Herself.*

inspired the author to make sense of them in terms of his own understandings of politics, society, and the African diaspora.[11]

Like many contemporary African American thinkers, Goings viewed the Civil War as inaugurating a revolution in the status of African Americans. He also viewed the progress of the war with some alarm, since that project was jeopardized by whites who fought, bled, and died for union rather than for a new birth of freedom. Goings's fourth chapter contains a manifesto, or exposition, on the then undetermined outcome of the Civil War and, with it, the destruction of American slavery. It was written after the Confederate Army of Northern Virginia invaded Maryland and Pennsylvania in the summer of 1863 but before President Abraham Lincoln's reelection in November, 1864. Like most African Americans, white abolitionists, and radical Republicans, Goings saw the Civil War as a war to end slavery. As late as 1864, however, the cause of union was paramount among most war supporters, and indeed many white supporters of the Union cause were opposed to ending slavery or extending civil rights to African Americans. Goings reports on the conditions of African Americans in Canada, and predicts that freedpeople would demonstrate the republican virtues of hard work, sound judgment, and self-restraint.[12]

Although he positioned himself as an African American spokesman, Goings's political thought was unconstrained by such categories as "race" and "nation." Goings viewed African Americans as having common cause with Irish nationalists seeking to end British rule. In Goings's view, freedom struggles for African Americans resembled freedom struggles for any who suffered oppression. He looked abroad to find historical precedents for post-emancipation societies, including the British West Indies, where slavery was abolished in the 1830s.[13]

As a self-taught student of literature and political economy, Goings was free of the practical political considerations that constrained others, such as Frederick Douglass and fellow Canadian expatriates Brown and Martin R. Delany, who were instrumental in recruiting and advocating

11. Clarke, *Odysseys Home*, 27–70; Saillant, "Aspirant Citizenship"; Jeffrey, *Abolitionists Remember*.

12. Blight, *Frederick Douglass' Civil War*, chaps. 5, 8; Nelson and Sheriff, *A People at War*, 204–9.

13. Levine, *Martin Delany, Frederick Douglass, and the Politics of Representative Identity*; Eudell, *The Political Languages of Emancipation in the British Caribbean and the U.S. South*, chap. 4.

for African American soldiers. He was not party to disagreements among African American leaders concerning, for instance, the merits of looking to Africa for freedoms denied black Americans in the United States. Goings did, however, have a very personal investment in the outcome of the Civil War. At age seventeen, his son Samuel H. Goings enlisted in the 102nd Infantry Regiment, U.S. Colored Troops, serving in Company C as a private from 1864 to 1865.[14]

Goings's fifth chapter is a tug-of-war between optimism and a sense of impending disappointment concerning the course of African American freedom. Composed following Lincoln's assassination in April 1865, it eulogizes the slain American president in biblical terms while arguing that Americans must take up the work of freedom that Lincoln had left unfinished. Slavery had died, Goings argues, but freedom had not quite yet been born. As he surveys the fortunes of the newly freed, made possible by the Union victory, he also is aware that they have fallen far short of their shimmering possibilities. To his African American countrymen the author counsels peace and reconciliation, in the spirit of Christian forgiveness. In the tone of a prophet, he exhorts African Americans to persist in their good works for the sake of "you and your posterity, yet unborn," to inhabit "a land of sunshine and gladness, where no mist or cloud or darkness shall ever obscure the brightness of the landscape." That optimism would soon dim.

In the appendix, written in 1868 or 1869, Goings loses patience with Reconstruction and despairs of black Americans ever becoming full citizens. "The place to which I kindly suggest to my emancipated brethren, the propriety of removing as a body would be the colony of 'British Honduras,'" he sighs. Central America, Goings contends, is more-fertile ground for African American rights and liberties than their homeland. He chose to stay in Canada. Like so many African Americans, Goings saw the promises of Reconstruction disappearing in the progress of reconciliation between white Unionists and whites of the former Confederacy.[15]

Instead of keeping the progress of freedom on track, Goings takes the view that whites have purchased reunification at the expense of blacks, tolerating black codes, racial terrorism, and the return of ex-Confederates to power in many areas of the South. As if to underscore the improba-

---

14. Blight, *Frederick Douglass' Civil War*, chap. 7; Levine, *Martin Delany, Frederick Douglass, and the Politics of Representative Identity*, chap. 5; National Park Service, *U.S. Civil War Soldiers, 1861–1865*.

15. O'Donovan, *Becoming Free in the Cotton South*, chap. 5.

bility of African American progress toward citizenship, Goings includes reports of violence in the Memphis, Tennessee, race riot of May 1866. His partial reprinting of two speeches by Freedmen's Bureau officials to freedpeople, one by Isaac S. Catlin and the other by Benjamin P. Runkle, highlights his outrage at the treatment by whites of the formerly enslaved. In their speeches, both Catlin and Runkle had argued that African Americans would have to work exceedingly hard to demonstrate that they were capable of being good citizens. Goings endorses the view, also shared by such African American civil rights activists as James McCune Smith and Sojourner Truth, who encouraged freedpeople to be diligent in their work, thrifty with their resources, and impeccable in their morals. Although by this time, Goings had resided in Canada for over a quarter century, he nevertheless wrote as an interested American, indicating that he had not abandoned his identity as a would-be citizen of the United States. Goings shared that attitude with, perhaps, the majority of the former bondmen who had remained in the United States, maintaining an identity as a member of that nation in which they all had been born slaves.[16]

Goings seems to give up, however, on the possibility of full African American citizenship in the country of his birth. Addressing his "unfortunate brethren," he argues in the appendix that "no act of Congress can pull down the social barrier erected by superstition and prejudice." African American men might get to vote or stand for office, Goings argues, but "the signs of the times do not justify any one of you to expect a single vote outside of our own race." The author then shifts to what amount to appendixes to his autobiography, recalling places he had visited in the service of his erstwhile owner Joseph L. D. Smith.

Perhaps illustrating his frustration with the progress of African American freedom, *Rambles* concludes with a darkly comical slaveholder's sermon in which a self-satisfied slave owner preaches to a gathering of his slaves on the extent of their duties to him. Goings claims he heard this "sermon" while passing through Tennessee, perhaps as a slave in Smith's company, but more likely on the Underground Railroad. It is clear that the owner's amassed slaves do not buy into his concept of mastery. He begins his talk with biblical injunctions that call for slaves to obey their masters, and then unfolds a catalogue of duties his slaves owe to him, the work regimen they are to undertake, and the privileges he will allow them as an ostensible reflection of his good will. Goings gives no gloss on this sermon

16. Hepburn, *Crossing the Border,* chap. 4; Cimbala, "Reconstruction's Allies."

except to say that it is worth repeating. The slaveholder's sermon, which returns the reader's focus to the recent slavery past, is a fitting conclusion to a book whose author was profoundly discontented with the course of African American freedom.

The transitions in tone and style from early to later chapters complement the author's own intellectual progress. Goings's spellings of names becomes more regularized after chapter 3, and he begins to mobilize a stock of biblical and literary allusions. He cites the New Testament, and alludes to authors, like Alexander Pope, and politicians, like Richard Lalor Sheil, who argued against characterizing Irishmen as "aliens" in Great Britain. He quotes passages from the King James version of the Bible, often in the tones of an evangelist. He also cites Thomas Cowper, Thomas Jefferson, Pope, Tertullian, and William Shakespeare. Besides copious allusions, Goings sometimes paraphrases memorable lines, alluding to the speech that opens Shakespeare's *Richard III*, but replacing "Grim-visaged war," for instance, with "grim visaged slavery."[17]

The growth of Goings's literary repertoire is also reflected in the publications he cites. Goings followed Canadian and international politics, reading African American newspapers such as Bibb's *Voice of the Fugitive*, religious periodicals such as the *Christian Recorder*, and mainstream newspapers such as the *New York Times* and *New York Tribune*. In the appendix to his narrative, he also attached a long travel narrative, including advice on immigration to Central America, taken from the *Christian Recorder*, and partly reprinted a pamphlet containing Catlin and Runkle's speeches, which had been published in Louisville, Kentucky, in 1868. By this point in the narrative, the author has traveled a long way from his primary education as a slave.

Goings was largely self-taught, listening in his formative years to the parlor discussions of his owners, employers, and those with whom they came into contact, gleaning the practical knowledge tucked between the double-meanings of conversations centering on land, politics, prices, and slaves: learning, as he recalled, "by stealth." Goings may have attended school briefly while in slavery in Virginia, but his lack of much formal education did not markedly separate him from a generation of contemporaries like Frederick Douglass and Harriet Jacobs. Also like Douglass and Jacobs, Goings was put to work at a young age in domestic rather than agricul-

17. Shakespeare, *Richard III*, 4.

tural labor, interacting with whites on a level of intimacy that allowed him special access to learning opportunities. We do not hear the substance of many conversations, but Goings could hardly have missed hearing about planters' aspirations and world views as they refashioned the Southern topography of old woodlands, Indian villages, and big sleepy rivers into a booming landscape of cotton plantations, entrepôt cities, and thriving commercial waterways.[18]

Goings does not detail how he learned to read and write in *Rambles*, but he leaves important clues. He had acquired aural literacy as a slave, and probably wrote from sound rather than from names read and recalled. In the first three chapters, Goings spells place-names and personal names phonetically, such as "Burnt Henry," which is how Goings recalled his one-time Virginia home of Burnt Ordinary (now Toano). ("Ordinary," which was the common term for a tavern in colonial America, pronounced with two syllables in a Tidewater accent, sounds like "Henry.") He recalls "Bogs-dale" for "Barksdale," "Doolands" for "Nowland," "Jerdan" for "Jordan," "Kemble" for "Kimbrough," "Hosman" for "Hosmer," and "Pricket" for "Pig-gott." Errors are primarily in the spellings of names the author remembers, in the accents in which he originally heard them.

Like most people deliberately deprived of an education, Goings had thirsted for knowledge. He was a precocious learner and had an excellent memory. Before leaving Virginia, a white child in his neighborhood gave him a spelling book, and he even sought the assistance of a schoolmaster in using it. James City County, Virginia, had an exceptional public school system for its day, and before 1831 there were few laws against teaching enslaved children to read. (Authorities, it seems, rarely enforced an 1805 Virginia law prohibiting the instruction of black or mulatto orphans in reading, writing, and arithmetic.) During Goings's youth, some Virginia slaveholders apparently thought it a good investment to have literate slaves. But as a slave, Goings never got the schooling he hoped to receive, and soon decided that it was better if he learned in secret. His second owner put him to work in a Halifax, North Carolina, hotel, and Goings's eagerness to learn helped keep him from fieldwork.[19]

---

18. Ayers, *What Caused the Civil War?*, chap. 6; Freehling, *The Road to Disunion*, vol. 1, *Secessionists at Bay, 1776–1854*, chaps. 1–2; Kirby, *Mockingbird Song*, chaps. 1–2; McFeely, *Frederick Douglass*, chap. 6; Yellin, *Harriet Jacobs*, chaps. 2–4.

19. Smallwood, *A Narrative of Thomas Smallwood, Coloured Man*, 14; Schiller, "Learning Their Letters"; Williams, *Self-Taught*, chaps. 1–2.

Goings and his sister Maria traveled with their owner to North Carolina, where Goings was taught one of the primary lessons most enslaved children learned early on: the cash a slave could bring to his owner through sale. In North Carolina, a man offered eleven hundred dollars for Goings and Maria. Goings's self-worth, then, had the dual character of self-esteem and also the realization of his market value.

Other lessons followed. Despite "often" being "flogged for my alleged incompetency" with horses, as a young man, Goings recalled, he learned how to handle them. That was essential in an age when travelers arrived and departed on horses or horse-drawn carriages. He was also given a job waiting tables, which was another component of his practical education. As he waited on the lawyers and other travelers to the county seat of Halifax, he attracted the attention of many visitors to the inn, who encouraged him to learn. "I was delighted to hear them frequently pronounce me one of the smartest of boys," he recalled. They also wanted to know "the money value put upon me by my master." After being sold to Smith, Goings's informal education took off, as he toured the country and listened to the conversations of planters and their circles. Learning involved assimilating the vocabulary, reading the signs, and understanding the grammar of political and social discourse. That part of his education was not categorically different than the self-education of many white Americans in an age before free public education was a widespread phenomenon. The difference came when Goings sought formal literacy. "I then thought how agreeable it must be to read," Goings recalled, "and wondered why the white man selfishly deprived me of so great and yet so harmless an amusement."[20]

Most slaveholders did not think reading was harmless, especially after David Walker's incendiary *Appeal . . . to the Coloured Citizens of the World*, a polemic against slavery that circulated among enslaved African Americans in 1830. A North Carolina native, Walker had been born free but traveled to Boston to escape the worst aspects of discrimination. His self-published *Appeal* argued for racial equality and urged violent means to destroy slavery. Walker heaped ridicule on whites, excoriated Thomas Jefferson, and ominously compared the United States to biblical Egypt under Pharaoh. Frenzied Southern citizens demanded laws against teaching African Americans—and especially slaves—to read and write. North Caro-

20. Johnson, *Soul by Soul*, chap. 1; Kett, *The Pursuit of Knowledge under Difficulties*, chaps. 2–3.

lina and Virginia tightened their laws against teaching African Americans to read and forbade gatherings of black people. In the wake of the 1831 Nat Turner rebellion in Southampton County, Virginia, in which rebels allied to that charismatic enslaved preacher killed scores of whites, state legislatures throughout the South tightened restrictions on teaching slaves and African Americans reading and writing. Word reached Goings of the uprisings in his native state while he was in Alabama.[21]

Any formal education would have to wait until freedom, but Goings's education as a slave involved gaining knowledge of the institution into which he was born and the world beyond its horizons. Like Charles Ball, Goings absorbed tales of far-flung places, and like Frederick Douglass, talk of abolitionists ignited his imagination. "I heard them tell of foreign travel," Goings wrote, "and have wondered what the hideous looking animal an 'abolitionist' was like." To most white Southerners, abolitionists were the witches and terrorists of their age: malignant, ubiquitous, and utterly real. Like Douglass, Goings hesitated to inquire. Of "abolition," Douglass recalled, "I did not dare to ask any one about its meaning, for I was satisfied that it was something they wanted me to know very little about."[22] Goings seems to echo that sentiment. In North Carolina, his second owner refused to sell him to a man who reportedly manumitted his slaves after they had reached twenty-one, dismissing the man as "too much of a tory and abolitionist." To the young Goings, that "was a great blow," since he had "become aware of the advantages of getting into the service of such a man." Goings would have heard abolitionists made scapegoats for all manner of evils, but he learned that there was a potential network of allies beyond the world of cotton and slavery. That was the Underground Railroad, which he would ride to quasi-freedom in the North.[23]

The authenticity of Goings's narrative is supported by contemporary accounts as well as the thoroughgoing accuracy of the people and places he names, albeit with variations according to his mnemonic memory. Goings's recollections are corroborated by other external evidence. For example, in chapter 1 of his narrative, Goings mentions the appearance on

21. Walker, *David Walker's Appeal* . . . ; Hinks, *To Awaken My Afflicted Brethren.*

22. Douglass, *Narrative of the Life of Frederick Douglass, An American Slave, Written by Himself,* 41.

23. Ball, *Slavery in the United States,* chap. 10.

the Tennessee River of the steamboat *Osage*. The *Osage* was indeed the first side-wheel steamer to make its way as far downriver as Humphreys County, Tennessee. The boat's appearance "caused immense excitement," and Goings recalls that Smith even attempted to charter it to transport 350 slaves downriver to Alabama (the master of the 149-ton vessel wisely refused). Other sources tell us that the *Osage* was built in Cincinnati in 1820, and sank on the Tombigbee River, in Alabama, in 1824, which establishes the fact that Goings traveled from Tennessee to Alabama between 1820 and 1824.[24]

Goings's recollection of overseers is particularly detailed, despite his being exempted from field work. He identifies a "Mr. Kemble," Elijah W. Kimbrough, an overseer on Smith's Alabama plantations who used excessive violence, and whose "debaucheries with the women are too vile to be recorded." Kimbrough, Goings recalled, "shot his father-in-law, a resident of Raleigh, North Carolina., for which he was hung." He is correct. Kimbrough was convicted in 1829 for the first-degree murder of his mother's husband, John Davis, and publicly executed in Raleigh in November 1830 for that crime. A crowd of some three thousand had gathered to watch. The bulk of Goings's 1855 interview with Drew focuses on the regime of "Mr. Kimball" (Kimbrough), whose brutality Smith tolerated because it made his cotton plantations more profitable. Goings chose not to revisit Kimbrough's atrocities at length in *Rambles*.[25]

Other details Goings includes could not have been known outside of Smith's family. He recalls with bitterness, after nearly two decades of service as a groom and manservant, how Smith had promised to manumit him upon his death. Instead, Goings recalled, Smith manumitted "Robin Purdy, an old field hand and gardener." He was the only enslaved person freed in Smith's will. "Old Robbin," Smith's will reads, was to be freed "in consideration of [his] faithful service." Besides instructing that Purdy should live with the deceased's brother, Henry D. Smith, Joseph Smith included a pension of "thirty five dollars annually for the support of Robbin and for his care and attentions of him during his life." Goings, who received

24. Lytle and Holdcamper, *Merchant Steam Vessels of the United States, 1807–1868*, 146; Neville, *Directory of Tennessee River Steamboats (1821–1928), with Illustrations*, 22.

25. Drew, *A North-Side View of Slavery*, 138–42; *State v. Kimbrough*, 13 N.C. 431 (N.C. 1830); *Raleigh (N.C.) Register*, November 8, 1830, 3.

no pay or pension, instead fell to Smith's widow, Mary Hannah Smith, and remained in slavery. His age, about twenty-seven, made him too valuable to set free.[26]

Goings's journey out of slavery took him nearly as far and wide as his rambles about the South. The Old Northwest was undergoing is own demographic revolution, as waves of migrants from the eastern seaboard and immigrants from northern and western Europe spilled across the Ohio and upper Mississippi Valleys during the 1830s, '40s, and '50s. From abroad, nearly 600,000 immigrants arrived in the United States in the 1830s, followed by 1.7 million in the 1840s, and nearly 2.6 million more in the 1850s.[27] The Trans-Appalachian West was a beacon for immigrants and a haven for runaways, but it was no paradise for either: many migrants—from eastern states as well as abroad—arrived to find the same grinding poverty that had caused them to move in the first place. People of color, free and enslaved, faced a raft of discriminations. Kidnappers plied borderlands looking for slave runaways—or anyone who could be sold as such. Others, of course, arrived, worked, and thrived, realizing the nineteenth-century American dream of property ownership and upward social mobility.[28]

Foreign-born white men could arrive and enjoy full citizenship, but African Americans faced significant constraints. The spread of democracy coincided with the advancement of black codes, as Jim Crow moved west in the antebellum period. States in the Old Northwest required free African Americans to post bonds and promise to keep the peace. They had few civil rights, but even so, there were some opportunities. Goings seized those after he made his way on horseback from Florence, Alabama, across Tennessee, and into Shawneetown, Illinois. From there, he headed east by steamboat up the Ohio River to Portsmouth, then north to Detroit, Michigan, then east again to Toledo and Perrysburg, Ohio, where he worked under the pretense of being free. During that period, he waited tables, cooked, and cut hair—part of the time in business for himself. In Perrys-

26. Will of Joseph L. D. Smith, Lauderdale County Will Records, 1835–58, vol. A (microfilm, LGM 00196, reel 26), Alabama Department of Archives and History, Montgomery [hereafter ADAH].

27. United States Immigration Commission, *Statistical Review of Migration, 1820–1910; Distribution of Immigrants, 1850–1900*, 5.

28. Howe, *What Hath God Wrought*, chap. 4; Gray, *The Yankee West*.

burg he stayed with a family active on the Underground Railroad, publicly concealing his identity as a runaway.[29]

Fugitives sometimes called Canada the Promised Land, but it too presented challenges for people of African descent.[30] Goings moved to Amherstburg, Ontario, in 1842, and after a month working for the army camp, he embarked on a career as a steward on passenger steamships plying Lake Erie and Lake Michigan. He did not record why he left Ohio, but when an opportunity seemed to open to rescue Maria White from slavery, he made a daring return to meet her there, only to be frustrated and very nearly returned to slavery.

Goings leaves few clues about the progress of his literary and political education in Canada, but his adopted home of Kent County, Ontario, where he lived from 1842 until about 1854, was a crucible of the African American expatriate community. The Reverend William M. Mitchell commented, with little exaggeration, "Chatham is the head-quarters of the negro-race in Canada." Following his escape and emigration to Ontario, Goings settled in Chatham, on the River Thames, from where he worked on passenger steamships and bought a house in the 1840s. About one-third of the town's population was black. Chatham supported an African American Methodist and Baptist Church (Goings identified himself as a Baptist), and many African Americans worked in skilled trades. Just north of Chatham, the Reverend Hiram Wilson and Josiah Henson (on whom Harriet Beecher Stowe patterned the title character in her novel, *Uncle Tom's Cabin*) founded the Dawn Settlement for African American refugees in 1842. In nearby Buxton, the Elgin Settlement flourished as well. In 1849, Goings published what was perhaps his first essay, a protest of white opposition to Elgin and the resettlement there of hundreds of African American families, most fleeing slavery.[31]

Following the Fugitive Slave Act of 1850, Ontario became a hub of African American agitation and resistance organizing. Henry Bibb published *Voice of the Fugitive* in Sandwich and Windsor between 1851 and 1853. As its name suggests, it was a forum for those who arrived in Ontario flee-

29. Middleton, *The Black Laws*, chaps. 4–5; Rael, *Black Identity and Black Protest in the Antebellum North*, chap. 4; Keyssar, *The Right to Vote*.

30. Franklin and Schweninger, *Runaway Slaves*, 116 and passim; Winks, *The Blacks in Canada, A History*.

31. Mitchell, *The Underground Railroad from Slavery to Freedom*, 141; Hepburn, *Crossing the Border*; Marsh, "From Slave Cabin to Windsor Castle."

ing slavery. In 1853, Mary Ann Shadd Cary and Samuel Ringgold Ward launched *The Provincial Freeman,* another important early African American newspaper; between 1855 and 1857, Cary and William P. Newman published the paper in Chatham. By then, Goings had left, but the intellectual atmosphere of the town continued to draw African American thinkers and abolitionist activists. Between 1856 and 1859, author, physician, and editor Martin Delany lived there and wrote his antislavery novel *Blake; or, the Huts of America.* It was also the terminus on the Underground Railroad. Harriet Tubman funneled settlers there, including a brother and a niece. Chatham also became a site for the planning of the most infamous slave insurrection plot of the antebellum era. John Brown arrived in 1858 and held a convention in which he sought recruits for his plan to cleanse the United States of slavery with the blood of slaveholders.[32]

By 1855, Goings was giving expression to his own experiences as a fugitive. He and his growing family, including second wife Martha Bentley, had moved to Galt, joining a settlement there of between forty and fifty African Americans. Bentley told her own story of far-flung travels across the American landscape, family separation, and escape from slavery.[33] With her, Goings raised a family and participated in civil rights struggles for refugees from American slavery. It is unclear whether he returned to the land of his birth, but he retained his identity as an American, following the fates of so many who had lived in bondage and then toiled in slavery's long shadows.[34]

Bentley could have written her own *Rambles* since she too had traveled a long, wandering road from slavery (see appendix B). Born about fifteen years after Goings, in the late 1820s, she was the daughter of an enslaved woman and the white man who had kidnapped her (under the pretext of buying her) as Bentley's mother was fleeing to New Jersey from her native Maryland. Martha, whose surname in slavery was Martin, recalled that her mother's maiden name was Bentley. Martha's father moved to Georgia and then to Mississippi, probably on the same trail of cotton

---

32. Olbey, "Unfolded Hands"; Rhodes, *Mary Ann Shadd Cary;* Clinton, *Harriet Tubman,* 102–4, 129–31; Levine, *Martin Delany, Frederick Douglass, and the Politics of Representative Identity;* Winks, *The Blacks in Canada, A History,* chap. 13; Ripley, Herrle, and Cimbala, *The Black Abolitionist Papers,* vol. 2, *Canada, 1830–1865,* 322–63; Wayne, "The Black Population of Canada West on the Eve of the American Civil War"; Drew, *A North-Side View of Slavery,* 136.

33. Drew, *A North-Side View of Slavery,* 138–46.

34. Blackmon, *Slavery by Another Name,* chap. 2.

riches Goings's owner Smith traveled. He fathered one other child with her mother, but it soon died, as nearly a fifth of slave infants did.[35] Her mother then married an African American man, contrary to her owner's wishes, and—Bentley guessed—remained in slavery as a consequence. When Martha was twelve, her father sent her to Cincinnati, Ohio, to attend school, with the stipulation that she not marry. He had plans to free his offspring by slave women (Bentley's mother was not the only enslaved mother of his children). Bentley's Cincinnati guardian, who was also entrusted with her half-brother and a half-sister, embezzled her tuition money and also the funds that should have gone for shoes, sending her to school for only one year instead of three. When the father found out, he started for Cincinnati but fell ill and died intestate in 1843. Like her future husband, Martha remained in the North for a few years before making her way to Canada. Also like Goings, Bentley had not seen her family for over a decade by the time she was interviewed in 1855. Deprived of schooling, she valued it for herself and her family. "I mean they shall have a good education," she said of her children, adding, "What little knowledge I have, has just made me hungry for more."[36]

Bentley and Goings settled first in Chatham, where Goings sold real estate in addition to serving as a steward aboard steamers. They and their three children, Samuel, Catharine, and Harriett, appear in the 1851 census for Chatham Township, Kent County, Ontario. All are listed as Baptist and Goings's occupation is "seaman." Catharine, named after her grandmother, was six; Samuel was four; and Harriett, three. The December 16, 1852, issue of the *Voice of the Fugitive* advertises the sale of farmland, for which Henry Goings acted as an agent (see appendix D). In about 1854, the family moved to Galt, but by 1861 the Goings family was living in a single-story wood-framed house in the town of Stratford, Perth County, Ontario. Goings was barbering and the family, each designated with an "M" for "mulatto," lived among many whites in the neighborhood. Curiously, the census taker recorded that neither Goings nor his wife could read or write. Samuel and Harriet were then attending school. Catharine, their oldest, was not. The youngest of their five children, James and Maria, ten and six, had joined the family. In her testimony to Drew in 1855, Bentley claimed to have five children, including three in school. Those were probably the children named in the census. Martha and Henry Goings had a large and

---

35. Klein, *A Population History of the United States*, 83.
36. Drew, *A North-Side View of Slavery*, 143–46 (quote at 145).

growing family in the 1850s, and perhaps Henry wrote his narrative—as so many former slaves did—to sell, in order to supplement his income. More likely, he chronicled the events of his life for posterity.[37]

What became of Henry Goings is unclear. He is listed in 1870 as a "laborer" in Stratford. By then, Martha and Henry Goings's children had already begun to move to the United States. In 1880, Civil War veteran Samuel H. Goings was living in Shannon, in the territory that would become South Dakota. James T. Goings, born in 1846, settled in Calumet, Michigan, in 1870. By 1886, he and his wife Agnes ("Minnie") were living in Grand Rapids, Michigan. He worked as a cook, and she as a hairdresser. In 1920, they both cooked for the state police. Catharine J. Goings, born in 1845, married North Carolina native Colwin Brown in 1884 and moved to Grand Rapids. Sister Harriet, born in 1850, married South Carolina native Joseph Adams in 1875 and was also living in Grand Rapids, Michigan, in 1900. They were still there in 1910. Whether Goings or Martha ever returned to the United States remains a mystery. Goings's despair over the future of African Americans' prospects in the land of his birth seems not to have extended to his children.[38]

37. 1851 Personal Census of Canada West, Enumeration District 2, Town of Chatham, Kent County, p. 8; 1861 Personal Census of Canada West, Town of Stratford, Perth County, roll C-1065, p. 2; Drew, *A North-Side View of Slavery*, 145.

38. Sutherland, *Counties of Perth and Waterloo Gazetteer and General Business Directory, for 1870 and 1871*, 122; 1880 U.S. Census, Enumeration District 104, Pine Ridge Agency, Shannon, Dakota Territory, roll 112, family history film 1254112, p. 513C, image 0790; 1900 U.S. Census, Enumeration District 177, City of Calumet, Houghton County, Michigan, roll T623-714, p. 15B; *Grand Rapids City and Kent County Directory, Vol. XIV*, 263; *Grand Rapids City and Kent County Directory, Vol. XVIII*, 446; 1900 U.S. Census, Enumeration District 45, Grand Rapids, Ward 1, Kent County, Michigan, roll T623-721, p. 3A; 1910 U.S. Census, Enumeration District 51, Grand Rapids, Ward 1, Kent County, Michigan, roll T624-656, p. 9A, image 250; 1920 U.S. Census, Enumeration District 95, Grand Rapids, Kent County, Michigan, roll T625-779, p. 25A, image 582.

Chronology

ca. 1810   Elijah Turner born on the estate of James N. Walker in James City County, Virginia, near Window Shades on the Chickahominy River south of Richmond

1815   Owned by Pearson Piggott at Burnt Ordinary, twelve miles from Williamsburg; briefly attends Bucky Dennis's primary school in James City County; begins work as groom for owner; separated from mother

1818   Piggott moves to Halifax, North Carolina, on the Roanoke River; takes Goings and sister, Maria, with him

1820   Bought by Henry Smith for his brother Joseph Lawrence Dawson Smith; removed to Raleigh, North Carolina

1821   Humphreys County, Tennessee, by way of Nashville; forced migration of 460 enslaved people, including neighboring plantation households

ca. 1821–22   Milledgeville, Georgia; meets and sings for William McIntosh

1823   Florence, Lauderdale County, Alabama; owned by Joseph Smith; notes the *Osage*, first steamboat on Tennessee River

ca. 1826   Visits New Orleans with Smith

1832   Married to Maria White, literate house servant, illegitimate daughter of wealthy planter and owner James Jackson

1837   Joseph L. D. Smith dies; ownership passes to wife Mary

1839   Assumes identity of Henry Goings; escapes

1839   Rolling Mills, Tennessee; first stop on the road to freedom

1839   Shawneetown, Illinois; on "free" soil

1839   Portsmouth, Ohio; works for a few days as a barber

1839   Detroit, Michigan; waits at the "American" restaurant, about one month

1839   Toledo, Ohio; engaged as a barber, about seven months

1840   Perrysburg, Ohio; stays about two years, including work at a hotel

1842   Arrives in Amherstburg, Ontario, Canada

1842   Living in Chatham, Ontario; working as a steward aboard boats on the River Thames

1843   Seaman on the steamboat *Kent;* commences maritime career

1843   Perrysburg, Ohio; returns for wife Maria

1844   Remarries to Martha A. Bentley, about age seventeen, a fugitive—also daughter of her owner—then living in Canada

1845   Porter on steamboat *Brothers,* at least through 1853

1849   Protests opposition to the Elgin Association, Buxton, Ontario

1851   Chatham, Kent County, Ontario; living with Martha (22), children Samuel (4), Catharine (6), and Harriett (3); lists his occupation as "seaman"

1855   Galt, Ontario (now Cambridge, Waterloo Region); interviewed by Benjamin Drew for *A North-Side View of Slavery;* two more children had been born

1861   Stratford, Ontario, Canada; working as a barber; living with Martha (33), children Catharine (16), Samuel (14), Harriett (12), Maria (10), James (6)

1869   Stratford, Ontario; publishes narrative

1870   Stratford, Ontario; working as a laborer

Rambles *of a* Runaway *from* Southern Slavery

Chapter 1

My birth and birth place in Virginia.—My name, Elijah Turner.—Changes
from one master to another,—In North Carolina,—Tennessee,—Alabama,
—Georgia,—Mississippi,—New Orleans,—Emigrating from plantation to
plantation,—My marriage,—Death of my last master.

I WAS BORN UPON the estate of James Walker, Esq.,[1] within three miles
of a place called Window Shades,[2] in the State of Virginia, and distant
some two and a half miles from James' River. Of the date of my birth,
I have no knowledge; the slave has no Family Bible in which to record
the births, marriages and deaths of his domestic circle. It is possible, the

1. James Norvell Walker, fl. 1784–1813, owned Burnt Ordinary, a plantation community at the crossroads of the Richmond and Chickahominy Roads (today, Virginia
Routes 60 and 631), in James City County, Virginia. In 1784, he sold the Blissland Parish
Church 2½ bushels of corn. The following year, Walker joined about 120 other county
freeholders to sign a petition asking for state tax relief. From 1782 to 1813, Walker paid
land taxes in that county, and by 1813, he owned or rented 465 acres. He also claimed
to own ten slaves in 1786. In 1790, Walker paid taxes on five slaves and three houses. By
the early 1800s, Walker had sold a substantial amount of his property to a neighbor. See
Chamberlayne, *Vestry Book of Blisland (Blissland) Parish, New Kent and James City
Counties, Virginia, 1721-1786*, 227; McCartney, *James City County*, 241, 262; *James
City County Personal Property Tax List, 1782-1799*; and Blackmon, *James City County,
Va. Land Tax Records, 1782-1813*, 292–306 and passim.
2. Window Shades is a plantation on the Chickahominy River two miles south of
New Kent Court House and now called "Windsor Shades." Locals recalled that the site
was an "Indian town" before Jamestown was founded by the English in 1607. It was
among the earliest plantations in the area and is associated with the Graves family. In
1795, that land, "Winsor Shades," was transferred, and by then it contained 109 acres.
By the nineteenth century, the land value had increased because of its proximity to the
navigable Chickahominy River. Ocean-going ships were able to dock at the plantation's
wharf. In 1862, during the Civil War, Union gunboats advanced as far up the Chickahominy River as Windsor Shades. During that invasion, enslaved people ran off, congre-
gating at Union-controlled land such as Sandy Point, at the mouth of the Chickahominy.
"Window Shades" appears on a Civil War–era military map. There is another "Windsor
Shades," which dates from the middle of the eighteenth century, on the National Register of Historic Places; that Windsor Shades is also known as "Ruffin's Ferry" and is
seven-tenths of a mile southwest of Sweet Hall on the Pamunkey River in neighboring
King William County. See Harris, *Old New Kent County*, 1:202–3; McCartney, *James
City County*, 315; and Abbot, "Williamsburg to White House" (map), 1862.

proprietors of a human herd may keep a registrar of births, just as an agriculturist records the annual increase of his farming stock.[3] But the commemoration of birthdays is a luxury unknown to expatriated Africans; in fact, there is little cause for grateful recollection of the day which added but another victim to a state of miserable servitude. My father and mother were named respectively Abraham and Catharine Turner,[4] and to me was given the Christian name of Elijah. How it came about that I afterwards changed my name, will subsequently appear.

My master died when I was quite young, and I therefore became the

---

3. Goings implies that Virginia slaveholders were breeding human beings in the same manner that pastoralists breed livestock. In personal property tax records from the area, enslaved people were listed alongside animals. In 1783, for instance, James N. Walker's personal property list read: "Frank, Ben, Lidy, Doll, Cutty; Clary, Moll, Sam, Jack," five men and four women; the next column claims the owner paid taxes on three horses; the next, twenty-one cattle. Other formerly enslaved authors recalled slave "breeding." Georgia native William H. Heard, for instance, wrote of his childhood in slavery: "A woman who had children regularly was called a 'breeder' in those days; and was allowed to go home at ten o'clock in the morning each day, again at twelve, and at three to nurse the child; for the child was reckoned as 'property,' and therefore valuable enough to be given this time." In his travel account of the antebellum South, Frederick Law Olmstead reprinted correspondence with a slaveholder who reported to him: "In the States of Maryland, Virginia, North Carolina, Kentucky, Tennessee and Missouri, as much attention is paid to the breeding and growth of negroes as to that of horses and mules. Further South, we raise them both for use and for market. Planters command their girls and women (married or unmarried) to have children; and I have known a great many negro girls to be sold off, because they did not have children. A breeding woman is worth from one-sixth to one-fourth more than one that does not breed." Despite anecdotal evidence, slaveholders' schemes to encourage fertility are belied by data on nutrition and family life under slavery, in which pre- and neonatal care is virtually absent for enslaved mothers, and by the fact that the family devastation caused by the domestic slave trade adversely affected enslaved people's social reproduction. See *James City County Personal Property Tax List, 1782–1799;* Heard, *From Slavery to the Bishopric in the A.M.E. Church. An Autobiography,* 21; Olmstead, *A Journey in the Seaboard Slave States,* 55; Richard H. Steckel, "Stature and the Standard of Living"; Coelho and McGuire, "Diets versus Disease"; and Troutman, "Slave Trade and Sentiment," appendix 3, p. 423.

4. James N. Walker claimed to own two enslaved people named "Cathy" and "Cate," in 1784 and 1786, respectively, one of whom may have been Goings's mother, Catharine Turner (county tax records began to omit slaves' names in 1787). Turners were among Goings's James City County neighbors: a John Turner had patented land as early as 1685. Mary Turner and John Turner paid taxes on slaves in 1782, and it was not uncommon for enslaved people to take the surname of owners. The eighteenth-century John Turner's estate was in Walker's neighborhood. See *James City County Personal Property Tax List, 1782–1799;* McCartney, *James City County,* 143; and Blackmon, *James City County, Va. Land Tax Records, 1782–1813,* 299.

property of one Pearson Pricket,[5] who was married to one of my master's daughters. Four other slaves, among whom was my sister Maria, were also devised to Mrs. Pricket. My mother and two brothers became the property of Mary Morris,[6] grand-daughter of my original proprietor. About nine months after Mr. Walker's death, my mistress died, and my master then removed from the farm to a small place on the Richmond road called Burnt Henry,[7] and distant some twelve miles from Williamsburg.[8] Here he kept a

5. Pearson was a member of the Piggott family of James City County and perhaps a descendent of the Pearson Piggott who died in 1782 or 1783. Part of that land and slave owner's estate fell to a John Piggott in 1794, who had paid taxes on one slave in 1782. In 1813, a Hannah Piggott paid taxes on lands adjoining William Bush's lands; Bush was James N. Walker's neighbor. A William Piggott signed the same 1785 petition in support of tax relief as James Walker, indicating he was a fellow freeholder. A Francis Piggott owned Huic and New Design plantations in James City County between 1813 and 1826. The Pearson Piggott to which Goings refers was perhaps a relative of that family, which also included Goings's contemporary, Nathaniel Piggott, a member of the Olive Branch Christian Church and a wealthy farmer in the county. According to the 1820 Census, Nathaniel Piggott owned eight slaves and was active in supporting public schools in the county. See McCartney, *James City County*, 257, 263, 264, 291, 355; 1820 U.S. Census, [place not stated], James City County, Virginia, roll M33-137, p. 112; image 121; Blackmon, *James City County, Va. Land Tax Records, 1782–1813*, 3, 18, 34, 302–3; and *James City County Personal Property Tax List, 1782–1799*.

6. Perhaps a relative of Mary Morris, or Morriss, fl. late eighteenth century, a local landowner who paid taxes on 295 acres of land and three slaves in 1782. See Blackmon, *James City County, Va. Land Tax Records, 1782–1813*, 3; and *James City County Personal Property Tax List, 1782–1799*.

7. Burnt Ordinary, now the town of Toano in James City County, was the county tavern. In April 1781, as they pursued Cornwallis's Army across Virginia's Lower Peninsula to Yorktown, Marie-Joseph Paul Yves Roch Gilbert du Motier, the Marquis de Lafayette, and his men stayed in the Chickahominy Church near an ordinary, or public house, locals later recalled as "Middle Ordinary," a stopover on the stagecoach road between Richmond and Williamsburg. When that ordinary burned during the same campaign, the area became known as Burnt Ordinary, which was the area Goings recalled as "Burnt Henry," the site of a post office by 1839. The town, forty-nine miles north and east of Richmond, was renamed Toano when the Chesapeake & Ohio Railroad was extended into that part of the county in 1883. See McCartney, *James City County*, 221–22; Chapin, *A Complete Reference Gazetteer of the United States of North America*, 46; Fisher, *A New and Complete Statistical Gazetteer of the United States of America . . .*, 89; and "James City County, 350th Anniversary," supplement to *The (Williamsburg) Virginia Gazette*, August 24, 1984, 5, 7, 15.

8. Goings's James City County was majority black and majority enslaved. Traveling about the county, a visitor would encounter two non-white residents for every white one. By 1820, the county was over 53 percent enslaved, and nearly 15 percent of the free population was "colored," a multiethnic mix of people of African, European, and

liquor establishment, and I was deemed capable of acting in the capacity of groom.[9] He was a great sportsman, and indulged in fox and deer hunting. His language was always mixed with excessive profanity. I think I have just cause to complain of his severity. He was more particular about his horses than his negroes; frequently upon his return from a journey at the hour of midnight, I would be compelled to spend nearly the remainder of the night rubbing his dirty and exhausted animal. I was often flogged for my alleged incompetency. Neither would he allow me to see my mother as often as I could have wished; I do not think that I was permitted to visit her on the adjacent farm of Mrs. Morris, more than two or three times during the space of nearly three years.

After the lapse of about a year, my master removed to Halifax, Roanoak River, North Carolina. He had sold all the slaves coming into his possession through his late wife, excepting only myself and sister. On our way to Halifax we stayed a fortnight at Petersburg. Here, a gentleman by the name of Leslie took quite a fancy for me and my sister, and offered the round sum of Eleven Hundred Dollars for us.[10] He said he should make a seamstress of my sister if he could effect the purchase. The offer, however, was indignantly refused. At Halifax, I was placed at a hotel kept by one

---

Native American ancestry. (State totals were 40 percent enslaved and about 3.5 percent free people of color.) Around the time of Goings's birth, some freeholders in the county were also people of African descent, including Elizabeth Allen, a "mulatto" woman who owned sixty acres of above-average farmland; a freedman named Clary, who owned four acres; a freedwoman named Jenny, who owned twenty acres; Mary Jones, sixty acres; a freedman named Mack, manumitted in a will, who owned six acres; and Christopher Robinson, a black man who owned one hundred acres of above-average land. Those several property holders were among a tiny minority of non-white residents who owned property around the time of the War of 1812. See Historical Census Browser, University of Virginia, Geospatial and Statistical Data Center; and Blackmon, *James City County, Va. Land Tax Records, 1782–1813,* 291, 298–99, 301, 304.

9. Goings's owner's decision to make him a groom gave Goings opportunities to travel, network, and even earn money. James City County's economy was overwhelmingly agricultural, so most of Goings's fellow slaves worked the land. Runaway ads do, however, mention enslaved people with skills like carpentry, transportation trades, and cobbling. Also, some slaves were literate. See Overton, "Farming Grew from Fallow to Fruit," 9; and McCartney, *James City County,* 484–88, 485.

10. When would-be owners offered sums of cash for him and his sister, Goings learned from an early age to view himself and other slaves as a saleable commodities. That often compounded the pain of family separation. See Johnson, *Soul by Soul,* 20 and passim.

Daniel Powell,[11] to act in the capacity of a waiter. For the two years that I was thus employed, I did my best to excel, and received much encouragement from the many travellers who visited this lively hostelry. During the Sessions of the Court, the house was crowded with guests, many of whom were lawyers of considerable local eminence; I was delighted to hear them frequently pronounce me one of the smartest of boys. Frequent enquiries would be made as to my name, the name of my owner, the probable chances of buying me, and the money value put upon me by my master.

I remember a lawyer named Hogg, from Talbot, saying that he would give eight hundred dollars for me.[12] He expressed a great desire to see my master when he came to town. I remarked that he generally stopped at some low tavern rather than frequent the company of lawyers and gentlemen at a respectable hotel. This little drive at my master raised a loud laugh at his expense from a large muster of gentlemen in the room. Mr. Hogg had evidently become interested in me, and enquired whether I could read. On my answering in the negative, he wished to know if I had never been sent to school. I replied that I had once attended a school kept by one Bucky Dennis,[13] in James' City, State of Virginia,—that a neighbor's boy named Wil-

11. In 1818 and 1819, two daughters of Daniel Powell of Halifax County married: Elizabeth Powell wed Benjamin Green in 1818, and Martha Powell married Thomas Green in 1819. See Gammon and Murphy, *Marriage Records*, 149, 150.

12. A Peter Hogg witnessed a will of William Burt of Halifax County, North Carolina, in 1804. Estate records of that county list members of a Hogg family who owned slaves, and a Martha Hogg was enrolled in county public school in 1843. The Hogg family had owned property in the town and county of Halifax since at least the 1760s. See Hofmann, *Genealogical Abstracts of Wills, 1758 through 1824, Halifax County, North Carolina*, 132; Gammon, *Records of Estates, Halifax County, North Carolina*, 41; Bradley, *Halifax County, North Carolina, Voters and Scholars, 1839–1862*, 14; Bradley, *The Deeds of Halifax County, North Carolina, 1758–1771*, 59; and Gammon, *Halifax County, North Carolina, Tax Lists*, 1:5, 59, 71.

13. Bucky Dennis could be a descendent of Matthew Dennis (d. after 1813) of James City County, Virginia, or of William M. Dennis, whose estates bordered each other. William Dennis's plantation adjoined the plantations of James N. Walker and William Bush in 1813. In 1820, William M. Dennis headed a household that included nineteen free people and held eighteen people in slavery. By 1823, nine primary schools were open in James City County, each enrolling twenty-five or so students, including about half from poor families. Henley Taylor, to whom James N. Walker sold much of his land, served as a commissioner, and Nathaniel Piggott compiled the schools' statistics. See 1820 U.S. Census, [place not stated], James City County, Virginia, roll: M33-137, p. 116, image 125; McCartney, *James City County*, 514; and Blackmon, *James City County, Va. Land Tax Records, 1782–1813*, 291, 294.

liam Bush[14] gave me a spelling book and endeavoured to make me believe that I was to be taught to read and write. I told the school master that I should be glad of his assistance as I had been put in possession of a spelling book.[15] I sat, however, a full forenoon without receiving any aid from the teacher. I therefore said to myself, if this is the way I am to get my education I may as well keep away from school altogether. This narrative of my educational experience raised another loud laugh from the assembled company. It is not safe for a slave to let it be known that he can read, when he is so far educated. It is for the interest of the slave-holding system, that the slave be free from education. Slaves learn by stealth. The interview closed with a renewal of the offer before mentioned, with the message to my master that Mr. Hogg desired to see him concerning the business. As soon as I saw my master I told him what Mr. Hogg had said and the offer he had made. He at once indignantly swore that no man should get me out of his hands for less than a thousand dollars. Just about this time my sister was levied upon in satisfaction of Graves, from Virginia.[16] She was learning to

14. That was perhaps William Bush (1801–1862), grandson of William Bush (d. 1810 or 1811). James N. Walker transferred five acres of land to the elder Bush in 1789 or 1790. That William Bush paid taxes on seven slaves, one horse, and sixteen cattle in 1782, and named six slaves on whom he paid taxes in 1784. He left a 484-acre estate that adjoined those of James N. Walker and William M. Dennis. The younger Bush bought "Windsor Castle" in 1840, which had been built between 1750 and 1775 and is on the National Register of Historic Places. It was located about three miles west of Burnt Ordinary. In 1860, a seven-year-old Willy Bush lived in the William Bush household, indicating that the family named successive generations of sons "William." See McCartney, *James City County*, 293; 1860 U.S. Census, [place not stated], James City County, Virginia, roll M653-1355, p. 687, image 34; 1860 U.S. Census, Slave Schedule, James City County, Virginia, images 1–2 of 23; Blackmon, *James City County, Va. Land Tax Records, 1782–1813*, 75, 245, 291; *James City County Personal Property Tax List, 1782–1799;* and National Register of Historic Places—Nomination Form for "Windsor Castle," Toano, Virginia, 1987.

15. An enslaved student acquiring a spelling book was unusual but important, since spellers held the keys to learning to read. Goings's near contemporary Frederick Douglass credited his acquisition of literacy with awaking in him a desire to escape slavery, which in turn was made possible by his procuring a school primer on oratory and a copy of *Webster's Spelling Book*. Goings's free neighbors did not apparently see his education as potentially subversive, and widespread fears of slave literacy did not take hold until after the distribution of David Walker's *Appeal* in 1830 (see the introduction to the present volume).

16. As moveable property, enslaved people were subject to being mortgaged. That was a widespread practice in colonial Virginia. See Martin, "'To Have and To Hold' Human Collateral."

be a seamstress under the care of Mrs Powell, who had become exceedingly attached to her.[17] A friend of Mrs. Powell's named McPherson, offered four hundred and fifty dollars to the trader, who, at the sale had given four hundred dollars.[18] He treated the offer with contempt, saying he had bought my sister for the South Carolina market and could realize at least six or seven hundred dollars for his recent purchase.[19] Mrs. Powell had hoped to raise the money for the purchase of my sister at the Sheriff's sale, but in this she had failed and was much distressed at losing her services. The trader remarked, that he would give 700 dollars for me as we seemed to be attached to each other, but as the sale of my sister had satisfied the claim I was not brought to the hammer. Our parting I need not say, was a bitter one. My mother had also begged of Mr. Picket that as we were so much attached to each other he would sell us together. The feelings or desires of the slave, however, are of little account to his merciless owner. Even where humanity would sometimes yield, the stern necessities of bankruptcy forbid its beneficent exercise.

During my stay at Halifax I was the object of keen competition. A lawyer named Drew took a great fancy to me and offered five hundred dollars in good notes and three hundred in cash, but his offer was refused.[20] This was three hundred dollars above the average price of boys of my age, but my master evidently appreciated his property, and determined that it should bring the highest market price. A competitor of Mr. Drew's was a

17. The Powell family of Halifax County, North Carolina, had owned land and slaves since at least the 1780s. See Hofmann, *Genealogical Abstracts of Wills, 1758 through 1824, Halifax County, North Carolina,* 180, 155, 147 (1st Mary Powell); 1820 U.S. Census, Halifax, Halifax County, North Carolina, roll M33-85, p. 159, image 140; Gammon, *Records of Estates, Halifax County, North Carolina,* 73; and Gammon, *Halifax County, North Carolina, Tax Lists,* 1:54.

18. John McPherson of Halifax County died around 1822. See Gammon, *Records of Estates, Halifax County, North Carolina,* 59.

19. Market price was primary to considerations of family when owners decided to sell slaves. See Tadman, *Speculators and Slaves,* chap. 6.

20. William Drew of Halifax County served as a witness to wills between 1797 and 1817, and gave testimony, or "proved," wills in the county between 1822 and 1824, indicating that he may have been a lawyer. In 1810, he was between twenty-six and forty-four years old. The Drew family owned land and slaves in the county since at least the 1780s. See Hofmann, *Genealogical Abstracts of Wills, 1758 through 1824, Halifax County, North Carolina,* 106, 157, 176, 184 [W. Drew], 148 [S. Drew]; 1810 U.S. Census, [place not stated], Halifax County, North Carolina, roll 38, p. 103 image 123.00 [W. Drew]; Gammon, *Records of Estates, Halifax County, North Carolina,* 24; and Gammon, *Halifax County, North Carolina, Tax Lists,* 1:7.

Mr. Burgess, who offered a thousand dollars, but how much of this was upon cash terms, I was never able to ascertain.[21] I greatly desired to fall into the hands of this gentleman as he was not only a kind master, but it was said he never kept a slave after he or she had attained the age of twenty-one. My master, however, determined that he would not sell me to Mr. Burgess, whom he denounced as too much of a tory and abolitionist.[22] This was a great blow to me as I had become aware of the advantages of getting into the service of such a man.

My master had knowledge of a mechanical business. He was an excellent gunsmith. He was, however, far too proud to work, and thus became involved in debt. My sister became converted into money, and it now became my turn to be seized by the Sheriff. I was negotiated as security for a lone of five hundred dollars to a Mr. Hives, of Halifax, North Carolina, who took me at once into his possession. Mr. Hives had authority to sell me for a sum not less than five hundred dollars. A Mr. Henry Smith took quite a liking to me in behalf of his brother Joseph,[23] then in New Jersey, and prevailed on Hives to keep me until his return. David Mason, a brother-in-law of the Smiths, also expressed a desire to get me.[24] One day he came over and asked me if I should like to go and live with him. Having heard that he was a severe master, I replied in the negative. He observed that he was one of those independent men who never bought a servant that did not wish to live with him. In about four months, Joseph Smith arrived home, and accompanied by his brother Henry, and his brother-in-

---

21. Lawyer Thomas Burgess of Halifax County owned ten slaves in 1820. He acted as executor of county wills in the 1810s and 1820s. See 1820 U.S. Census, Halifax, Halifax County, North Carolina, roll M33-85, p. 140, image 121; Gammon, *Records of Estates, Halifax County, North Carolina*, 13; Hofmann, *Genealogical Abstracts of Wills, 1758 through 1824, Halifax County, North Carolina*, 160, 161, 164, 173; and Gammon, *Halifax County, North Carolina, Tax Lists*, 1:22, 24.

22. Slaveholders were not immune from charges of being abolitionists, and such a charge was among the worst insults. After calling Richmond editor John H. Pleasants an "abolitionist" and a "rank coward" in 1846, rival Richmond editor Thomas Ritchie Jr. fought a duel with Pleasants, fatally wounding him. See Grimsted, *American Mobbing, 1828–1861*, 89.

23. Joseph Lawrence Dawson Smith (December 24, 1797–October 26, 1837), who married Mary Hannah (1802, Ireland–October 18, 1843) on May 14, 1823, had a daughter, Jane Smith (b. August 15, 1830). See *Lauderdale County Marriage Book*, 3:141 (microfilm), ADAH.

24. David Mason witnessed the marriage bond of Rebecca J. Smith and Robert Williams on February 14, 1815. See Neal, *Abstracts of Vital Records from Raleigh, North Carolina, Newspapers*, vol. 1, *1799–1819*, 541.

law Daniel Mason, came over the river to look at me.[25] Mr. Joseph Smith enquired of me whether I should like to go and reside with him, I promptly answered that I should not. The fact was, my great desire had been to be purchased by Mr. Burgess, but of course I did not allege this as my reason for expressing myself unfavorably towards Mr. Smith's service. He then tried coaxing, and patting me on the head said: "My boy, I would like to buy you, you are just the lad to suit me. For what reason do you refuse to consent?" I then told him that I should like Mr. Burgess to buy me because that gentleman would give me chances to go and see my mother in Virginia where I came from. He replied: "If that is all, I will buy you and give you opportunities to visit your mother. I travel a great deal in various parts of the country, and you will be able to see her very often." The bargain was therefore soon concluded. He paid Mr. Hives $500, and took me to his mother's residence. It was agreed between them that I should be called Elijah Smith. It is customary to give the slave the surname of his master and in many cases both names, where but one slave is kept. The old lady seemed pleased with me, and gave me a good dinner, informing me that I should always take my meals in the house.*

My master then showed me to his stables in which were two very fine horses. He told me that I must feed and clean these animals, keeping them as sleek as butterflies. One of the animals, a fine black horse, he said, he gave me, the other was used by himself as a "sulky" horse. A few days afterwards he brought me home a new suit of clothes.[26]

On one occasion my master took a trip to Raleigh the capital of North Carolina where his sister Mrs. Williams resided.[27] We stayed there, I should think, some six months. My master instructed Mrs. Williams to keep me well employed when I was not attending to the horses, and most faithfully she followed her instructions. She would keep me rubbing furniture till nine or ten o'clock at night. The servants were all treated with much sever-

25. "Colonel" Daniel Mason (b. 1776) of Northampton County, North Carolina, married Dorothy Laurence Jane Smith on April 19, 1808, his second marriage. Dorothy was the daughter of Jane Smith and Colonel Lawrence Smith (d. 1812).

*Slaves usually have their own small houses made of boards or logs, to live in, separate and apart from the main dwelling in a farm or plantation. —*Author's note*

26. A new suit of clothes often marked a passage in an enslaved person's life, either the beginning or end of a year-long labor contract or a change in position.

27. Rebecca J. Williams (née Smith) married Robert Williams in Northampton County, North Carolina, in February 1815, reported the *Raleigh (N.C.) Register.* She was the daughter of the late Colonel Laurence Smith.

ity. The cook, of course a slave, was almost a daily victim to severe floggings. Many a time I have heard him express the wish that the Lord would take him out of the world, for death would be a relief from such unmitigated cruelty. A woman they called Nancy was said to be half sister to Mrs. Williams, an illegitimate daughter of her father's, and consequently treated with considerable leniency.[28] I came very near getting a severe whipping myself as a penalty for a somewhat mischievous freak. Much of my leisure time was spent collecting withered leaves in a wheelbarrow from a handsome grove adjoining the house. One day when I was not in the best of humors, I drove my loaded wheelbarrow in among the horses, which being frightened, kicked it sadly to pieces, but I managed with hammer and nails to patch it up as well as I was able. Next morning, however, Robt. Williams sent his servant, to use the barrow in fetching a barrel of flour, but alas! the damage was of too serious a nature and I was summarily charged with being the author of the misfortune.[29] The trick was told to my master and he told General Williams to take me into the garden and whip me to his heart's content. Next morning he took me into the garden, and threatened to skin me alive for the next offence, taking care to tell me that my master had given him full permission to flog me to his own satisfaction. It was a narrow escape, and I took care to avoid a second offence. Raleigh is a very beautiful place—It is situated on high ground, the capital overlooking the town from a very lofty eminence. The streets are wide, and there are many substantial buildings, not the least of which is a handsome residence for the Governor of the State.

I was glad, however, when we turned our backs upon the town for I was subject to all the severity exercised by General Williams to his own slaves. Even on Sundays, I was deprived of the liberties usually accorded to family servants. There always seemed great manifestations of affection between

28. Offspring of enslaved women and white men were common, although, like Nancy, most were not recognized as heirs.

29. Lawyer and Adjutant General Robert Williams of the North Carolina militia was appointed judge of the Superior Courts of Law and Courts of Equity in 1808; he married Rebecca J. Smith in 1815, was named Clerk of the North Carolina Senate in 1816, and died of a heart condition in Knoxville, Tennessee, in 1821. See the *Raleigh (N.C.) Star* for December 15, 1808 (p. 27), and for December 6, 1816 (p. 3); Neal, *Abstracts of Vital Records from Raleigh, North Carolina, Newspapers*, vol. 2, *1820–1829*, 759; Powell, *Dictionary of North Carolina Biography*, vol. 6, *T–Z*, 213; and Boylan and Boylan, "A roster of the names and dates of commissions of the several major-generals, in command of the Militia of North-Carolina, as enrolled on the first of January, A.D. 1813."

these parties. The old lady, Mrs. Smith, perfectly doted on her youngest son Joseph and this unequivocal expression of maternal love could not but make me sad when I thought of the unfulfilled promises with regard to myself, which seemed to have been forgotten by my master as soon as I had become his property. The matron spoke to me very kindly, shaking me by the hand as if I had been something more than a saleable chattel. They had but two sons Henry and Joseph, the former had added to his estate by marriage and was the possessor of one hundred and fifty slaves. His farm was close to Harper's Ferry and was subsequently sold by him, it was said, for the sum of thirty thousand dollars.[30] Situated upon the Roanoak river, it was a splendid place for carrying on fishing to a very heavy extent. At this point the river was shallow and the bed rocky. During the month of August the slaves would frequently be put to fishing with nets. Rock fish were as fine in size as they were abundant in quantity. I have seen some specimens weighing from sixty to seventy pounds.[31] Shadd were also found below what was called the Muscle shoal, as also Sturgeon in large quantities.[32] For these facilities combined with unusual agricultural productiveness, the farm of Mr. Henry Smith in North Carolina, had a notoriety rarely surpassed in the Southern States.[33]

30. Daniel and his wife Dorothy moved from Northampton County, North Carolina, to Humphreys County, Tennessee, in about 1820. Goings here mistakes Harper's Ferry for another ferry on the Roanoke River.

31. Rockfish, or striped bass *(Roccus lineatus)*, were and are plentiful on the Roanoke River, and spring fishing on the rapids west of Weldon, North Carolina, supplemented the diets of local populations of Native Americans before European settlers began to harvest the fish. It was not uncommon to find fish weighing sixty to seventy-five pounds, and on occasion, fish exceeding a hundred pounds were caught in North Carolina waters. They are plentiful throughout the year, but are caught primarily in late April and early May when they run upriver to spawn. See Hairr, *North Carolina Rivers*, 38–40; and Smith, *The Fishes of North Carolina*, 2:271–72.

32. Shad, or white shad *(Alosa spadissima)*, are a silvery fish, three to five pounds on average, and are found on the rivers emptying into North Carolina's Albemarle and Pamlico Sounds. Runs are plentiful in May when the fish return from the ocean to spawn upriver. Sturgeon, or sharp-nosed sturgeon *(Acipenser oxyrhynchus)*, averaged about five feet in length, but could be twelve feet long and exceed five hundred pounds. These bottom-feeders were plentiful on the Roanoke River, where they began to run as early as February. Adults typically appeared in April, after the main run of shad. See Smith, *The Fishes of North Carolina*, 2:55–57, 125–26.

33. An 1816 will filed in Halifax, North Carolina, mentions Henry Smith's property as being adjacent to the estate of the late Daniel Weldon (of the family who founded Weldon, North Carolina), to the lands of William Eaton, and to the Halifax Road. See

It will thus readily be perceived that the Smiths were influential people in their immediate neighborhood. They were a more energetic money
seeking race of men than the ordinary planters of the south. The most efficient means were adopted to render their property productive. They could
not content themselves in the easygoing slip shod style of many of their
neighbors. They fed and clothed their slaves well from motives of sound
policy. The slaves might attend Church on Sundays, and except during the
busy seasons, a week's work was completed on Saturday at noon. Public
sentiment in this part of the country was not in favor of undue cruelty.
Severe floggings were of rare occurrence.

The "Western fever" is sometimes, however, as likely to show itself in
the South as in the North. The Smiths were not the kind of men to rest satisfied with doing well if they could see a reasonable hope of doing better by
migration. Daniel Mason, who had married, one of the Misses Smith, was
a strong advocate for going West.[34] He succeeded in inducing Henry and
Joseph Smith, together with William Dancey,[35] who had married Mason's

---

Hofmann, *Genealogical Abstracts of Wills, 1758 through 1824, Halifax County, North
Carolina*, 160.

34. Daniel Mason's plantations expanded rapidly. In December 1819, he bought a
440-acre property on the north bank of the Tennessee River in Humphreys County, Tennessee, for $3,520. That lot bordered Mason's existing property, to which he then added
a 220-acre property in Humphreys County, Tennessee, in January 1820, for $1,100. For
$500, Mason also bought two parcels totaling 170 acres in March 1820, which were also
on the bank of the Tennessee River. Daniel and Dorothy L. J. Mason sold Joseph L. D.
Smith, then in Lauderdale County, Alabama, their 900-acre farm in Northampton
County, North Carolina, for $15,000 in July 1822. In 1826, Mason received an enslaved
woman named Marion and her children Chancy, Peter, and Nathan as surety for a debt.
By 1828, Mason was in the land business as "Daniel Mason & Co."; in that year, he
bought nearly 90 more acres on the Tennessee and collected debts owed to his company
by other landowners. In 1830, Mason bought more land, this time bordering the mouth
of Bear Creek on the east bank of the Tennessee River, and another parcel adjoining his
riverfront lands. In 1830, census takers counted thirty-seven slaves belonging to him in
Humphreys County, Tennessee. See Hutchings, *Humphreys County, TN Deeds, Books
A–D, July, 1810–June 1832*, 1:42 (second quote), 43, 47 (first quote), 60, 88, 94 (third
quote), 100, 103, 107–8; and 1830 U.S. Census, [place not stated], Humphreys County,
Tennessee, roll 176, p. 306A–B, image 15–16.

35. William E. Dancey was a Justice of the Peace for Lauderdale County, Alabama,
from the late 1820s through at least the mid-1830s. He bought nearly 235 acres of land
near Florence, Alabama, in January 1830. He witnessed a transfer of land to Jones Glover
for his service in the Continental Army; Mason was the warranting party. Dancey solemnized a marriage in 1835, and perhaps others. See Garrett, *A History of Humphreys
County, Tennessee*, 83; Whitley, *Tennessee Genealogical Abstracts*, 34; Cowart, *Old Land*

sister, to accompany him to Tennessee. The journey was a formidable one, as the distance to be travelled was, I believe, a thousand miles, and the railway had not yet been built upon the route.[36] There were about 460 slaves including old and young; it therefore required a very considerable caravan to move so large a body of people and to provide provision and tent equipage for the journey.[37] The worst feature of this species of migration arises from its being an involuntary act on the part of the slaves, who were the large body of the emigrants. It involves not merely the dissolution of life long friendship, but it severs the most sacred ties of domestic relationship. Not only is the child separated from the parent, but not unfrequently the husband is separated from the wife. This is one of many of the dark sides of the picture which cannot be treated with too much severity. To the slave, the marriage service is little more than a farce. The husband, the property of one person, and the wife, the property of another, what security is there that the marital relation shall be upheld until death severs the relationship? A bankruptcy, a death, or a removal, may produce a score or two of involuntary divorces. Surely the present age hath not this parallel of cruelty? There was quite a scene at this unusually large parting. The number of persons present must have been a thousand. Some of the slave-holders themselves who were looking on, could hardly refrain from tears. As only some twelve miles were accomplished, the first afternoon, many, contrary to orders, returned during the night to accomplish one more short interview with those to be for ever left behind. There were some twenty white men in the travelling company, and the most expert and responsible of the colored men were appointed to overlook the welfare of the rest. Apple brandy was freely distributed, and every means adopted to make the journey agreeable and to drown in forgetfulness the friends and kindred left behind. We halted some three or four days at Nashville to take in a full supply of winter clothing and provisions. From this place, we had

---

Records of Lauderdale County, Alabama, 166, 199; Campbell et al., *Lauderdale County, Alabama*, vi; and Jones and Gandrud, *Alabama Records*, vol. 217, *Lauderdale County* (microfilm), reel 7: 67, 70, ADAH.

36. The distance was about seven hundred miles, yet walking overland over crude or non-existent roads it could easily seem like a journey of a thousand miles.

37. That coffle of 460 enslaved people was part of a great forced migration from the older Upper South to the new lands of the Lower South. Between 1820 and 1829, some 155,000 enslaved people crossed state lines, part of a total of 1.1 million enslaved forced migrants who crossed state lines between the framing of the Constitution and the onset of the Civil War. See the introduction in Johnson, *Soul by Soul*.

to travel about one hundred and ten miles through a sparsely settled and most dismal country. After passing a mill some one hundred and ten miles from Nashville, we travelled some thirty miles not seeing more than two or three houses within that distance, Charlottesville[38] was the last and only village on our route after leaving Nashville, from which, for a distance of some seventy miles, we frequently had to "blaze" a road through the forest. The new settlement was in a heavily timbered and hilly section of country. The cabins were built of logs on the edge of a mountain. This mountain extended a mile and a quarter in length. Those who have experienced the hardships of pioneer life in Canada, can form some conception of the courage and endurance essential to keep up the spirits of the emigrant. But in this instance must be added, the enervating effects of a harder climate and a greater frequency of unhealthy swamps. Besides this, the poor slave has not the hope which cheers toiling Anglo-Saxon emigrants, the hope of early independence. Beyond the reach of old established laws and a partial human public opinion, the backwoodsman relying upon slave labor, too frequently takes advantage of his isolated position. The difference in this case was at once perceptible. The only rule established with regard to labor seemed to be to extract it to the fullest possible amount, destroying or seriously impairing the life of the slave. The women would frequently be put to grubbing and ploughing under task work, according to their strength. Work commenced at daylight, lasting until night, with only a short intermission for a meal at noon, denominated "breakfast." The manager named Howell Edmonds was decidedly a model overseer.[39] He wished himself to be known, to the slaves by the name of "Damnation," his horse he call "Thunder," and his dog "Thunderbolt." The end of the heavy raw-hide that he carried was loaded with lead. His will was law. His only arbitrator,— brute force. Mr. Mason and himself would breakfast together by candle light in order to see all the slaves at work at the earliest hour of dawn.

38. Charlotte, Tennessee, was the Dixon County seat; it was established in 1804 and named after Charlotte Reeves Robertson, wife of pioneer James Robertson, who—like Mason and the Smiths—arrived in search of profitable farm land. Goings notes that the coffle traveled about 180 miles from Nashville on their trip and that "Charlottesville" was the last village. That was 180 miles in a westerly direction, close to the present western border of Tennessee. Goings later passed through Charlotte during his escape in 1839. See Miller, *Tennessee Place Names*, 43.

39. Howell Edmunds witnessed the deed for the purchase of Daniel Mason's 220-acre property in 1820. See Hutchings, *Humphreys County, TN Deeds, Books A–D, July, 1810–June 1832*, 1:42.

At first sight Edmonds might have been taken for an easy good natured man, but continued connexion with the cruel system seemed to have corrupted and destroyed every seniment of humanity. The first time I heard the doleful effects of flogging, was under direction of this heartless brute. I was not within four hundred yards of the scene of cruelty, yet I still seem to hear the agonizing "Oh ! pray, sir," of the helpless victim, as if the act occurred but yesterday. It was an occasion that set me thinking of what might happen to myself, and I silently nurtured the stern resolution to escape so soon as my plans could be prudently and effectually matured.

By the stern system thus pursued, it would be imagined that many slaves must die from exhaustion. There seemed to be, however, a safe margin preserved, as the deaths were considerably below the average of a newly settled country. As a general rule the bulk of the slaves were healthy. Within a year and a half they had cleared up a farm some two miles in length by one and a half in breadth. They had also fenced the same with a heavy rail fence fifteen rails high. Those who had acquired knowledge of a mechanical business, had put up the houses and buildings.[40]

A foundation had thus been laid for a prosperous and wealthy colony, but the wandering propensities of my master were never satiated. He determined to make an exploring expidition to Alabama.[41] His restlessness of character exceeded even the national propensity to change, which so pre-eminently distinguishes the American people. There were all the outward signs of success in the Tennessee investment, but for reasons probably satisfactory to himself he prepared to migrate. Howell Edmonds was

40. Southerners on the cotton frontier divided lands up on grids, and compelled slaves to make the land conform to property boundaries rather than natural ones. Cotton fieldworkers labored in gangs, with slaves working and foremen and white overseers superintending. Goings recalled that enslaved women were given tasks, such as "grubbing" (digging up root vegetables or roots and stumps), which varied according to their strength and abilities and which were overseen by enslaved men. Although he reports that the slaves with whom he traveled from North Carolina to Tennessee and Alabama were generally healthy compared to new arrivals on the frontier, sicknesses he associated with moisture, including debilitating diseases such as hookworm, affected workers at picking time. See Coelho and McGuire, "Biology, Diseases, and Economics."

41. Slaveholders rushed into the territory that would become Alabama and Mississippi before they became states in 1819 and 1817, respectively. Smith bought lands in Alabama beginning in 1818. To an interviewer in 1855, Goings mentioned that he had firsthand knowledge of "two plantations" in Alabama, staffed by "one hundred and fifty, and one hundred and thirty" slaves, respectively. See Drew, *A North-Side View of Slavery*, 138.

displaced from his position as overseer, in order that he might accompany my master in search of a new place of settlement. I also was of the party in the capacity of groom. I remember that our first night was spent at the house of a Mrs. Doolands,[42] whose daughter subsequently married a Mr. Fulton.[43] This gentleman became somewhat notorious afterwards in the South as the appointed Governor of Arkansas Territory, under the administration, of President Andrew Jackson.

For about fifty miles we travelled upon the old military road laid out by General Jackson during the war of 1812.[44] Our journey, a distance of 230 miles was accomplished on horseback. The country through which we passed was tolerably well settled. In about a week we reached our destination,—the Village of Florence, Lauderdale County, Alabama.[45] It was then, but a small village, but I have been informed has since become

42. Rebecca Nowland (ca. 1768–1833) was the mother of Matilda Frances Nowland, who married William Savin Fulton in 1823. R. Nowland died on the steamboat *Little Rock* on the Arkansas River. See Lucas, *Obituaries from Early Tennessee Newspapers, 1794–1851*, 276.

43. William Savin Fulton (1795–1844), of Maryland, served as Andrew Jackson's personal secretary during the 1818 Seminole War in Florida. He moved to Tennessee in 1820, and then to Florence, Alabama, where he edited a Democratic newspaper and served as judge of the Lauderdale County Court. In 1829, President Jackson appointed him secretary to the Arkansas Territory, where he also served as governor in the absence of John Pope and installed family members in political posts. The "notorious" behavior of which Goings writes was Fulton's controversial opposition to Arkansas statehood after Jackson appointed him territorial governor in 1835. For his loyalty, Jackson, despite intense criticism, appointed Fulton to serve as the U.S. senator from Tennessee in 1836, a post which Fulton occupied until his death eight years later. See Baker, "Fulton, William Savin"; and Campbell et al., *Lauderdale County, Alabama*, vi.

44. "Jackson's Military Road" was a federal internal improvement project funded in 1816, begun in 1817, and completed in 1820. It linked Columbia, Tennessee, to Madisonville, Louisiana, via Columbus, Mississippi, and was constructed by the Army Engineers under Major General Andrew Jackson. It was built to facilitate rapid transportation from eastern Tennessee, down through northern Alabama and eastern Mississippi, and on to eastern Louisiana and the Gulf of Mexico. See Bauer, *Zachary Taylor*, 35–36; and Nelson, "Military Roads for War and Peace, 1791–1836."

45. Located in the northwestern corner of Alabama on the banks of the Tennessee, Florence was named after the flourishing capital of Tuscany on the Arno River, a center of Italian commerce and culture. Florence, Alabama, was laid out on a grid according to land plats drawn up by the U.S. Land Office. The English traveler Anne Royall visited in 1821 and recorded that Florence was "one of the new towns of this beautiful and rapid rising state. It is happily situated for commerce at the head of steamboat navigation, on the north side of Tennessee river, in the country of Lauderdale, five miles below the port of the Muscle Shoals, and ten miles from the line of the state of Tennessee." Echoing Smith's expectations, Royall wrote, "Florence is to be the great emporium of the north-

a flourishing city. We stayed in it about six weeks. During the time of this visit, my master spent a good deal of time at the residence of James Jackson, Esq., an Irish gentleman, who was a large dealer in lands, and at that time held about forty slaves.[46] His residence was at the Forks of Cypress.[47] This is a beautiful ridge between two streams, and nature has made it one of the most beautiful places I have seen.

From this place, I accompanied my master on a trip to Georgia. Our destination was Milledgeville the capital of that state.[48] Through this

---

ern part of this state. . . . It has a great capital and is patronized by the wealthiest gentlemen in the state." Smith bought lands surrounding Florence and also built a fine house for himself and his wife in town. "Florence is inhabited by people from almost all parts of Europe and the United States," Royall wrote. "Here are English, Irish, Welch, Scotch, French, Dutch, Germans, and *Grecians*." As Royall's description suggests, immigrants from across the Atlantic arrived to stake their claims alongside transplanted Southerners. See Royall, *Letters from Alabama on Various subjects*, 144–46; and Howe, *What Hath God Wrought*, 352–55.

46. James Jackson (1782–1840) was a native of Monoghan, Ireland, and moved to Alabama from Nashville, Tennessee. He formed the Cypress Land Company in partnership with several other investors, which company bought up 5,515 acres of land on the north of the Tennessee River for over $85,000 in 1818 and sold them off in parcels. After the Panic of 1819, the Cypress Land Company could not collect its debts, though it was helped by congressional action to ease the financial burden of buyers who bought land on credit. With his partner John Coffee, Jackson is also credited with importing "Carter's Improved Gin" into the Tennessee Valley between 1822 and 1824. Carter's cotton gin did not tear the cotton fibers while removing the seeds. Coffee moved the federal land office from Huntsville to Florence in 1821. After the panic, in the period 1820–22, Jackson patented more lands, including islands in the Tennessee River. James Madison and Andrew Jackson were stockholders in the Cypress Land Company. Madison owned thousands of acres by 1827; Jackson at least six hundred. See Abernethy, *The Formative Period in Alabama, 1815-1828*, 81; Cowart, *Old Land Records of Lauderdale County, Alabama*, 49, 51, 124, 129, 171, 172, 197, 201, 202, 213, 251, 252, 254–60, 262, 265, 296, 299, 300, 306, 307, 333, 334, 356; and Jill K. Garrett, *A History of Florence, Alabama*, 4–7.

47. Forks of Cypress plantation was built in 1820 on some three thousand acres of land. Its house was in Greek Revival style, and James Jackson was later buried in the adjacent cemetery. His widow, Sarah Moore Jackson, lived through the Civil War, at which time the invading Union army occupied the plantation house. It survived occupation, but burned in 1966.

48. Named after Georgia governor John Milledge (1757–1818) and located just west of the Oconee River, Milledgeville was founded in 1804 as the Georgia state capital, and continued to be so until 1868. It is the Baldwin County seat, and after 1815 it became a commercial center, as the cotton economy of the state took off. When Goings visited in the early 1820s, the landscape of Baldwin County reflected the plantation regime that took over the lands ceded by the Muscogee-Creek Indians in the 1802 Treaty of Fort Wilkinson. In 1820, Baldwin County was majority black and majority slave, with enslaved people making up nearly 55 percent of a population of over 7,700; by 1830, over

country there were many settlements of Cherokee Indians.[49] We found them peaceable and most of them occupied good farms tilled by slaves.[50] I should think, from all I saw, that they were much better masters than the white people, as the colored people seemed more contented than any I had ever seen. At one of our stopping places a Mrs. Wolfe who was half Indian, treated us well, but I could not fail observing that my master was a little suspicious, and would have preferred staying with a person of his own

62 percent of the population was enslaved. See Wilson, "Milledgeville"; and Historical Census Browser, University of Virginia, Geospatial and Statistical Data Center.

49. By the early 1820s when Goings witnessed events, the Cherokees of northern Georgia, southwest North Carolina, southeast Tennessee, and northeast Alabama were being deluged by men like Smith, hungry for their land. The State of Georgia had implemented an aggressive policy of expropriation of Cherokee owners. The Cherokees responded in 1827 by establishing their own constitutional government and demanding that the United States recognize them as a sovereign nation. Georgia answered by seizing the Cherokees' lands, dismantling their courts, and outlawing their government. In 1830, the U.S. government aided that policy by passing the Indian Removal Act, which gave President Jackson, an enthusiastic supporter of Removal, the power to negotiate Removal treaties. The Cherokee nation sued, and in 1831, in *Cherokee Nation v. Georgia,* the tribe lost its argument, that the United States government should nullify Georgia state law subverting Cherokee sovereignty, in the U.S. Supreme Court. A year later, in *Worcester v. Georgia,* the U.S. Supreme Court held that the Cherokee Nation was a sovereign entity in legal possession of its own territories, and that Georgia laws to the contrary were illegitimate. Georgia and President Jackson refused to comply, and by 1835, one Cherokee faction agreed to move. Three years later, the U.S. army invaded Cherokee territory, rounded up most of the population that had refused to vacate their lands, and forcibly marched them to present-day Oklahoma, along what has been called the Trail of Tears. See Garrison, "Worcester v. Georgia"; and Perdue and Green, *The Cherokee Nation and the Trail of Tears.*

50. A small minority of Cherokees, men and women, adopted Anglo-American labor practices and enslaved Africans and African Americans. Some were small slaveholders, but others followed the custom of white grandees and deployed large gangs of slaves to work plantations. By 1809, the Cherokee Nation numbered 12,395 members, who held 583 slaves; by 1810, the state of Georgia contained many times that number of African American slaves, some 105,218. That was before large-scale white incursion into Cherokee territory (341 whites resided in Cherokee territory in 1809). By 1820, Georgia had a slave population of 149,656, or nearly 44 percent of a total population of 340,989. Racial boundaries were less pronounced on the contested borderlands between white Georgia and the Cherokee Nation, since many slaves and slaveholders could count Cherokees among their ancestors. Cherokee slavery was less a permanent intergenerational status than a condition that could be improved through adoption into a lineage, but social flexibility worked in another way as well, since some Cherokees avoided forcible removal by adopting Anglo-American culture, accepting American "civilizing efforts," pledging allegiance to the United States, and creating a plantation system within the Cherokee Nation itself. See Miles, *Ties That Bind,* 36–43; Perdue, "Cherokee Planters"; and Historical Census Browser, University of Virginia, Geospatial and Statistical Data Center.

blood. There were some thirty slaves about the house, and I spent a very pleasant evening with them. I was brought out to dance, and my master accepted an invitation to witness our enjoyment. He seemed more at home with the colored merrymakers, than he did with the Indian proprietor of our temporary stopping place.

We stayed some three months at Milledgeville; here my master visited several of his relatives living in the vicinity.[51] One of the houses frequently visited by my master, was a Mr. Hunt's,[52] who kept a large plantation, occupied by a large number of healthy and contented slaves. This gentleman had a good reputation among all his people; he had but one child, a daughter of whom Mr. Smith was evidently in search. Unfortunately this handsome and intelligent girl had already given her hand and heart to some one else, and he became the victim of disapointed love. During this time my master visited at the houses respectively of Abner Jerdan,[53] Benjamin Jerdan,[54] and Hezekiah Jerdan,[55] all wealthy planters and owning a large number of slaves. The two first mentioned were bachelors, but lived in

51. Henry Smith married Mary Jordan of Greensville County, Virginia, on July 26, 1820, which tied Joseph L. D. Smith into the Jordan families originally of Greensville County, Virginia. See Vogt and Kethley, *Greensville County Marriages, 1781–1853*, 114; and Knorr, *Marriages of Greensville County, Virginia, 1781–1825*, 66.

52. Perhaps members of the Hunt family that included property owners Henry, John, and Turner Hunt of the Monticello area of Georgia. John Hunt lived in Jasper County, and Turner Hunt was a commissioner of Monroe County in 1823. See Hartz and Hartz, *Genealogical Abstracts from the Georgia Journal (Milledgeville) Newspaper*, vol. 2, *1819–1823*, 288, 540, 564, 568, 745, 763, 787, 797, 856, 867, 959, 987; and Evans, *Milledgeville, Georgia, Newspaper Clippings (Southern Recorder)*, 1:130.

53. Abner Jordan (ca. 1795–1826) was a slaveholder who owned an 800-acre plantation on Sugar Creek, Morgan County, Georgia. A native of Greensville County, Virginia, Jordan advertised for a runaway slave named Ben in 1819. According to his obituary, "Capt." Jordan left a wife and "a train of relations and friends" when he died. See Hartz and Hartz, *Genealogical Abstracts from the Georgia Journal (Milledgeville) Newspaper*, vol. 1, *1809–1818*, 21; and ibid., vol. 3, *1824–1828*, 443 (quote), 778.

54. Benjamin S. Jordan, of Milledgeville, Georgia. Brother of Abner, Jordan was also a former tavern keeper and slaveholder living in Jasper County within five miles of Hillsboro, Georgia. He was planting cotton in Georgia by 1816, and advertised for a runaway woman named Charlotte in 1826. He sat on grand juries in Monroe County in 1826 and for the Baldwin County Superior Court in 1834, was a stockholder in the Bank of Milledgeville by 1839, and was granted lands in Baldwin County, Georgia, in 1842. See Hartz and Hartz, *Genealogical Abstracts from the Georgia Journal (Milledgeville) Newspaper*, vol. 1, *1809–1818*, 530; ibid., vol. 2, *1819–1823*, 397, 752, 787; ibid., vol. 4, *1829–1835*, 729; ibid., vol. 5, *1836–1840*, 545; and Evans, *Milledgeville, Georgia, Newspaper Clippings (Southern Recorder)*, 1:243.

55. Hezekiah Jordan married Lydia Wright in 1816. Upon his death sometime before 1839, he left an estate in Wilkinson County, Georgia. Benjamin and Hezekiah Jordan are

good style and seemed to be kind and indulgent masters. Hezekiah being a married man, did not live in so great style, and had the character of being a hard taskmaster. The bachelors household, was always the picture of neatness, the servants of Hezekiah seemed dirty and ragged, except upon occasions of having company at the house. I saw evidences of cruelty and mismanagement not soon to be forgotten.

From Milledgeville we went to Indian Springs, a fashionable place, and also the retreat of invalids that sought the beneficial effects of Mineral Springs.[56] We stayed at the house of General Macintosh;[57] he took a fancy to my dancing and musical talent, and offered in exchange for me money sufficient to cover the amount of three thousand dollars. No bargain was struck, and therefore I bade a final good-bye to Indian Springs.

Our journey back to Tennessee was accomplished in about three weeks, I cannot tell the year in which this occurred, but I remember it as being the first time when a steamboat had navigated the Tennessee river. She

---

mentioned in Joseph L. D. Smith's will. See Cook, *History of Baldwin County, Georgia*, 262; and Hartz and Hartz, *Genealogical Abstracts from the Georgia Journal (Milledgeville) Newspaper*, vol. 5, *1836–1840*, 288.

56. That would be the Indian Springs Hotel, built by William McIntosh and another man in 1821–22, the main structure of which still stands. Indian Springs was an auspicious place for an ambitious planter to speculate in lands opening up for cultivation. William McIntosh's plantation was in Carroll County, Georgia. See McMichael, *History of Butts County Georgia, 1825–1976*, 6–9.

57. William McIntosh Jr. (ca. 1778–1825) was a Muskogee leader of the Lower Creeks. Smith was probably introduced to him by James Jackson or John Coffee. Born in Coweta when it was a Lower Creek town, he was raised among the Creeks and spent time in Savannah, moving comfortably between societies. McIntosh supported Andrew Jackson in the Creek War against the rival Red Stick faction in 1813–14, and signed the Treaty of Fort Jackson ceding some 22 million acres of Creek land to the United States. He was also a U.S. ally in the First Seminole War of 1817–18. He owned the Acorn Bluff plantation in Carroll County, and Indian Springs in Butts County. In 1821, McIntosh agreed to cede Creek hunting grounds between the Flint River and the Ocmulgee River, for which he received a 640-acre plantation around Indian Springs. The Muskogee land later became Dooly, Fayette, Henry, Houston, and Monroe counties. On February 12, 1825, he signed the treaty of Indian Springs on the behalf of the Creek Indians, ceding more lands to the United States. That caused bitter divisions between the Lower Creeks and Upper Creeks opposed to ceding lands. In the 1825 cession, McIntosh signed over some 4,700,000 acres to the United States in exchange for compensation and agreeing to remove to an equivalent tract of land elsewhere. After the Creeks signed the agreement, an angry Hopoethleyoholo, representative of the Upper Creek leader Big Warrior, vowed revenge. McIntosh was murdered on May 1, 1825, and his plantation burned. See Stock, "William McIntosh"; and McMichael, *History of Butts County Georgia, 1825–1976*, 6–9.

was called the "Old Sage" (Osage), and her appearance caused immense excitement.[58] This steamer could bear no comparison with those built in later years, as the Captain on account of the small size of his vessel refused to fetch my master's slaves to Florrence, so that Mr. Smith had to embark his servants upon some half dozen keel boats on his removal from Humphries County to his new house in Alabama.[59] This was a journey of about 300 miles. We camped out every night. Although the season was winter, it was not cold enough to render this mode of travel disagreeable. There must have been some 350 slaves on this journey, as my master had under his charge not only his own slaves, but also those belonging to his brother Henry, his sister Mrs. Williams,[60] and Mr. Frank Dancer, his brother-in-law. On arrival at Florence the slaves were all put to work on the farm, and I continued in my position as groom. The first overseer was

58. The *Osage* was a side-wheel steamboat displacing 149 tons. It was built in Cincinnati, Ohio, in 1820, and its home port was Louisville, Kentucky. It was snagged near Coffeeville, Alabama, on the Tombigbee River, and sank on February 14, 1824. Use of the steamboat illustrates that the forced migration of enslaved people was undertaken on the most advanced transportation technology available. See Lytle and Holdcamper, *Merchant Steam Vessels of the United States, 1807-1868*, 146; and Neville, *Directory of Tennessee River Steamboats (1821-1928), with Illustrations*, 22.

59. Between 1818 and 1835, Joseph L. D. Smith was assigned or bought more than 1,800 acres of land in Lauderdale County, Alabama. He was among the first in the land bonanza of March 1818, being assigned 80.25 acres north of Florence on March 7, and another 160.48 acres in the same area two days later. He patented both properties on July 25, 1825, and bought another 160.48 acres adjoining that property in March and April of 1830. On March 9, 1818, he became the assignee of 600 acres north of the Tennessee River, which he patented in May 1824. Those are probably the lands Goings mentions. Smith was the assignee of two parcels of 80.25 acres each west of Florence on March 11, 1818, and he patented one of those in May 1824. Smith was the assignee of approximately 160 more acres in the same area sometime after 1818, and the assignee of 80.25 additional acres on September 13, 1821, after the original assignee gave up the claim. That parcel was adjacent to one of Thomas Kirkman's estates. In 1830 and 1831, Smith expanded his landholdings, buying 81 acres southeast of Florence on March 23, 1830, which parcel adjoined the lands of Sarah Hanna, his mother-in-law. He also bought approximately 80 acres in the northwest of the town of Florence on April 20, 1830. Those had been James Jackson's lands. He also bought approximately 80.45 acres just to the northwest of Florence on July 25, 1831, and 80.45 acres adjoining that property in November. Finally, Smith bought 84 acres of river improvement land on the north bank of the Tennessee River on June 1, 1835. Smith's will also mentions financial interests in Texas lands. See Cowart, *Old Land Records of Lauderdale County, Alabama*, 197, 201, 202, 208, 209, 213, 258, 259; and the Will of Joseph L. D. Smith, Lauderdale County Will Records, 1835-58, vol. A (microfilm, LGM 00196, reel 26), ADAH.

60. Rebecca, or Rebekah, J. Williams.

Anthony Olmstead, sent out by Henry Smith, who remained on the farm until there was a division of the different gangs among their respective owners.[61] When this took place Mr. Olmstead accompanied the slaves of Henry Smith to a plantation some fifteen miles distant, at a place called Colbert's Reserve.[62] The departure of this kind overseer was deeply regretted by the slaves who were left behind.

Mr. Olmstead was replaced by a Mr. Thomas Williams, more commonly known, among the slaves as "old buster."[63] He was a short thick set man. Like most little men he had a great deal of bluster. He would flourish his whip and even pull out his revolver at a refractory laborer, but he never slashed with much effect and I doubt if ever his pistol was placed on full cock. Indeed, he was too good natured for my master who had great faith in the lash, and therefore discharged "old buster" at the expiration of the year. At last my master got a man to his choice. His name was Kemble and

61. That was Sweet Water Plantation. On March 20, 1822, Henry Smith bought two tracts, of 160.57 and 160 acres, north of the Tennessee River in the eastern part of Colbert's Reserve, and patented both on October 1, 1823; on May 14, 1824, Smith bought 80.62½ acres (patented October 2, 1824) also in the former Colbert's Reserve, Lauderdale County, Alabama. Henry Smith married Rebecca M. Beckwith on June 14, 1842, and died in 1849. In November of that year, Henry D. Mason and James Caruthers became executors of the will of Henry Smith of Sweet Water. See Cowart, *Old Land Records of Lauderdale County, Alabama*, 301, 305; *Lauderdale County Marriage Book* 5:36 (microfilm), ADAH; and Gandrud, *Alabama Records*, vol. 43, *Lauderdale County*, 51.

62. To encourage Chickasaw leaders George and Levi Colbert to sign a treaty with the United States ceding Chickasaw land, in 1816 a portion of the land three to four miles by twelve miles was set aside for their use. Containing about 30,000 acres of prime farmland opposite Colbert's Ferry on the Tennessee River, it was called Colbert's Old Reservation, and later, Colbert's Reserve. In that agreement, the Chickasaws ceded all of their lands north of the Tennessee River. The Colberts sold the Colbert Reserve to the United States in 1819, and the government sold it to private buyers the following year. See Cowart, *Old Land Records of Lauderdale County, Alabama*, ix.

63. Virginia native Thomas Williams (b. ca. 1780) lived in Lauderdale County, Alabama, in 1830 with six children under fifteen and a wife, Elizabeth, a Kentucky native; he owned two slaves, one male and one female, both twenty-four to thirty-six. In 1850, he was farming in the county, owned $100 worth of real estate (and apparently no slaves), and his household included five daughters, aged ten to twenty-three. In his will, Smith left $500 to his "friend Thomas Williams of Miss." He was perhaps another Thomas Williams. See 1830 U.S. Census, [place not stated], Lauderdale, Alabama, roll 1; p. 195; 1850 U.S. Census, Division 2 East of The Military Road, Lauderdale, Alabama, roll M432-7, p. 325, image 646; and Will of Joseph L. D. Smith, Lauderdale County Will Records, 1835–58, vol. A (microfilm, LGM 00196, reel 26), ADAH.

I believe he was a native of North Carolina.[64] He came down to Alabama seeking a situation as an overseer. I remember his being introduced to my master by the Hon. James Jackson, for many years a member of the State Senate and near neighbor and connection of my master. Mr. Kemble seemed to me so much of a gentleman in his personal appearance that I had no suspicion of his business. My opinion was soon, changed, however, for while waiting at table, I overheard a remark which satisfied me, he was to be the new overseer to commence his labor on the ensuing first of January. He came to the day, and drove up in good style, accompanied by a handsome and ferocious looking animal of the bull dog breed. He was a tall heavy man. Shortly after his arrival, the slaves were ordered to the master's house (called by the slaves the "great house") to make the acquaintance of their new overseer. This happened on a Sunday. Each gang of slave laborers has a foreman who superintends the whole number of those engaged in any particular employment. For instance, there is a foreman among the plow gang, who is generally proficient as a laborer, and is to a certain extent responsible to the overseer for the amount and quality of the labor performed.

My master at the interview above mentioned did his utmost to impress his Negroes with his intended plan of leaving the overseer to the entire management of the farm, and that all disagreements must thereafter be settled by Mr. Kemble and not as had previously been the case, brought before the master or mistress for hearing and settlement. Mr. Kemble in accepting the charge paid his attention at once to Donerson, one of the foremen, of whom he inquired whether he had a watch. To this, Donerson replied in the negative. The overseer then asked,—"If you had one could you tell the hour by it." To which Donerson said, "I dun know, but 'spose I can learn." My master then instructed me to bring a silver watch belonging to him hanging in the parlor, which I handed to the overseer, who at once proceeded to instruct poor Donerson as to the easiest method of acquiring the requisite information. He began by pointing out the numerals, IIII. "This" he said, "is the time at which you must rise. Whenever the hand of the watch points to this place, you must turn out of bed, blow the horn, and commence preparations for work. He then addressed the slaves collectively, and said: "I have heard that some of you are fighting characters, but I tell you once for all, if you want to fight me I will give you a white man's

64. Elijah W. Kimbrough (d. 1830).

chance. I guess I should soon convince that I am a match for any mothers' son of you." He further added, that anyone failing to get to work, by six o'clock, they would be followed by the lash from the place of their loitering to the spot appointed for their day's work. He faithfully promised to lash every one into subjection and to convince them he would enfore his rules with the utmost severity. His ultimate conduct proved the faithfulness of his promises.

On the following Tuesday the Flogging commenced and continued during the entire year. His debaucheries with the women are too vile to be recorded. His plan with both men and women was generally to strip the upper parts of their garments from their backs and draw their blood at almost every blow of the lash. One of the foremen at the plow was lashed almost to death upon a log, because he did not get work enough from the people under his charge. Of these latter, two women were tied to a stake though in a state of pregnancy, and their backs were literally hacked until they were completely raw. My master must have been well satisfied with Kemble, for severity was joined with general good management of the affairs of the farm. Mrs. Smith, however, who was a kind-hearted and religious woman, was much opposed to the undue harshness of the cruel Kemble.[65] I had heard her express her dislike to his conduct in her conversations with the house servants. She took great pains, especially when her husband was off on a journey, to instruct her servants in matters of religion, and this tended to secure for her, the love and esteem of all, except the concubines, of her lewd and loathsome husband. I think it was through her influence that Kemble was discharged at the expiration of a year, and his place filled by a Dr. Bogsdale, who however, turned out to be but a little improvement upon his immediate predecessor.[66] He was I think equally as severe as Kemble, but not so cruel. I omitted to mention, that shortly after Kemble had left, he shot his father-in-law, a resident of Raleigh, North Carolina., for which he was hung.[67] My master read the statement from

65. Mary Hanna Smith.

66. Alexander Barksdale married Mary S. Scruggs in 1823. He oversaw Smith's plantations in Mississippi. See Gandrud, *Alabama Records*, vol. 43, *Lauderdale County*, 40 [marriage record]; and Jones and Gandrud, *Alabama Records*, vol. 217, *Lauderdale County* (microfilm), reel 7: 23–24, ADAH.

67. In 1829, Elijah W. Kimbrough was convicted in Raleigh, North Carolina, of murdering John Davis by strangling him with a rope and stabbing him, for which Kimbrough was executed by the state in November 1830 after losing an appeal. Some three thousand spectators gathered to see Kimbrough hanged, along with a slave identified

the newspaper in my hearing, and afterwards told the incident to many of the slaves.

It will be well here to give the reader some of my own experiences from the time of my arrival at Florence. I should think I was about 16 years of age at the time of our removal from Tennessee. My duties were exclusively, confined to the house and stables. I attended my master in his dressing room, waited on him at table, accompanied him in his travels, and until his marriage, occupied a corner of his sleeping-room at night. There was frequently company at the house, and I was a diligent listner to the conversations at the table. I then thought how agreeable it must be to read, and wondered why the white man selfishly deprived me of so great and yet so harmless an amusement. I heard them tell of foreign travel, and have wondered what the hideous looking animal an "abolitionist" was like. As year by year rolled on, the longing for freedom increased. I had enough to eat and drink, and the many presents that I received from visitors were spent to gratify my own vanity. Still there was the consciousness that I was but a "slave," a piece of property controlled, and owned by another, the same as a horse or cow or waggon. I felt that I had no will of my own, that to contradict was to render myself liable to the lash, and to refuse to labor, was but to expose myself to punishment, or even death. An incident that occurred about this time made a deep impression upon my mind. Within a few miles of Florence on the plantation of Captain Keys, two slaves died from the effects of severe whipping, and one was shot down by the overseer for disobedience to orders.[68] The perpetrator of these cruel acts was amenable to no law. We could only stifle our convictions of the deed. Woe be to us if we dared to comment on the heartlessness of our oppressors. On another occasion, Dr. Hill of Colbirl Reserves, had returned home drunk, and under such circumstances was exceedingly violent.[69] He was the

---

as "negro Carey." See *State v. Kimbrough,* 13 N.C. 431 (N.C. 1830); and *Raleigh (N.C.) Register,* November 8, 1830, 3.

68. "Captain" James Key (December 24, 1795–February 27, 1878). With a partner, Key bought 75 acres northeast of Florence in 1847. See Jones and Gandrud, *Alabama Records,* vol. 123, *Lauderdale County* (microfilm), reel 7: 48, ADAH; and Cowart, *Old Land Records of Lauderdale County, Alabama,* 156.

69. Dr. George Hill advertised his services as a physician in 1827. He bought 156 acres of land near Colbert's Reserve on January 30, 1830, and 79 more in the same area on April 23, 1830. Besides two adult females and four children under ten in his household, Hill claimed to own three slaves in 1830, one male twenty-four to thirty-five, one male thirty-five to fifty-five, and one female between ten and twenty-four years old. Anne Royall commented on the prevalence of physicians: "Every town is flooded with them. They

owner of a married slave and two children. His man Dick had given some trifling cause of offence, and was thereupon tied to a couple of sleepers in a building then being erected. From the effects of the flogging his poor victim never recovered. Within a few minutes of the rope being untied, poor Dick had become a corpse! This was frequently commented upon at my master's table. As near as I could learn, the doctor became frightened at what he had done, as there is a statute in Alabama against killing a slave. In his alarm he sought the advice of Mayor McKinlay a prominent lawyer in the place, who recommended him to leave the neighborhood.[70] He very soon made himself scarce, but no attempt was made to arrest him or to prevent his escape as a fugitive from justice. The pro-slavery argument that self interest will deter men from destroying their own property, is erroneous as it is in opposition to a hundred facts. Few men will flog their horses to death but cruelty to animals is itself a crime too frequently left unpunished. How much more then are the uncontrolled passions of the hot blooded Southerner vented upon his human Chattel. He laughs at the law because he knows it will never reach him. His brother slaveholders do not care to see the enforcement of an act which some day might reach themselves. The slave himself can only brood in silence on the wrongs and persecutions of his race.

During the time of Mr. Bogsdale's superintendence, I accompanied my master to Pontotoc in the State of Mississippi.[71] This was a new village

---

are strung along the roads like so many blacksmith's shops. You can neither walk nor ride, but you have a physician on each side, one in front, and one in rear. Here are seven in Florence—seven more went away, for want of room" (Royall, *Letters from Alabama on Various subjects*, 148). See also Garrett, *A History of Florence, Alabama*, 13, C-71; Cowart, *Old Land Records of Lauderdale County, Alabama*, 144, 152; and 1830 U.S. Census, [place not stated], Lauderdale County, Alabama, roll 1, p. 224.

70. John McKinley (1780–1852) was a U.S. senator, representative, and associate justice of the United States Supreme Court. Born in Culpeper County, Virginia, he moved to Kentucky and practiced law in Louisville. He then moved to Huntsville, Alabama, where he served in the state House of Representatives from 1820 to 1822. McKinley filled a vacant U.S. Senate seat from November 1826 to March 1831, and afterwards moved to Florence, where he was elected to another term in the U.S. Congress, from 1833 to 1835. He was a Jacksonian and a Democrat, and later served briefly as U.S. Senator from Alabama, in 1837, before being elevated to the Supreme Court by President Martin Van Buren, where he served for fifteen years until his death in Louisville, Kentucky. See *Biographical Directory of the United States Congress*, s.v. "McKinley, John, (1780–1852)," http://bioguide.congress.gov/scripts/biodisplay.pl?index=M000519.

71. By 1840, Pontotoc County, Mississippi, had a slave population of over 1,500, or 35 percent of a total population of just under 4,500, in a state whose 195,211 slaves made

in the midst of the woods, and the land was then occupied by Indians. My master speculated largely in the lands of the neighbourhood, setting apart about five hundred acres for his own occupation.[72] Upon my master's return to Florence, Mr. Bogsdale accompanied by all the farming hands, was sent to the new settlement, and the farm near Florence was sold; my master, family, and servants removing into the town of Florence, where he rented the best house in the place.[73] I always accompanied my master on his visits to the farm, and was astonished to see the effects of Mr. Bogsdale's management. The field hands often told me of their hardships in clearing the primitive forests. At the first removal to this new country many of the slaves died from fatigue and disease. The loss was so rapid that much improvement was made in the diet and housing of the field hands. Coffee and molasses were added to the rations.

In the first year a large piece of ground was prepared for cotton, and the crops soon became abundant.[74] On the low lands corn was planted, and potatoes and other vegetables were produced for home consumption. The

---

up 52 percent of the population. Alexander Barksdale was an overseer in the service of Joseph L. D. Smith. See Jones and Gandrud, *Alabama Records*, vol. 217, *Lauderdale County* (microfilm), reel 7: 23–24, ADAH; and Historical Census Browser, University of Virginia, Geospatial and Statistical Data Center.

72. In his will, Joseph L. D. Smith mentioned "lands on the Mississippi River which I own in partnership with Thomas Kirkman" that he wished to be sold. Those were likely in Yalobusha County, one county to the west of Pontotoc. (John Coffee was involved in treaty negotiations with the Choctaws and Chickasaws in the area; that John Coffee was also a partner with Thomas Kirkman in the Cypress Land Company.) See Will of Joseph L. D. Smith, Lauderdale County Will Records, 1835–58, vol. A (microfilm, LGM 00196, reel 26), ADAH.

73. Once Smith bought lands in north-central Mississippi, perhaps his lands in Pontotoc County, he moved most of the enslaved agricultural workers to Mississippi and moved himself to the town of Florence, Alabama, where he lived as an absentee landlord. In his will, Smith named several enslaved people in Florence but merely mentioned what must have been the majority of his slaves, in Mississippi. In that will, he advises his executors "to continue my negroes on the same plantations in Mississippi where they are now another year." At the expiration of that year, he directed the executors to "sell the negroes plantations tools stock &c." for the benefit of his heirs. See Will of Joseph L. D. Smith, Lauderdale County Will Records, 1835–58, vol. A (microfilm, LGM 00196, reel 26), ADAH.

74. Short-staple cotton was the cash crop that built the South, and slaves built plantations along river bottoms or wherever planters could get access to transportation to market. Between 1820 and 1825, American production of raw cotton soared from 334,378 bales per year to 532,915. By 1840, the U.S. was producing over 1.3 million bales a year, and by 1860 the total was more than 3.8 million. See Gray, *History of Agriculture in*

sight of a field of cotton, ready for picking, is most beautiful. The stems are some five feet apart when planted, but at maturity they all meet, and the ground seems covered as if with snow. The heat of our August sun, however, is not the usual accompaniment of that which is seldom seen in a Southern winter. There are generally three pickings in a season.[75] The slave has to repair to work long before the dews which are very heavy, are off the cotton. These dews are so heavy that the lands are kept moist, so that the crops seldom fail for want of rain. Their bad effects upon the pickers often showed themselves in fevers and other miasmatic diseases. Each hand is required to pick a given number of pounds per day. An able-bodied man or woman must generally gather 150 pounds, and children less in proportion according to their age.[76] The cotton at night is brought home in baskets and weighed and placed inside the "Cotton house." Next morning each basket is brought out and emptied on a scaffold, where it is spread for the purpose of being thoroughly dried. The spreading and subsequent housing of this, is attended to by two or three old or partially disabled slaves. After a few hours it becomes thoroughly dry and is removed to the "gin house" for separation of the cotton from the seed. These gins are generally worked by horse power.[77] The cotton falls from the gin into the packing room, where it is at once placed in the press and formed into bales of about 500 lbs each. These bales are generally repacked at the shipping ports by steam power compressing a much larger quantity, into a much smaller bulk. A good hand is supposed to cultivate 15 acres of cotton and 10 acres of corn.[78]

There is but little wheat grown in the country, and flour is a rarity at the table of the slave! In these States the "picking" begins some six weeks before Christmas, and ends before the Easter following.

I happened to arrive with my master at his farm just one week after

---

the Southern United States to 1860, 2:1026; Stoll and Davis, *Southern United States*, 121–28; and Eltis, *Economic Growth and the Ending of the Transatlantic Slave Trade*, chaps. 3 and 11.

75. O'Donovan, *Becoming Free in the Cotton South*, chap. 1.

76. Engerman and Gallman, *The Cambridge Economic History of the United States*, vol. 2, *The Long Nineteenth Century*, 337–38.

77. Many cotton gins were operated by horses. See Lakwete, *Inventing the Cotton Gin*, 59–60, 78.

78. Antebellum cotton planters did not practice monoculture. Maize and other foodstuffs were commonly cultivated, especially on frontier areas where food was not always available for purchase.

much excitement had been created by the shooting of one, "George," a slave owned by Mr. Kirkman a cousin to my mistress.[79] George had been so badly treated by the overseer that he concealed himself in a cave some three miles from the residence of his master. His suspected concealment had been disclosed by a man named MacDonale, who for some five weeks had furnished him with food.[80] His fears becoming excited for his amenability to the law, he informed Kirkman's overseer that he had observed smoke issuing from a cleft in the rock where there was no recognized habitation. Immediately a search was made, and the hound and bull dog were at once in requisition. Too many residents in a constitutionally governed and Christian country, have probably supposed these negro hunting expeditions to be the mere extravagances of ingenious romancers and novel writers. They will not believe that human nature is sufficiently depraved as to subject a fellow being to the savage torture of infuriated and ferocious

79. Thomas Kirkman (ca. 1800–1864) was born in Ireland and moved to Alabama in his teens. He was among the first speculators in Lauderdale County, Alabama, lands. Kirkman married Elizabeth McCulloch of Tennessee in 1827, and they had nine children. Kirkman bred racehorses and listed his occupation as "merchant." He was a cousin of Mary Hannah Smith and executor of J. L. D. Smith's will. He claimed more than 1,500 acres in the initial land assignment of March 1818, patenting lands in the east of the county in 1824. Kirkman bought nearly 240 more acres in Lauderdale County in 1842 and 1844, and more than 275 more in 1856. He likely grew cotton and was a slaveholder. In 1830, he owned seven slaves in Alabama. By 1850, he was one of Florence's wealthiest residents, claiming $80,000 worth of real estate, and his two sons, Thomas and Samuel, were "clerks." Thomas Jr. would later be wounded during the First Battle of Bull Run, fighting for the Confederacy during the Civil War. By 1860, Kirkman was retired and reported owning eight slaves among his $132,000 in personal property, and $110,000 worth of real estate. His youngest son, Jackson—perhaps named after his neighbor and sometime business associate, James Jackson—was in 1860 a "student in Germany." See Cowart, *Old Land Records of Lauderdale County, Alabama,* 51, 89, 90, 158, 164, 172, 186, 187, 258, 260, 356; Garrett, *A History of Florence, Alabama,* 23, C-66; 1830 U.S. Census, [place not stated], Lauderdale County, Alabama, roll 1, p. 203, images 33–34; 1860 U.S. Census, Florence, Lauderdale County, Alabama, roll M653, p. 32 image 33; and 1860 U.S. Census, Slave Schedule, Florence, Lauderdale County, Alabama, p. 13, image 5.

80. William McDonald was a justice of the peace in the late 1810s and justice of the quorum of the Orphan's Court. He died in 1828, leaving his property in Florence, "where Col. James Benham formerly lived," to his wife and family; included in the inventory were McDonald's "medical books." See Gandrud, *Alabama Records,* vol. 104, *Lauderdale County,* 2, 3, 4, 5; and Jones and Gandrud, *Alabama Records,* vol. 213, *Lauderdale County* (microfilm), reel 7: 53–54, 55, 67, ADAH.

dogs. Yet such is the actual fact. The chase after poor "George" must have been an exciting affair. There were but two horsemen on this memorable occasion,—the overseers af Kirkman, and Bogsdale, who superintended my master's plantation.[81] The sport commenced shortly after sunrise. On arrival at the expected cover of the game, it was found the bird was flown. The well-trained hound, however, soon caught scent of his prey. It might be instinct or it might be reason, that led George who heard the shouts of the pursuers, to run for an adjacent river. He effected a crossing to the other side on logs, where the cane was thick enough to shelter him from the observation of his pursuers. For hours he kept his followers at bay. The excitement grew stronger and the peril proportionally increased. At last a gun was heard. A rifle ball had done its deadly work. The wound in the breast prevented a successful defence from the immediate attacks of the accomplished dogs. By the time these sporting gentlemen had come up with their prey, poor George was in the agonies of death. Before his body could be borne to its former earthly home, the vital spark had fled. It appeared that at least forms of law were more respected here than in Alabama. In a formerly mentioned incident of murder there was no judicial inquiry into the cause of the death of Dick, the property of Dr. Hill. But in the State of Mississippi, the form of a coroner's inquest was undertaken. I never heard the verdict, but as none of the accomplished hunters on this eventful occasion were ever punished or confined, it, is safe to presume that the jury found a verdict of "justifiable homicide!"

During the time of my residence at Florence, I twice accompanied my master to New Orleans.[82] The journeys were made by the river Mississippi, and accomplished in about ten days. I remember the position of Vicksburg, so famous now in the annals of the American revolution or rebel-

81. Whether Goings witnessed this firsthand is unclear, since the incident took place in Mississippi.

82. New Orleans's strategic location on the Mississippi River was its key to the Cotton Kingdom. Before the opening of the Erie Canal in 1825, most of the goods produced west of the Appalachians that found their way to market passed through that port city. In 1810, the city's population was 17,242; in 1820, it had grown by more than half, to 27,176. By the end of the 1820s, the decade in which Goings first visited, the population had soared to 46,082. In the 1830s, the population more than doubled again, making the city of 102,193 the third largest in the nation by 1840. It would remain that way until the twentieth century. See Gibson, "Population of the 100 Largest Cities and Other Urban Places in the United States, 1790–1990."

lion.[83] I should say the river is here about a mile in width. On each side are high ridges, but the town itself is situated in a hollow. When within 300 miles of New Orleans the scenery becomes most beautiful. The moss on the trees and bushes has the appearance of the weeping willow. It is used for mattresses, and is as soft and pliable as hair. The process of curing for use, is that of boiling, otherwise it would grow after being stripped from the tree. The six miles of shipping at the levee in New Orleans, was to me a truly wonderful sight. I noticed a large number of French and Spaniards.[84] We were in this bustling city during the winter months, when all is activity. The restrictions here placed upon my colored brethren, made a deep impression upon my mind. They are all locked up after about the hour of eight in the evening, and if afterwards found upon the streets must produce a "pass" or give a satisfactory account of themselves.[85] There are a large number of free colored persons in this city who seemed to have more privileges than the same class in the more northern of the Slave States. Many colored men near New Orleans are the owners of large plantations, and employ white men as Overseers. It is said that as much severity is fre-

83. Founded in 1811 and incorporated in 1825, Vicksburg was a thriving commercial city on the Mississippi River by the time Goings visited in the late 1820s or early 1830s. It was strategically located at the crossroads of railroads beginning in 1831, which made it a key entrepôt city for the Cotton South. The U.S. Census for Warren County, Mississippi, which included Vicksburg, counted 7,861 people in 1830; 57 percent were enslaved. See Historical Census Browser, University of Virginia, Geospatial and Statistical Data Center.

84. The French founded New Orleans in the early eighteenth century as the principal outpost of a plantation economy that failed. France surrendered it to Spain in 1763, but it reverted to French control (secretly) in 1800, just three years before the United States bought the Louisiana Territory. Colonial governments had attempted to regulate slavery using a variety of laws and customs, and until Americans asserted control in the early nineteenth century, slavery in Louisiana bore little resemblance to the institution Goings experienced. Slaves in colonial Louisiana had legal rights under the French Code Noir and the Spanish Siete Partidas, including the right of self-purchase known as *coartación*. Through the failure of the early eighteenth-century plantation regime, which was overshadowed by that of the sugar islands of the Caribbean, enslaved people had bargained for and achieved customary privileges. They often traded on their own account, sometimes bore arms, could petition colonial officials for redress of grievances, and enjoyed relatively broad freedom of movement. See Berlin, *Many Thousands Gone*, 87–90, 196–214.

85. The Anglo-American possessors of New Orleans in the early nineteenth century attempted to clamp down on the movements of anyone who could be a friend to slaves. Despite restrictions, people of African descent, free and enslaved, gathered in corners

quently practised upon these plantations as upon those owned by the white race.[86] The ladies generally promenaded the city between 5 and 6 o'clock in the evening.[87] All kinds of amusements are in vogue in this extraordinary place, and the dresses and equipages of the people are frequently of the most extravagant character. On my second visit, I observed that several handsome churches had been erected. The Methodist Church I found to be well attended by persons of color, intermixed with the poorer class of white. The preacher was a colored man, and was popular and talented.[88] I accompanied my master on several occasions, to the theatre which was generally the most crowded on Sunday evenings.[89]

I now come to a not unimportant part of my history, to wit, the seeking and finding a wife. My courtship lasted about four years. My choice fell upon a servant of Mr. James Jackson, an Irish gentleman who resided a short distance from my master's house, whose name I have before mentioned. Her name was Maria White, and she was the reputed illegitimate

---

of the city like Congo Square (where slaves congregated from the mid-eighteenth century until city officials banned such gatherings in the 1840s), trading, visiting, making music, and exchanging news and information. See Sublette, *The World That Made New Orleans*.

86. Recent scholarship confirms this observation. One such African American slaveholder of Louisiana was Andre Durnford, who owned seventy-seven slaves when he died in 1859. See Lightner, "Were African American Slaveholders Benevolent or Exploitative?," 543.

87. Goings could have witnessed winter Carnival balls, masquerades, or perhaps "Quadroon" balls, in which young women who had recognizably African antecedents yet who were light skinned, met white men. No other American city had absorbed so many influences, from the western coast of Africa to the Iberian Peninsula, and from the Caribbean to the British Isles. While so many flocked to New Orleans seeking their fortunes, many—if not most—migrants arrived involuntarily.

88. The Methodist church mentioned had been founded by Benjamin M. Drake (1800–1860) in 1825, though it is not clear how long the church survived. Drake and his co-religionists perhaps tolerated an integrated church in a polyglot and multiethnic city. Drake corresponded with the American Colonization Society, which suggests that his congregation may have been multiracial. In the late eighteenth century and early nineteenth century, Methodists integrated their class papers, or lists of members, and congregations that included black and white members persisted even if whites assumed a more authoritative leadership role and blacks increasingly favored black-run churches, such as the African Methodist Episcopal Church, which was founded in 1816. See Hill, *Religion in the Southern States*, 136; and the Drake Papers, J. B. Cain Archives of Mississippi Methodism.

89. This was the American theater on Camp Street, which opened in 1823. See Louisiana State Museum, "Antebellum Louisiana: Politics, Education, and Entertainment."

daughter of her master. She had been taught to read and was a great favorite in the family. Thus it was that Elijah Turner the property of Joseph Smith became united in the bonds of matrimony to Maria White the property of James Jackson.[90] The ceremony was performed by a colored Baptist Minister, who was also a slave, but in consequence of his religious attainments he had the privilege of travelling among the surrounding plantations for the purpose of preaching the Gospel to his fellow bondmen. He was unable to read, yet many white persons attended his occasional ministrations, and were favorably impressed with his natural ability. The marriage of a favorite slave is made quite an occasion of excitement and jubilation. The house servants from adjoining plantations were present, and even some of the relatives of my mistress participated in the conviviality of the evening. A substantial supper was provided at Mrs. Jackson's expense, and there was a plentiful supply of excellent wines, liquors, and fruits. Some 50 or 60 persons partook of the festivities, and for the time being, all sorrow was banished.

The reader must not, however, imagine that the joining together of two pieces of chattel property embodies the full enjoyment of all the rights and amenities, and securities, of married life as possessed by free men in a free country. I could visit my wife only with the express permission of my master, and was liable to be sold away and separated at any moment. My wife continued in her position of house servant, and I was only permitted to visit her twice a week. This limitation was frequently restricted by being forbidden to go when there was company, or the weather was wet. I was so frequently deprived of the rightful enjoyment of my marital rights, that I used to take clandestine means for running over to spend an hour or two in the society of my much beloved wife. After I had been married some six years my master died. He called me to his bedside, and, in anticipation of death, said he had always intended to bequeath me my freedom, but as my

---

90. Many of the names of the original property owners are Irish or Scottish, including James Jackson, who lived at the "Forks of Cypress" plantation. Jackson was also the natural father of Maria White, Goings's first wife. Jackson, along with U.S. surveyor John R. Coffee, who would serve as President Andrew Jackson's agent of removal for the Choctaws, was a principal in the land company that surveyed and parceled the lands in northern Alabama. Like most slaveholders, James Jackson did not recognize White as his daughter. James Jackson's will does not mention Maria White, but wills that slave property be sold to pay debts and leaves generous amounts of property to his wife, daughters, and grandchildren. See Will of James Jackson, Lauderdale County, Alabama, Will Book (microfilm, LGM 00196, reel 26), ADAH.

services to my mistress would be greatly needed, he had thought better of his intention. He added that she would remain a kind mistress to me, and would arrange for my ultimate freedom, should my life outrun her own. The widow soon recovered as she was the possessor of a comfortable property.[91] Only one child survived, a little girl, some eight or nine years old.[92] She was the heir to $50.000, and, I have heard, ultimately married a wealthy gentleman, of Nashville.[93] One slave only was the recipient of his freedom—this was Robin Purdy, an old field hand and gardener.[94] The fact of my having to remain in serfdom was a serious blow to my happiness—I

---

91. From the will of Joseph L. D. Smith: "To my wife Mary Smith I bequeath all my household and kitchen furniture carriage and horses and the following negroes Leige[?] Wenning[?] and her children who are near in Florence Nancy and Joe and during her widowhood to be supported out of the proceeds of my estate with the same ease and comforts that she was accustomed to during my life—Should she marry I bequeath to her Five thousand dollars. The property above mentioned vis. The household and kitchen furniture carriage and horses Liege Wenning and her children in Florence at this time Nancy and Joe to be included as part of the Five thousand dollars to her and her heirs for ever." See Will of Joseph L. D. Smith, Lauderdale County Will Records, 1835-58, vol. A (microfilm, LGM 00196, reel 26), ADAH.

92. In his will, Joseph L. D. Smith provided that, "I wish my daughter Jane to be educated in the best practicable and experimental branches of education which the United Sates can offer and to facilitate her in the French language which I desire her to acquire. I wish her to live as for two years with a respectable French family and further more that she may acquire a good education. I desire that she should continue in school until she arrives at the age of eighteen years." It is unclear whether Jane Smith went to France, but she did go to school in Tennessee, probably from the early 1840s to the mid-1840s. One Ann Pope was appointed guardian for Jane Smith and filed accounts beginning in 1845, including board at the Nashville Academy in 1846 and 1847, along with other charges. See Will of Joseph L. D. Smith, Lauderdale County Will Records, 1835-58, vol. A (microfilm, LGM 00196, reel 26), ADAH; and Jones and Gandrud, *Alabama Records*, vol. 221, *Lauderdale County* (microfilm), reel 7: 80, ADAH.

93. Jane Smith (1830-1894) married George Augustine Washington (1815-1892) of a plantation called "Wessyngton," in Tennessee on June 21, 1849. Washington was one of the South's largest tobacco planters during the 1850s, the president and receiver of the Edgefield Kentucky Railroad by 1871, and an elected director of the Louisville and Nashville Railroad in 1874. See Washington Family Papers, Tennessee State Library and Archives, Nashville.

94. In his will, Joseph L. D. Smith instructed: "In consideration of the faithful service of Old Robbin I will and bequest to him his freedom and desire that he shall live on the plantation or elsewhere with Henry D. Smith under his care and direction and that my Executors do pay to Henry D. Smith Thirty five dollars annually for the support of Robbin and for his care and attentions of him during his life." See Will of Joseph L. D. Smith, Lauderdale County Will Records, 1835-58, vol. A (microfilm, LGM 00196, reel 26), ADAH.

had always expected my freedom at my master's death. His conduct led me to confide in his bequeathment. But now the cloud assumed its darkest hue. Verily, there was no hope but in the "under-ground railroad." Here was I, the property of a person about 30 years of age, who might leave me my freedom to be only enjoyed at the period of decrepitude, or, which was much more likely, the mistress might outlive her slave. For two years, however, I had no extra cause of complaint. We remained in Florence during this time, and I paid semi-weekly visits to my wife. At the expiration of two years my mistress spoke frequently of removing to Mississippi. There was a general suspicion that a Mr. Thompson, from St. Louis, was falling in love with the captivating and handsome widow. Her family connections were evidently opposed to the match. I suspected that an elopement to Mississippi would take place, as I had of late been informed of a scheme to that effect. This would not only separate me from my wife, but would also, in all probability, lead to an entire change of service and employment. My fears were more fully excited from the fact that I had been charged by my mistress with overlooking her bed-room, under decidedly suspicious circumstances. From that moment I decided to escape, for I foresaw that banishment was speedily to be my fate, and I now therefore come to the most momentous period of my life. I was about to engage in an enterprise in which failure would be punishment, probably punishment to the death. I must summon courage, for I was now to fight the battle of life.

CHAPTER 2

My Change of Name and Escape from Slavery,—Through Tennessee,—
Kentucky,—Illinois,—Indiana,—Ohio to Michigan,—Employed at various
places, and at Perryburg, (Ohio.)

SOME FEW YEARS before the death of my master, I had purchased of a
mulatto, named "Henry Goings," his free paper.[1] He was a well-known
character, and upon representing that this document had been lost or
stolen he could, easily have it replaced. I had always surplus cash in my
pocket, and knowing that from Henry's love of drink, he might strike a
bargain upon easy terms, I offered him $15 for his certificate of freedom,
and, to my surprise, a trade was at once effected.

I immediately took it to the residence of my wife, and tacked it under
the table, covered by a piece of buckskin. This was one day to be used as a
passport to freedom, a guide book on the highway to Canada. Banishment
to Mississippi seemed imminent.[2] The time had come when this investment of $15 should begin to pay some interest. My mistress had evidently
resolved to get me away, and I was equally resolved to turn my steps in an
opposite direction.[3]

One evening in the early spring, I had orders to visit Mr. Kirkman, my
mistress's cousin, on the following morning. This gentleman informed me
that he was going on to the farm, and that having to go to Tuscumbia, he

1. There was a Nancy Going in Lauderdale County (white?) who married Littleton
Richardson in 1827. Perhaps he was a relative or former slave who took her name. See
Gandrud, *Alabama Records*, vol. 199, *Lauderdale Co.* (microfilm), reel 7: 16, ADAH.

2. Goings was not among the half-dozen enslaved people mentioned in Smith's will
as being candidates to stay in Florence. Accordingly, he was probably slated to be moved
to Mississippi to work on one of his erstwhile master's cotton plantations there.

3. Goings was not the last of Smith's slaves to flee. On August 8, 1840, the *Huntsville
(Ala.) Democrat* reported: "Stewart County, Tenn. Committed to jail, runaway slaves;
1 belongs to Andrew Jones of Ala. and one to Joseph Smith near Florence. Wm. Cook,
Jailor." Cited in Gandrud, *Alabama Records*, vol. 12, *Newspapers, "Huntsville Democrat,"
1833–1840*, 12:82.

desired me to meet him at Buzzard Roost,[4] as he might have something to send back to my mistress, upon whose business he was going to Tuscumbia. I could clearly see this was but a trap to draw me away to the distant South,—and I now determined to strike for liberty or death.[5] Of course I agreed to be at Buzzard Roost at the appointed hour. I had already secured my free paper, and taken farewell of my wife, to whom I said that as I suspected I was going to the Mississippi, it would be the last night of my seeing her. I only communicated my design of running away to my wife's stepfather and to another friend, both of whom were the property of Mr. Jackson. I put my best clothes on my back, and about $40 in my pocket.[6] I trusted the places that then knew me, would know me no more for ever. I was ordered to take my mistress's horse to Buzzard Roost, but as I preferred making my escape upon the horse which was called my own, and which was always ridden by me, I had to use a little stratagem to accomplish my object. At Mr. Jackson's I found a boy whom I sent into town for my own horse, giving him 50 cents for his trouble. I took care to meet the boy on the road between Mr. Jackson's and Florence. After watching the boy out of sight, I turned into the adjoining thicket with both horses to wait until night had set in. I then turned my mistress's horse adrift carefully adjusting the stirrups on the top of the saddle and also lashing the rein of the bridle to the saddle, I thought if they caught me they should not have to charge me with stealing my mistress's horse. I then started

4. Buzzard Roost lies three miles west of Cherokee, Alabama, in Colbert County, and was used as a hotel during some time in its existence. The main building was constructed between 1800 and 1824. See Buzzard Roost, "National Register of Historic Places" (no. 76000157).

5. Most runaways did not seek freedom in the North or beyond the U.S. border in Canada. Families were all most had, and to desert them was to lose the chance to protect them. Most runaways were young unmarried men in their teens or twenties, and those with skills or experience with horses or wagons were most likely to make good their escape. As mothers, women tended to have small children with whom traveling presented difficulties. The majority of fugitives escaped to get a break from relentless toil, to protest working conditions, or simply to visit a spouse, friends, or relatives. See Franklin and Schweninger, *Runaway Slaves*, 119; Frazier, *Runaway and Freed Missouri Slaves and Those Who Helped Them, 1763–1865*, 98–99.

6. Fugitive slaves who had a chance to plan their escapes gathered their portable resources and did their best at passing for free men and women. Runaway ads of the period regularly mention enslaved people believed to be wearing fancy clothing, often purloined from an owner's closet. See Meaders, *Advertisements for Runaway Slaves in Virginia, 1801–1820*, 15 and passim.

on the Bolivar Road, making perhaps for the first night some 50 or 60 miles.[7] About 10 o'clock, I stopped at a country tavern and, fed myself and horse at a cost of 75 cents. After a short rest I went on to Charlotteville,[8] where I arrived early in the afternoon. As I had been in this village before, I deemed it prudent to make no stay. My object was to reach the Rolling Mills where I could cross the Cumberland River and get into Kentucky, thence to the Ohio river into Iillinois. A short distance from Charlotteville, I received sufficient information to enable me to find the road to the Rolling Mills.[9] It was not a well travelled road and was therefore exactly suited to the purposes of a fugitive. I stopped at the house of a small farmer (a white man). No questions were asked, as I tendered compensation without grumbling. I believe I paid 62½ cents for my entertainment, and started early next morning on my route. It was Saturday evening when I reached Rolling Mills. On my enquiring at the log house of a colored man, on the outskirts of the town for a night's lodging, he informed me that the laws were very strict with regard to colored people, but if I could satisfy him of my freedom, I was welcome to become a lodger in his house. I stated that I had "free papers" in my pocket, which upon my offering to produce them, he at once expressed himself satisfied and extended his hospitality. Next morning I had to start in good time, for I was on dangerous ground. I feared recognition by Mr. Vanlear,[10] the proprietor of the Mills, as I had frequently seen him in Nashville and had no desire to be put through a series of questions to which answers might not only be difficult but also disagreeable. I saw the gentleman early as it was, but he was fortunately a little too far off to recognize me. I crossed the river upon the Ferry, and

7. Goings started out to the northwest, toward Bolivar, Tennessee, and his sojourn on horseback from the Deep South to Illinois covered about 270 miles in 1839.

8. Goings tacked to the northeast, returning to Charlotte, Tennessee, the Dickson County seat. His initial move from North Carolina to Tennessee ended in neighboring Humphreys County.

9. Dickson County's population included 1,687 slaves in 1840, nearly 24 percent of the county's population. Goings could have found allies among the enslaved or other locals who gave him directions to the Rolling Mills. In 1830, Rolling Mills was established by the Woods-Yeatman Company on the Cumberland River five miles east of Dover, on the Kentucky-Tennessee border, Stewart County. See Hawkins, "Forts Henry, Heiman, and Donelson."

10. Anthony Wayne Vanleer (1783–1863), of Tennessee, was the owner and operator of the Cumberland Furnace in Dickson County, Tennessee, beginning in the early 1820s. That ironworks employed 114 mostly male slaves by 1840. See Vanleer Papers, Chester County Historical Society.

no questions were asked as to my right to travel. I reached a considerable town in the afternoon where I enquired for the intersection of the Ohio river. The road was pointed out to me which I found to be a well travelled highway. I made quite a distance this day and passed through a couple of prosperous looking villages. I stayed with a colored horse trainer, where I passed myself off as a traveller, looking about me for my own pleasure, now on the way for Canada, where if I liked the country I should make it my permanent residence.[11] He was not at all inquisitive. If he had any suspicions as to my being a runaway, he did not manifest them. My host's wife, upon hearing that I was bound for Canada, became immediately interested, as she stated she had sisters and brothers in some part of British North America, and desired me to make inquiry concerning their welfare and report if I was successful. These runaways had been the property of General Taylor.[12] The son of their former master had traced these people to Amherstburg in Upper Canada, where he had made efforts to induce them to return to slavery.[13] The colored people in Amherstburg made great exertions to secure and punish, if not to kill the slave-catcher, and he owed his life to his former slaves, who aided him in escaping to the other side, but they prudently declined his invitation to accompany him back to Kentucky. I subsequently found the people in Amherstburg doing well, and thoroughly satisfied to reside upon the domains of Queen Victoria.[14] Next day I made a good many miles and just at dusk in the evening, called at a respectable looking tavern where

11. Recent scholarship suggests twenty thousand or so African Americans settled in Canada before the Civil War. See Hepburn, *Crossing the Border,* 10–11.

12. Zachary Taylor's biographer does not mention runaways, commenting instead that during the 1830s he left oversight of his plantations to "good managers." See Bauer, *Zachary Taylor,* 73.

13. Amherstburg, Essex County, Ontario, is situated on the mouth of the Detroit River where it enters Lake Erie. Founded in 1798 as a garrison town after the evacuation of Detroit, below Fort Malden, it was a shipping and steamboat port town. The steamboat *London* stopped there en route from Buffalo to Detroit, and Brothers provided service to and from Chatham, where Goings settled. The population was 985 people, 174 of whom were "of colour," or 18 percent in 1846. The town had five churches, including Episcopal, Catholic, Presbyterian, Methodist, and Baptist denominations. There were also breweries, mills, schools, woolen mills, blacksmiths, and ten taverns, including the "British North American." See Smith, *Smith's Canadian Gazetteer . . . ,* 4–5.

14. Victoria (1819–1901) was Queen of the United Kingdom of Britain and Northern Ireland from 1837 to 1901. Canada was a British possession until independence in 1867, and remains in the British Commonwealth.

I received very courteous treatment. During my preliminary inquiries at the door I was evidently taken for a "white man." When I entered the house I noticed some surprise on the countenance of the landlord, but as by subsequent conversation with himself and the numerous loungers about the "bar," he became satisfied all was right, and found no disposition to suspect my character. Some of them expressed surprise that I should choose so cold a country as Canada for a residence, but I silenced all suspicion by telling them I should return if not satisfied with the country, and I supposed I might be able to stand the climate just as well as the colored people already there. Next morning I was directed into a well travelled road, by which I reached the Ohio river at noon. Before reaching the river I enquired my way of a gentleman who conversed with me some little, and suggested that I had better shew my certificate to the keeper of the ferry, as it might save him harmless from trouble. When I reached the ferry the boat was coming from the other side, and finding me a passenger we started without delay for the opposite shore. As I was not asked to produce my certificate, I told the keeper of the ferry what the gentleman had told me, and at once produced the document. Of course this was satisfactory, and in a few minutes I stood upon the soil of a "free State," the State of Illinois.[15]

I now felt partially safe, only partially, for no State of the Union is "free' as regards slaves. I imagined I was at least to some extent breathing the air of freedom, although I knew that if my former owners caught me, I should quickly be returned to slavery. I also felt that I was getting nearer to Canada, and that now the chances of a complete success were in my favor. My first day's experience however did not give me a favorable impression of the free States. Upon starting next morning for Shawneetown,[16] I found I must cross over the Saline river, a branch of the Ohio.[17] This had to be

15. An 1874 map of the area described here notes a ferry crossing which fits the location from Kentucky into Illinois and corresponds to Goings's route through Kentucky. The ferry is identified as Berry's Ferry on the map and crosses into Golconda, Illinois. See Asher and Adams, "Illinois" (map), 1874.

16. Shawneetown was a village in Gallatin County in southeastern Illinois across the river from Kentucky. In 1840, the county's population was 10,760, among whom 671—or just over 6 percent—were people of color. Illinois, like most Northern states, placed considerable restrictions on free people of color. In 1829, Illinois passed a law requiring that African American residents post a bond of $1,000 and promise not to violate any laws. This was ostensibly to protect localities from having to support black indigents, but it had the effect of discouraging black emigration. See Historical Census Browser, University of Virginia, Geospatial and Statistical Data Center

17. The Saline River is a tributary of the Ohio River.

crossed by a ferry, and previous to reaching the river I had to go something like a mile and a half to ford an overflown creek. The persons who
directed me as to the shallow part of the stream to be crossed, had gone
over on logs and reached the Ferry house before I had accomplished my
circuitous route. When I arrived at the Ferry house there was evidently
a consultation concerning me. The ferryman desired me, however, to go
down to the ferry and he would be with me in a few minutes. These few
minutes must have been at least a score, when getting impatient I returned
to the house and demanded to know why I must be so needlessly delayed,
as I was somewhat in a hurry. They promised to follow immediately, but
instead of putting me across the river, demanded to see my authority for
travelling as a free man. I denied their right to demand or see my papers,
but if I could not be taken across except upon condition of proving my
right to the privileges of a free man, I would accompany any or all of them
to the nearest Justice of the Peace. For the moment they seemed abashed
with my boldness and the oldest gentleman present, who seemed to be
proprietor of the ferry, expostulated with the rest, remarking that I was a
freeman, and that he had told them I was free. My object in refusing to
shew my paper to such a crowd, was a fear lest they might destroy it and
leave me in the lurch. The state of society is such generally, where a colored
man is involved, that there is not much dependence on common justice
being measured to him. The old gentleman, who had just spoken seemed
so thoroughly disposed to be just and merciful, that I quietly gave him a
peep at my certificate, which he pronounced all right, and immediately
ordered the men to put me across the river free of all charge. This they did
promptly, and when I thanked them, they said my gratitude was unnecessary, as they had caused me a good deal of needless delay.

I reached Shawnee town in the evening where I found a colored board-
ing house. Within a short time of my arrival I saw a crowd of people among
whom was a "white man" who had formerly been a butcher at Florence,
where he had married a colored woman at one time his slave.[18] I was not
recognised, however, but determined to leave by first boat going up the
Ohio. Early next morning I offered my horse and his accoutrements for

---

18. This was perhaps the Greek butcher whom Anne Royall mentioned in her diary
some two decades earlier. Whatever the butcher's views on race and slavery, his presence
posed a risk to Goings. Anyone who recognized a fugitive could turn him in, even inad-
vertently, and there were men who earned a living catching fugitive slaves and kidnapping those they could claim were.

sale. I was obliged to sell for anything I could get. Not feeling inclined to participate in unnecessary risk I took the first I could get—some twenty dollars, and watched my opportunity to embark for Portsmouth some distance above Cincinnatti.[19]

The steamboat Lexington was due next morning.[20] I determined to take passage on her for Portsmouth.[21] Before embarking I took a quiet peep at the passengers who generally run ashore for a few minutes while the boat is getting on wood. As I was taking my unobserved survey I recognised a large cotton dealer of New Orleans, known as Major McMicking.[22] He had often stayed at my master's house during his periodical business journeys, and would consequently have remembered me. To avoid this disagreeable dilemna, before going on board I bound a handkerchief around my head, and made a feint of being unwell. I found the Captain of the boat, and negotiated for a passage. I also pulled out my documentary evidence of freedom which he declined to read, saying, "all men are free here." It is not so, nevertheless. I told him I was very unwell, and would thank him for a berth at once. Thereupon he called the Steward and told him to allot me a place forthwith. I requested the Steward to furnish me with soup as I felt unable to partake of the ordinary daily meals. The Major went ashore at Louisville, the second day of my unfortunate illness.[23] After this I rapidly recovered; in fact as the boat stayed two hours at the Commercial Metropolis of Kentucky, I very nearly run myself into the lion's den. I went out to take a peep at the busy city, but I had not gone far before I observed a Mr.

19. Cincinnati, Ohio, on the north bank of the Ohio River from Kentucky, was established in 1819. It was the hub of steam transportation on the Ohio River. See "Map of Cincinnati and Suburbs and Covington & Newport," 1880.

20. In June of 1861, a river steamer called the *Lexington* was converted to a "wood-clad" U.S. gunboat in Cincinnati, along with two others, the *A. O. Tyler* and the *Conestoga*. See Symonds and Clipson, *The Naval Institute Historical Atlas of the U.S. Navy*, 88.

21. Portsmouth, Ohio, the Scioto County seat, was established in 1815 at the confluence of the Ohio and Scioto Rivers. See "Outline plan of Portsmouth, Ohio. (with) Sciotoville, Haverhill, Ohio" (map), 1877.

22. No "McMicking" appears in either *Gibson's Guide and Directory of the State of Louisiana* . . . or *Kimball & James' Business Directory for the Mississippi Valley: 1844.*

23. Louisville, Jefferson County, Kentucky, was part of Virginia when the town was incorporated in 1780 on the south bank of the Ohio River. By the time Goings arrived, it was indeed a "Commercial Metropolis" southwest of Cincinnati, Ohio. In 1811, the first steamboat to reach Louisville paddled down from Pittsburgh, and by 1815 a steamer from New Orleans reached Louisville, opening that commercial artery to steam navigation.

Webb,[24] of Florence, who would have known, me, if I had not fortunately disguised myself in the habiliments of a sailor. Other familiar faces soon appeared, and I deemed it the part of prudence if not of valor, to return to the boat. At Cincinnatti I renewed the experiment hoping for more success, but here again I noticed faces that I had seen in the South and therefore curtailed my observations in this city. Although I was on what is called "free soil," I knew that informers might be the means of my being arrested and brought to trial as a fugitive, from bondage.[25]

I had no more attacks of sickness, as there was no arrival of passengers calculated to disarrange my nervous system. We duly reached Portsmouth where in a couple of days I got employment in a barber's shop. I made no permanent engagement, as I was anxious to get on to Cleveland. Just previous to my starting, the Captain of one of the Portsmouth and Cleveland Canal boats, entered the shop, and hapening to state that his cook had absconded, I deemed it a good chance to get at least a cheap passage to Cleveland. I told the captain I could not boast of my culinary skill, but with a little assistance I thought I might be able to fill the place of a more experienced hand. He accepted my offer and upon reaching Cleveland paid me $19 in cash, and offered me $25 per month upon my agreeing to remain with him. As I felt no real safety South of Canada, (for there is none to the colored man in slavery) I was compelled to decline his offer. I stayed at Cleveland a couple of days, but not feeling comfortable in a city where Southerners frequently visited during the summer season, I engaged passage on the steamer Bunker Hill for Detroit, Michigan.[26] At Detroit, where

24. John Webb, d. ca. 1849. Webb bought 80 acres north of Colbert's Reserve, Lauderdale County, Alabama, in 1833, and had been assigned 160 acres in 1818, which he patented in 1827. He was also involved in legal proceedings in the late 1820s. See Gandrud, *Alabama Records*, vol. 43, *Lauderdale County*, 49; Stewart, *Lauderdale County, Alabama, Marriage Records, 1820–1840*, 70; Cowart, *Old Land Records of Lauderdale County, Alabama*, 324, 351; and Hageness, *Alabama Genealogical Sources, Series, Abstract of Equity Record Book C (1808–1830), Lauderdale County, Alabama*, 46.

25. Ohio had banned slavery in its 1802 Constitution, but in 1804 and 1807 it passed laws requiring blacks to post a $500 bond, to promise not to violate laws under penalty of forfeiting the bond, and requiring them to obtain certificates testifying to their freedom. The codes also forbade employment for African Americans without certificates attesting to their free status and compliance with residency laws, and forbade the harboring of fugitives. See Middleton, *The Black Laws*, 74–75.

26. There was a side-wheel steamboat, *Bunker Hill*, built in Charleston, Ohio, in 1837. It displaced 457 tons, and its home port was Cleveland, Ohio. See Lytle and Holdcamper, *Merchant Steam Vessels of the United States, 1807–1868*, 23.

I was within sight of Canada, I engaged myself as waiter at the "Ameri-can."[27] There I remained only a month. All accounts of Canada were so dis-couraging that I accepted an offer to go to Toledo,[28] (Ohio) where after an engagement with a barber for about a month, I opened a little shop on my own account, I remained here some six months, but did not feel contented in a town where there were scarcely any colored people.[29]

I was advised to go to Fort Wayne, a town in Indiana,[30] but on my way

27. Detroit, Michigan, began as a French fort along the Detroit River in 1701. After struggles with local Indian nations and the French, the British took control of the area in 1760 and defended it three years later when the Ottawa leader Pontiac, as part of a coalition, laid siege to it. Detroit was incorporated as a city of the Northwest Territory in 1802, but it nearly burned down. Michigan's territorial law of 1827 contained both a black code and an anti-kidnapping statute, simultaneously requiring people of color to register with a county court to certify that they were free, and also forbidding the kidnapping of such persons. In 1833, a race riot in Detroit caused many African Ameri-cans to flee to Amherstburg and other towns in Ontario, across the Detroit River. By 1840, about half of Michigan's small population of people of color (707, or 0.3 percent of the population) was concentrated in the southeast: Monroe, Oakland, and Wayne Counties (including Detroit). Despite the territorial requirements to, in effect, license black Americans to live in the state, Michigan lacked the hard edge of southern Ohio's anti-black culture. There were fewer whites with Southern sympathies, and in the years following the 1833 riot, Detroit established a free school for black children (in 1842) and vigilance committees were formed to protect against slave-catchers. By 1850, Michigan's non-white population was just above 2,500 (0.6 percent of the population), in a state in which nearly 14 percent of the population was born outside of the United States and more than half of the state's residents had been born in other states. See Hine, *Black Women and the Re-construction of American History*, 61–62; Gray, *The Yankee West*; Jones and Shreve, "Detroit African-American History Project"; Winks, *The Blacks in Canada, A History*, 145; and Historical Census Browser, University of Virginia, Geo-spatial and Statistical Data Center.

28. Goings found the prospect of entering Canada dispiriting because, at the time, anti-black sentiment in Ontario was on the rise, in part because initially accepting Cana-dians viewed the arrivals as lazy or profligate and felt they attracted kidnappers to the area. See Winks, *The Blacks in Canada, A History*, 144.

29. Most black migrants to the Upper Mississippi and Ohio Valleys faced a double-bind. If they arrived as fugitives from slavery, they were often desperate, destitute, lack-ing in formal education, and rootless. If they were among the small proportion of Afri-can Americans who prospered, they sometimes became targets of white violence. See Rael, *Black Identity and Black Protest in the Antebellum North*, 207.

30. Indiana had anti-immigration statutes, including black codes, requiring that African American arrivals post a bond and promise to obey laws. The 1831 law required the posting of a $500 bond, and also required that any person of color who failed to do so would be sold at auction for a six-month term of service. See Hurt, *The Ohio Frontier;* and Davis, *Frontier Illinois.*

thither I met the keeper of a hotel at Perrysburgh, (Ohio) who made an engagement with me for a year.[31] Afterwards I was in business myself for a year. At this time I caught sight of Judge Whately formerly of Florence, Alabama, who was attending a large convention during the presidential campaign, in which the lamented General Morrison was the successful candidate.[32] Fearing he might recognise me I thought I had better travel to Canada as soon as possible. I took steamer to Erie. Pennsylvania, on Lake Erie, where a convention was being held, but where I managed to escape detection by any of the familiar faces of the Southern delegation.

31. Perrysburg was a station on the Underground Railroad and when Kentucky slave Henry Bibb escaped in 1837, he "found quite a settlement of colored people, many of whom were fugitive slaves." Bibb later wrote that after telling his story, "they sympathized with me," and despite the fact that he was "a stranger . . . they took me in and persuaded me to spend the winter in Perrysburgh, where I could get employment and go to Canada the next spring, in a steamboat which run from Perrysburgh, if I thought it proper so to do." He chopped wood in order to buy a suit of clothes. Like Goings, Bibb's "intention," he recalled, "was to go back to Kentucky after my wife." See Bibb, *Narrative of the Life and Adventures of Henry Bibb, Written by Himself,* 55.

32. William Henry Harrison (1773–1841) ran as the unsuccessful Whig Party presidential candidate in 1836, and won the presidency in 1840. He could be the "lamented General." The Virginia native owned a farm at North Bend, Ohio, to which he retired in 1829. See Peterson, *The Presidencies of William Henry Harrison and John Tyler,* 18, 32.

CHAPTER 3

Landed in Canada,—Nearly victimized into slavery again,—Returns after his wife,—Trial at Perrysburg,—Escape to Canada,—Marriage of second wife.

T HE FIRST REALLY "free soil" that my feet touched, was in Essex County at Fort Walden now called Amherstburgh, in Canada on the Detroit river.[1] There I stayed about a month, securing employment with the Major of the 42nd Regiment Infantry. While here I found the persons who were mentioned to me by the horse trainer in Kentucky. I afterwards entered into an engagement with the Captain of the steamboat Kent running from Amherstburgh to Chatham on the river Thames, Counties Essex and Kent, in Canada. The following season she was purchased for the Lake Erie trade, and I luckily declined to accept an offer of the steward's place after she had changed her route. The second season of her being on the Lake she was run down by the steamer London,[2] and sank in about ten minutes, losing many of the lives on board.[3] I remained on the River Thames as steward of the Steamer Brothers for nine seasons.[4]

1. After agreeing to evacuate U.S. territory under the terms of the Jay Treaty, the British constructed Fort Malden, opposite Detroit, between 1797 and 1799, to protect the Amherstburg Navy Yard. During the War of 1812, the Shawnee leader Tecumseh met British General Isaac Brock there, and the fort was used as a base of operations against Detroit. Fort Malden was later burned by the British fleeing American forces, but a smaller fort was rebuilt on the ruins of the first one following the American evacuation on July 1, 1815, when the land reverted to the British. See Collins, *Guidebook to the Historic Sites of the War of 1812*, 31.

2. The steamboat *London* displaced 432 tons, was built in 1845 in Chippewa, Canada, and operated out of the port of Detroit, Michigan. It was seized and condemned by the Treasury Department. See Lytle and Holdcamper, *Merchant Steam Vessels of the United States, 1807–1868*, 115.

3. The steamboats *London* and *Kent* collided at 3 a.m. on the morning of August 12, 1845, about twelve miles from Rondeau, Ontario. The *Kent* had left Detroit the previous evening with many passengers and sank in Lake Erie. See the *Ohio Statesman*, published as the *Tri-Weekly Ohio Statesman*, August 18, 1845.

4. The steamer *Brothers* was based in Chatham, Ontario, in the 1840s. During the passenger season, it left Chatham for Detroit and Amherstburg on Mondays, Wednes-

It was during this time that I became victimized into an adventure as perilous as my escape from slavery. At Chatham I formed the acquaintance of a colored man named George Wilson who had recently purchased a couple of hundred acres of land in the vicinity of the town. He was considered a reliable and respectable man. Having always been a free man, he had accumulated considerable means. During a conversation that I had with him he happened to mention Alabama, and upon further inquiry I found he had been in Florence, in that State, and was acquainted with some of the prominent "white" citizens, whose names were quite familiar to me. He stated that he had left some money behind, which required him to re-visit his former residence and settle the claims. I thought this a good chance to send for my wife, and therefore I told him all my former history which seemed to excite his interest and induced him to offer to rescue her from slavery.[5] I thereupon agreed to give him one hundred and fifty dollars upon his delivering her to my charge at Chatham. He claimed to be a little short of funds, and I therefore gave him twenty dollars on account.

I heard nothing of him for six months. At about the expiration of that time he returned, and told me he had fetched my wife to a town which was about a day's travel from Detroit. She was taken sick and could travel no further, but he was willing to accompany me back to the town where she had been left. I had some difficulty to induce my employers to let me away, but this I attributed to their dislike to be inconvenienced rather than to any fear that I might be ensnared into an unpleasant trap. With considerable reluctance they supplied me with funds to pay our expenses, and I accompanied him by way of Detroit to the town of which he had forgotten the name. From Detroit he insisted upon taking the stage as he pretended

---

days, and Fridays, returning on the alternate days. From Chatham, the boat steamed down the Thames River into Lake St. Clair, then stopped at Detroit to exchange passengers before docking in Amherstburg in a channel at the mouth of the Detroit River created by Bois Blanc Island. It was overhauled and its size enlarged during the winter of 1844–45. As a steward, Goings would have been responsible for preparing and perhaps serving meals, again plying his trade as a domestic servant for transient customers. The *London*, reputedly the fastest steamer on the upper Great Lakes at the time, met the *Brothers* at Detroit, continuing the passenger route to Buffalo, New York, by way of several Canadian ports. See Smith, *Smith's Canadian Gazetteer . . .* , 31.

5. Betrayal of fugitives was common. After his own escape from Maryland in 1838, Frederick Douglass recalled learning that "the black people of New York were not to be trusted; there were hired men on the lookout for fugitives from slavery, and who, for a few dollars, would betray me into the hands of slave-catchers." See Douglass, *My Bondage and My Freedom*, 338.

we might miss the village if we traveled by boat. The alleged distance from Detroit was only a day's travel, but instead of this we were traveling on a heavy road for three days and two nights, until we arrived much to my astonishment at my old residence, the town of Perrysburg, Ohio. I of course, recognized the place, and upon reaching the suburbs of the town suggested that I would stay at the house of an old acquaintance, which I pointed out to him, while he might go and fetch my wife. We arrived shortly after midnight, and he agreed to return about break of day.

I succeded in waking up my old friend who gave me a bed. I had not waited long before Wilson, (the villain, that he was,) came to the door and said he had found my wife all right, and would come down with her about sunrise. I then rose for the purpose of being in readiness, as day had commenced to dawn. As I watched for the arrival of my long lost wife, I was a little surprised at so early an hour to see five or six apparently well dressed gentlemen arrive at the corner of the street and hold a consultation. Two of them only came towards the house where I was staying. As they approached the dwelling, I recognized one of them as the Town Constable, and the other as some one I had seen before. Immediately the terrible thought flashed across my mind that one of my own race and color, adopting the wicked teachings of more civilized "white" people, had laid a wicked and treacherous scheme for my capture. The creatures of the law were at the very door and escape was impossible. To run was out of the question, my only hope lay in firmness and resolution. They came to the door and on the invitation of my friend Langford,[6] the occupant of the house, they entered the room. The first enquiry was made by Constable Smith: "Have you any strangers here ?" My friend said "No, except those you see around you, and my own family." Smith then turned into two of the adjoining rooms but returned without finding the property he expected. As he reentered the room, his companion gave him a knowing look, then a glance at me and ultimately a nod. Thereupon the Constable tapped me on the shoulder, saying : "Mr. Goings, I have a warrant for you." "For me? What do you want with me ?" said I. "Oh" says he "we will soon show you,

6. Joseph Langford, or Lankford, was one of a small minority of African Americans who lived and worked in Wood County (0.6 percent of the population), where Perrysburg was located. He was a conductor on the Underground Railroad, and Goings roomed and boarded with the Langford family of four in 1840. The Langford household included one male, ten to twenty-four, another male twenty-four to thirty-five, and two females, one ten to twenty-four and the other twenty-four to thirty-five. See 1840 U.S. Census, Perrysburg, Wood County, Ohio, roll 434, p. 401.

get on your boots quickly, and go with us to Brigham's tavern." Then for the first time, the tongue of the constable's companion was at least partially unloosed. Giving me a severe look he says with a peculiarly nasal twang "E-E-E-E—lijah d-d-d—don't you k-k-k—know me !" "No." I answered promptly. Shaking his fist he replied : "You r-r—rascal you. I k-k-k—know you very w-w-w—well." The light already dawned upon me as to who this old stammering creature was, but I determined not to pretend to recognize him. There was no alternative however, but for me to accompany them to the tavern. I did not feel the alarm which I would otherwise have felt if this had not been the town of my former home.

The person accompanying the local constable was named Fields.[7] I remembered him as one of the constables for Lauderdale County, Alabama. I should think he was more respected than many who hold that somewhat disagreeable office. He could neither be considered a drunkard or a blackguard, but brought up among the corrupting influences of slavery he would chase a slave with the pertinacity of a blood-hound.

By the time of our arrival at the tavern the news had evidently begun to spread, that a slave catching case was to come off before the magistrate. A large number of people had already assembled, and as I was well known in the town, much sympathy was expressed in my behalf. First and foremost among my friends on the occasion, was the Hon. William Hollister commonly called Judge Hollister.[8] He had never supposed I was a runaway and therefore expressed much surprise to find me in such an unfavorable position. He desired a few moments consultation with me in private, to which Constable Field demurred, but as the judge agreed to be responsible for my redelivery, Constable Smith knew better than object to so good a surety. The Judge asked me, "How is this that you are in this predicament ? Were you ever a slave ?" I replied that "I had been in slavery in Alabama, but that separation from my lawful wife had disgusted me so much that I had succeeded in making my escape. Since leaving Perrysburg I had been living in Canada and had employed a colored man named Wilson to fetch my former wife as he had been on a visit to the county in which I had

7. John G. Fields married Mary Devit in August 1830. As a justice of the peace for Lauderdale County, Alabama, he solemnized other marriages in the 1830s. See Jones and Gandrud, *Alabama Records*, vol. 213, *Lauderdale County* (microfilm), reel 7: 9, 28, 32, 87, ADAH.

8. John and B. F. Hollister are listed as pioneers or founders of Perrysburg. See Leeson, *Commemorative Historical and Biographical Record of Wood County, Ohio*, 360, 366.

once resided. He had returned to Canada and informed me that my wife had fallen sick by the way, and by such misrepresentations, had entrapped me into this dilemma. I had been, in my own estimation, a free man for between five and six years, and trusted that I should not be allowed to fall into the hands of my former "tyrants." He expressed a sympathy on my behalf, which gave me much encouragement. He said I must employ a lawyer. I therefore asked his advice as to a selection, and he suggested the well-known name of Spink.[9] The Judge kindly consented, at my request, to see Mr. Spink on my behalf. In a short time I had an interview with this gentleman, who, after, hearing my case, regretted that as he was just then a candidate for public office, he deemed it prudent not to imperil his position by touching so dangerous a subject, as the rights of the colored man, but he would send Mr. Hosman his partner with whom I might entrust my case with every confidence.[10]

Constable Fields was evidently a little surprised to find so much sympathy among the populace on my behalf. He spoke of my trustworthiness as a slave and the confidential character of the service in which I was engaged. The cause of my running away from so much kindness was inexplicable. Such conduct must be made use of as an example, and therefore he had resolved to carry me back to my former mistress. At ten o'clock we all repaired to the court-house where Squire Harrington presided. I should think upwards of five hundred persons had assembled, this being as I was informed, the first case of the kind ever tried within the County, Mr. Coffinbury, the District Attorney, appeared on behalf of the State and demanded a jury of 12 pursuant to the laws of Ohio.[11] The affidavits in possession of Fields were introduced and read under objections from my

9. John C. Spink was a resident of Perrysburg by 1839 and died before 1862. An early settler to the area, he appeared in courts in Defiance, Fulton, Lucas, Sandusky, Williams, and Wood Counties in Ohio, and was known by a colleague as an excellent advocate and a man of outstanding personal character. See Leeson, *Commemorative Historical and Biographical Record of Wood County, Ohio*, 78, 363–64.

10. Hezekiah L. Hosmer (1814–1893) was a resident of Perrysburg, Ohio, by 1839. A justice of the peace as well as a lawyer, he later served as chief justice of the Montana Territory. Hosmer wrote a novel, *Adela: The Octoroon*. See Leeson, *Commemorative Historical and Biographical Record of Wood County, Ohio*, 78, 363–64.

11. William Coffinberry, later a banker and newspaperman as well as a jurist remembered as a "brilliant advocate," put the case against Goings: he was a fugitive slave and according to U.S. law, Ohio was obliged to deliver him up. But in 1843 Coffinberry was still a young lawyer, with only three years' experience at the bar, which could explain his being taken by surprise by Hosmer. See Leeson, *Commemorative Historical and*

attorneys. There was no oral testimony offered, and the question on my side being one purely of law, the main features of the case were confined to the arguments of counsel.

Mr. Coffinbury relied upon his citations from the laws of Congress. My own attorneys had quite a struggle to get an adjournment. Mr. Coffinbury resisted the application as he claimed there could be no question as to the proper decision in this case. Mr. Fields, however, considered it best policy to consent to an adjournment, as he repeated his confidence in securing my return. My own lawyer desired time for investigation as the case presented several novel and intrinsic features and questions of law. The hour to which the case was adjourned was two o'clock in the afternoon of the following day. During this temporary suspense, my lawyer told me, that if the decision went against me there was such an anti-slavery feeling in the place that there would be ample assistance to secure my escape. Upon the re-assembling of the Court Mr. Hosman made a powerful address in my behalf taking the legal ground that under the laws of Ohio all men were free, and that since the year 1835, no Justice of the Peace had jurisdiction in any case of application for the return of a fugitive slave. Mr. Coffinbury disputed the assertion, until my counsel showed the statute in question. Thereupon Mr. Coffinbury seemed taken aback and admitted having overlooked this, to me, very fortunate legislative act.[12] There was not then the fugitive slave law.[13]

I suppose that Mr. Coffinbury having become convinced that a Justice of the Peace had no jurisdiction, consented I believe, to take what the lawyers call a "nonsuit." This did not, however, relieve me from the peril of further detention by the process of some superior court. No sooner was the Court over than I received instructions from my lawyer to mount the first

---

Biographical Record of Wood County, Ohio, 363; and *History of Hancock County, Ohio,* 279.

12. Hosmer outwitted Coffinberry, arguing that, under an 1835 Ohio law, Fields, being a constable, or justice of the peace, could not recover a fugitive slave in that particular court. Ohio had passed an anti-kidnapping statute in 1835, mostly because of concerns that white residents were vulnerable to being kidnapped and sold into slavery south of the Ohio River. Coffinberry conceded the point and agreed to a non-suit. If Fields wanted to take Goings back to Alabama, Goings would have to be arrested again and the matter would have to be taken up by a higher court. See Leeson, *Commemorative Historical and Biographical Record of Wood County, Ohio,* 76; and Middleton, *The Black Laws,* 92–93.

13. The Fugitive Slave Act of 1850 overrode state laws enacted to protect African Americans from kidnapping and transport out of state as slaves.

horse I could find and take route for Detroit, thence into Canada as speedily as possible. He said that a person would follow me and return with the horse as soon as I had got out of harm's way. As I was going down the stairs I heard Fields shouting to detain me just for one half hour. He promised two hundred dollars in gold to any one who would accomplish the daring feat. Unfortunately for Fields, he had been entrapped more successfully than his unfortunate victim. In this little town of Perrysburg a strong anti-slavery feeling existed, or at least a decided opposition to aid slave catchers in their nefarious operations. Apart from this, I had resided some eighteen months among the people of this town, and they had a sympathy for me which completely frustrated the shrewd and nearly successful plans of my undaunted pursuers. Wilson would never have drawn me to this town if he had been told my position among the inhabitants. No one seemed tempted even by the gold of my pursuer, for as soon as I reached the door, I found a horse, in fact several horses, ready to be mounted. I took the one opposite the entrance, held by my friend Langford, and in a few moments amid the shouts of the assembled crowd, I was galloping on towards Toledo. In about ten minutes my friend Langford overtook me, and we drove along at a rapid rate some eighteen miles.[14] Feeling myself now out of danger, I bade good bye to my old friend who turned back with the horses, and I walked on for several miles, until, being tired, I called at a farm house where I obtained accommodation free of all expense. Next morning I walked on to Monroe (Michigan), where I waited until the arrival of the stage. On stating my case to the keeper of the hotel he directed the driver to take me to Detroit and charge me nothing for the fare. I duly arrived at Detroit, and took the steam ferry forthwith to Windsor, Canada, thence by stage to Chatham, where my employers expressed some surprise at my long absence. I think they somewhat doubted my story until a letter arrived

---

14. That was not the first time Langford had aided a fugitive whom the local authorities refused to hand over to kidnappers. A Wood County historian contended that "on one occasion a Kentuckian arrived" in Perrysburg "and found his human chattel." Like Fields, the man took the matter to court in order "to prove his ownership before he could take" the fugitive back to slavery. As in Goings's case, "the slave's lawyer found a flaw in the indictment, or information, and this necessitated the making of new papers." Meanwhile, the Underground Railroad "'conductors,' seeing a chance to save the slave, soon had a fleet horse at the door of the justice's office, upon which the negro mounted and rode off, Langford, the colored owner of the horse, exclaiming: 'Here is a dead horse or a free nigger!'" See Leeson, *Commemorative Historical and Biographical Record of Wood County, Ohio*, 368–69.

from my lawyer, enclosing a bill for something over three hundred dollars. At this time I had purchased a one acre lot and house in Chatham, for which I had paid four hundred dollars, leaving one hundred dollars due upon an outstanding mortgage. My employers thought the legal charges exorbitant and advised me not to pay them. I felt, however, that my advisers had worked so faithfully for my release that they were justly entitled to their charges. I therefore raised the money by selling Messrs. Ebards my homestead subject to the mortgage which had become due, and they liquidated my lawyer's bill.[15]

I have thus attempted to give a brief but correct statement of my escape from slavery upon two several occasions. This last time I was victimized by the treachery of one of my own color. The villain who deliberately planned my recapture, has never to my knowledge returned to Canada. I heard of his subsequent settlement in Cincinnati, where I believe he has since died. The last information that I have been able to gain of my first wife, was, that she had been married to another slave of the family with whom she resided. I married a second wife in Canada, and have a family. I suppose also that I have a brother and sister still in bondage. I heard of the former some ten years ago. He was then living (if any slave may be said to live) in New-Kent County, Virginia. It is more than twenty years ago since I heard of my sister. If they still survive it is to be hoped that they may yet obtain their freedom.[16]

15. Before being lured to Perrysburg, Goings had saved $400 and had bought a house and a one-acre lot by 1843, borrowing the balance of the $500 purchase price. Like nearby Amherstburg, Colchester, St. Catharines, and Toronto, Chatham was home to a large refugee population of African Americans. Canada set no onerous restrictions on people of African descent like Goings, and the law made no distinction between white and black residents. Like white men in Canada, black men could vote (after meeting a three-year residency requirement, just like whites) and enjoy other benefits of citizenship, including access to public accommodations, military service (in separate units), jury duty, and testifying in court. From time to time, white Canadians sought to bar blacks from the polls or refuse service on an equal footing. Afro-Canadians organized protests and did not hesitate to defend their rights in the courts and in the press. See Hepburn, *Crossing the Border,* chaps. 3–5.

16. The mention of the brother still in slavery indicates a drafting date before Emancipation, and the first three chapters make no reference to the Civil War.

CHAPTER 4

Observations on Slavery,—The present War,—The Church,—The Irish Orator, Shiells.

IT IS THE OPINION of many eminent discerners of the times that the death knell of slavery is now being rung.[1] The slaveholders themselves have long trembled for the fate of their despotic institution. Jefferson forewarned the people of its downfall, and the sword is now dealing its foretold destruction.[2] I remember while in Alabama, that my master received occasional visits from a Mr. Harris, who had been a wealthy slaveholder, but in consequence of undue speculation had become a bankrupt. He was a man possessed of much information, and I often listened to his conversations at table with close attention. Upon the occasion of his return from a trip through the State of Ohio, I recollect his observations upon the false economy of the slave system, produced a great impression upon the guests surrounding the table of my hospitable master. He argued that the average profits of the labor of an able bodied slave did not exceed from twenty-three to twenty-five dollars per annum over and above expanses and interest of money upon the cost of the slave. He showed that the voluntary labor of the North was performed more skillfully by the men who received a fair day's wage for a fair day's work, and he was eloquent upon the thrift and progress everywhere apparent upon the North side of the Ohio river. I was astonished to hear him confess that he expected that within fifty years every slave would be free upon the principle that any system must fall so soon as people are satisfied it does not pay. When among themselves the Southern Slaveholders would not only argue this question with calmness but would assent to the reasonableness of such an argument as that used by Mr. Harris.

1. This section was written during the Civil War, probably during or after the summer of 1863.
2. Jefferson, *Notes on the State of Virginia*, query XIV.

I little expected at that day to taste the fruits of my own labor in a free land, much more could I have hoped to watch the approach of deliverance to three millions and more of my enthralled brethren of the South. Yet surely the day of redemption draweth nigh.[3] Gradually though positively, events are working to the accomplishment of the glorious consummation of a people's hopes. At the commencement of the fearful struggle still going on upon this continent, there seemed danger of a compromise with the detested system.[4] For at least a twelvemonth, few would admit that slavery was an issue in the war. Even the proclamation of the President came hedged and surrounded by the specious apology of "military necessity."[5] Yet who can doubt the final working of all events to the certain emancipation of the Slave? These are not days of retrogression when, the Emperor of Russia has humanely considered the necessity to move the schackles from off his serfs, and when Spain herself (and she is the oldest slave holding nation, I believe) is trembling lest she be compelled to follow in the wake of freedom.[6] The votaries of the iniquitous system who are still declaiming in

---

3. Gospel of Luke 21:28.

4. The Crittenden Compromise of December 1860 was a final attempt to forestall disunion. Senator John J. Crittenden of Kentucky proposed six new constitutional amendments regulating slavery and its territorial extension, including an un-amendable constitutional amendment sanctioning slavery in perpetuity in the Federal Union, a reinstatement of the Missouri Compromise line of 1820 extending it to the Pacific, federal reimbursement for fugitive slave property not returned to owners because of active interference, the right of territorial inhabitants to decide whether slavery would be legal in the territories south of the compromise line, and protections for slavery in the District of Columbia. The proposals were unsuccessful and the secession crisis of 1860–61 deepened. See Ayers, *In the Presence of Mine Enemies*, 98–99; and Crofts, *Reluctant Confederates*, chap. 8.

5. The Emancipation Proclamation of 1863 relies on the president's constitutional authority as commander in chief, freeing the slaves as a "fit and necessary war measure for suppressing" the rebellion. The proclamation freed only those slaves in areas then in rebellion against the United States and not those in Union-occupied territories, yet it established emancipation as a war aim.

6. Czar Alexander II of Russia issued the Emancipation Manifesto on March 3, 1861 (the day before Abraham Lincoln became president of the United States). It legally freed Russian serfs, transferred between one-third and one-half of all private estate land to those newly freed, to be distributed to families through peasant communes, and provided that recipients would pay for the land by repaying one-fourth of the original price over an extended period, the government reimbursing owners for the balance. After a fierce abolition movement by slaves and former slaves in the Spanish Caribbean, Spain abolished slavery in Puerto Rico in 1873 (compensating owners). By 1880, Cuba was

the North will be silenced by the rolling tide of an enlightened public opinion. Even as politicians, they will become convinced that the longer continuance of an indefensible system is a source of constant irritation between the two sections of the country. Those who have held property in slaves will soon make favorable comparison between the results of a compulsory system of labor and the willing service of a free man. By degrees they will arrive at the conviction, that national prosperity can only be attained by the maintenance of national justice,—a justice based upon the principle: "no property in man."

It is cheering also to note the gradual change which is working in every section of the Christian Church. The pulpit is being aroused after its participation in slavery, to the real merits of the slavery conflict. Nearly half a century ago the great John Randolph of Virginia inserted a clause in his last will and testament to the following effect: "I give to my slaves their freedom, to which my conscience tells me they are justly entitled."[7] The foregoing narrative has shown conclusively that according to the case of the Slave States, the bonds of matrimony are a sham, and the possession of a family of children, a misfortune. Surely the Divine Author of the universe would not have given any of the human family the feelings and faculties of men, unless he also intended them to assume the responsibilities, and appreciate the pleasures of domestic life. The whole tendency of our blessed Saviour's preaching was the moral and social elevation of the human family. The proclamations of His Gospel seem specially intended to reach the ear of the helpless and oppressed. Better, far better, would it be if the pretended successors of the Apostles of each and every denomination throughout Christendom, would give louder utterances to the precepts of their Lord and Master, rather than attempt the elucidation of enexplicable doctrines, or practice the pernicious quackery of prophetic interpretation. Surely they might array a portion of their artillery against the drunkenness that stalks in every street, the extravagance which is leading individuals

---

committed to abolishing slavery, which accelerated a gradual and grudging transition to free labor there. See Wortman, *Scenarios of Power*, chap. 2; and Scott, *Slave Emancipation in Cuba*.

7. This sentence is contained in the will of John Randolph of Virginia (1773–1833). He freed some 385 slaves upon his death and also willed them money to settle in Ohio. The quote had circulated widely by the time Goings wrote this passage, including in Helper, *The Impending Crisis of the South*. See Russell, *The Free Negro in Virginia, 1619–1865*, 85.

and nations to hopeless bankruptcy, the trickery which colrurs the dealings of modern society, and the "slavery" which has cursed a continent. Too frequently these theological disputants have been the apologists for national voluptuousness and the defenders of human oppression. They heap their curses upon innocent amusements, or brand as a heretic the patron of free thought, while they rarely utter words without which we should have no Gospel: "Whatsoever ye would that men should do unto you, do ye even so unto them."[8]

The issue of the present gigantic American war, which is in truth a revolution, is watched with hopeful interest by every friend of human progress. It daily becomes more apparent that the morning Star of Freedom has arisen upon my benighted brethren. The numbers are rapidly increasing of those who favor the total abolition of slavery. They see in slavery the cause of their terrible revolution, and will advocate the removal of that cause. The proclamation of freedom has gone forth and no statesman of the free north will dare to pronounce it a nullity. That which was all a "military necessity" will ripen into a "moral right." The great question is as to the possibility of ultimate conquest. So long as the Southern Confederacy maintained a defensive attitude, they seemed to have the best of it. But the aggressive policy of General Lee is taming the tide in favor of the federals.[9] The full effects of these southern movements will only be gradually developed. They must tend to rouse the north as it has never been roused before. If men were lately getting tired of the war, they will become awakened to their true position when the enemy, whom heretofore they have not seen, is threatening to devastate their own homesteads.

But the ultimate failure of the north to subjugate the south, is a possibility not to be entirely overlooked. Even under such circumstances it is unlikely that slavery will long survive. The Southern Confederacy can receive but a tardy and a short recognition from many of the freedom loving countries of Europe, even if such, a thing was done, which is not so likely.

---

8. Gospel of Matthew 7:12.

9. In early June of 1863, the 80,000-man Confederate Army of Northern Virginia invaded Maryland and Pennsylvania under the leadership of General Robert E. Lee. On June 28, General George G. Meade's 112,700-man U.S. Army of the Potomac entered Pennsylvania to repel them. The two armies clashed at the Battle of Gettysburg on July 1–3, 1863, with 57,000 casualties on both sides, including casualties suffered during the campaign. The Confederate army retreated to Virginia. See Sears, *Gettysburg*, 95, 149, 496–98.

It will be asking admission to the brotherhood of nations with a constitution the "corner stone" of which is slavery. Heretofore the federal powers at Washington have shirked the responsibility, and declared the system to be peculiarly and exclusively a "State" institution. In fact, each slave State made its own laws applicable to slavery. But the national charter of the Confederacy has dealt openly and explicitly, however wrongfully, with the subject of chattel property in man. It seeks not to hedge round the dangerous theme with the tender words of "persons held to servitude"![10] It enters into league and covenant with the accursed crime. A country basing its social system upon the enslavement of a portion of its inhabitants, cannot secure the sympathies of enlightened Christians. Perversion of Christianity itself, has alone screened the slavery system. Even policy alone will insure a final abolition of slavery by the people of the Confederate States. It is not likely that any guarantees would be given by any contiguous government or country for the return of fugitive slaves. The United States will be as safe an assylum to the escaped runaway from the Southern Confederacy, as Canada has heretofore been the only haven of security to the colored wanderer. The result of separation will be the wiping out the stain of slavery upon the territory of the United States.

From the signs of the times there is everything to hope, nothing to fear. The cry of the oppressed is not uttered in vain. The Great Arbiter of human events is at the helm, and will evolve beneficent results in a manner not to be forseen by the imperfect observations of sinful humanity. He will overrule the commotions which everywhere prevail, to the advancement of His own glory and the welfare and happiness of the human family. May that time be at hand!

On the other hand, there are those who believe that nothing short of conquest and subjugation can uproot a system so thoroughly interwoven into the local institutions of Southern Territory. It is argued with much truth and plausibility that the cause of the revolution was slavery from the beginning, and that the extinction of the foulest blot that ever darkened a nation's history, is now the object contemplated by nine-tenths of the people of the North. Already where the Northern Army has secured and reclaimed possession of Southern soil, the philanthropists of New England are establishing schools for the training of colored children, with a view to

---

10. Here, Goings is paraphrasing Article IV, Section 2 of the U.S. Constitution, concerning "persons held to service," that is, slaves.

their better preparation for a new and improved position in Society.[11] Furthermore, the establishment of Freedmen's Societies under the direction of prominent abolitionists, aided by Congressional appropriations, gives tokens of an interest in the cause of emancipation never before so practically manifested by the American people.[12] The ready manner in which the Yankee nation can adapt itself to great and fundamental changes in the policy of their government, has been exemplified in instances too numerous to mention. Take for instance the periodical financial disasters which have so frequently brought sudden and inevitable ruin to the hearths and homes of thousands of happy families. The banks have suspended specie payment under legislative approval, and courts of law have sanctioned unjust delay if not direct repudiation between creditor and debtor.[13] Such a defiance of honest principle would not be tolerated in the better governed and older established countries of Europe. Yet with this pliant people such unconstitutional intervention is looked upon with cool complacency, as if they exercised a universal faith in Pope's immortal words: "Whatever is, is right."[14]

To come to more recent times and more immediately to the subject of the work it is interesting to notice the ready acquiescence in the people of the United States to every proclamation or decree of the presiding Officer of the Republic. Step by step, the rights of the colored race, have been recognized by the Edicts which have emanated from Washington. A growl or a threat is the extent of the opposition that has been encountered. If it were anything but the declamation of a small minority, the accomplished work must have been retarded if not indefinitely posponed. Men who a few years or even a few months ago, were crying out against an interference with slavery, are now sustaining their illustrious Chief in every edict that makes an inroad on the once serf trodden territory of a proud and overbearing dynasty.

But the question even now is sometimes asked: What is to, be done with

---

11. As early as September 1861, the American Missionary Association had begun work among the contrabands at Fort Monroe in Virginia. See Drake, "Freedmen's Aid Societies and Sectional Compromise."

12. Goings is referring to Freedmen's Aid Societies.

13. The Panic of 1837 was among the worst financial panics to date. It was followed by a bust in the cotton economy, widespread bank failures, suspensions of specie payment, frozen credit, and the loss of 45 percent of their assets by state-chartered banks. See Rousseau, "Jacksonian Monetary Policy, Specie Flows, and the Panic of 1837."

14. See Pope's *An Essay on Man and Other Poems,* 12 (the last line of first epistle).

the three or four millions of emancipated slaves? Common sense would seem to reply: "Let them alone." Give the colored race an equal chance of competition in the labor market of the world and they will be ready to bear the responsibilities of their social existence. If they are made the recipients of honest wages, they will cheerfully engage in honest labor. They are easily to be actuated by the emotions of hope and self-respect, as any other branch of the human family. The numbers who have already made experiment of freedom are a living testimony to the capabilities of the race. Thousands are earning an honest and peaceable livelihood in Canada, while many have accumulated wealth in every section of the Northern States. If capable of leveling forests and reclaiming swamps, while in a state of bondage, which, they unquestionably were, why should they be less fitted for hardy toil when they are emancipated from an infamous and debasing thraldom. They will surely remain equal to the task of the cotton field and the sugar plantation. In slavery they have been peaceable, industrious, and orderly, and as free men they will be loyal, diligent, and frugal. The poor and the feeble are to be found among every people, but they are the exception and not the rule. On this great continent where labor is generally abundant, every man can find something to do. All may not be fitted for work of the severest kind, yet each one can pursue some calling for which he possesses sufficient natural ability.

The same hue and cry was raised before the successful emancipation of the slaves in the West Indies. No better testimony to the results as it affects the colored race in those islands can be cited than that of Governor Hincks[15] of Barbadoes, who was once M. P. and member of the Government in Canada, who says: "There can be little if any difference of opinion among well informed persons as to the satisfactory change in the condition of the African race. The improvement which has taken place in the religious condition of the people of all classes and the progress of education is

---

15. Sir Francis Hincks (1807–1885) was a Canadian journalist and statesman who had been born in Ireland. Entering the Canadian legislative assembly in 1841, Hincks was twice inspector general (or finance minister), from 1842 to 1843, and again from 1848 to 1851. Hincks served as the British governor of Barbados and the Windward Islands from 1855 to 1862, and of British Guiana from 1862 to 1869; he then returned to Canada to serve as minister of finance (1869–73) in Sir John A. Macdonald's coalition government. In 1869, he was knighted. Hincks published a pamphlet, *The Results of Negro Emancipation*, which was based on a speech he gave in London in August 1859 celebrating the twenty-fifth anniversary of emancipation. See Ormsby, "Hincks, Sir Francis."

quite equal to what could reasonably have been expected. The Creoles are advancing rapidly in cultivation and it is no longer pretended that emancipation has ruined the British West Indies.["]

The condition of the race must have ample legal protection against the contumely and imposition to which they are at first likely to be exposed. Such will be the suddenness of a change from abject serfdom to constitutional liberty, that many may be tempted into paths of idleness and debauchery. Yet it will behove a professedly Christian people to treat these new created sons of freedom with consideration and even generosity. Let them feel that they are no longer a proscribed and outlawed race, and they may be expected speedily to adapt themselves to their improved condition.

Compulsory colonization in a foreign soil has been suggested, and even partially tried by a few earnest advocates of anti-slavery feelings. Such a step is as cruel as it is unnecessary. By no principle of justice can it be argued that the colored man shall be forced from the land of his birth. The Southern States are eminently adapted for his residence. So soon as it has become free soil, there will have become created an additional bond of attachment to a country so suited for his physical condition. Thoroughly acclimatized he can successfully compete in the labor market under the newly established regime of political economy. Heretofore the white man has been to him a remorseless, greedy and cruel tyrant. Under a reformed and better state of things, his former oppressor will exhibit a new and nobler side to his character. The colored race have had to water the soil with their tears, and enrich it with their blood. Surely it would be cruelty unparalleled to drive them from the country made wealthy by their exertions. They will occupy no larger territory as "freemen" than they did as "slaves." There are no competitors who are eager to take their places in the cotton fields, or "till" the land which they have helped to redeem from the primeval forest. There is no such competition.

Any attempt at such a vast system of emigration would be as futile as it is inexpedient. The navies of the world might be employed for years and yet the tide of natural increase would be flowing ever onward. The colored man is found alike upon the prairies of Minnesota or at the seat of commerce in the modern "Gotham;" in the battle field, or in the workshop, he has toiled to make himself a name.[16] Our commerce and our agriculture have been improved and increased by the labors of the poor slaves.

16. "Gotham" is a satirical term for New York City popularized by Washington Irving in the early nineteenth century, which in turn was based on the poem "Gotham," a satire

Verily, the language of the illustrious Shiel, the compeer of the great O'Connell, might be transposed to meet the argument we fain would bring.[17] Alluding to a charge that Lord Lyndhurst had brought against the "alien" sons of Erin, the florid orator burst forth in a torrent of words that have immortalised his memory:—"Methinks it ought to be remembered that the negro soldiers with whom your armies were filled were the inseparable auxiliaries to the glory with which your unparalleled successes have been crowned. Whose were the athletic arms that drove your bayonets at Chattanooga, through the phalanxes that never reeled in the shock of war before?[18] What desperate valor climbed the steeps and filled the moats of Vicksburg?[19] Tell me, General Grant, (for you were there,) when the artillery of Southern chivalry levelled with the precision of the most deadly science played upon them; when her legions, incited by the voice,

---

on the relationship between the king, his supporters, and slaves, written by the Englishman Charles Churchill (1731–1764). See Paulding, Irving, and Irving, *Salmagundi*, 48 and passim.

17. Richard Lalor Sheil (1791–1851), an Irish lawyer and nationalist, was admitted to the Irish Bar in 1814. He was one of the founders in 1823 of the Catholic Association, supporting the movement of Daniel O'Connell (1775–1847) for Catholic emancipation or the right to hold senior government offices or to sit in the British Parliament. O'Connell was instrumental in passing the 1829 Emancipation Act and worked to dissolve the union of Great Britain and Northern Ireland, for which he was arrested in 1843. See Flaherty, "Richard Lalor Sheil."

18. At the Battle of Chattanooga, Tennessee, November 23–25, 1863, the Union victory laid the groundwork for General William Tecumseh Sherman's campaign to Atlanta and the sea. From late September until October 1863, Confederate forces pinned down the Union army in Chattanooga, cutting their lines of supply in an attempt to starve them. Taking command of the western U.S. forces, General Ulysses S. Grant directed Major General George Thomas to assume control of the Union army besieged at Chattanooga and reestablish a supply line. He moved in Union forces under William T. Sherman, who assaulted the Confederates on November 23–24, capturing Lookout Mountain. On the 25th, they captured Missionary Ridge and routed the Confederacy's western army. The victory in Chattanooga complemented the taking of Vicksburg and furthered the Union military strategy of dividing the Upper South from the Lower South. Sherman's army used Chattanooga to stage his march to Atlanta in late 1864. See McPherson, *Battle Cry of Freedom*, chap. 22.

19. The Siege of Vicksburg took place in the summer of 1862 when Union naval forces under Flag Officer David Farragut assaulted the city, which was the key to controlling the Mississippi River after the fall of New Orleans in April 1862. A two-pronged Union assault in December 1862 also failed to take the fortified city and the Confederate army that guarded it. In May of 1863, Union forces under General Ulysses S. Grant were

inspired by the example, of their mighty leader, rushed again and again to the contest—tell me, if for an instant, (when, to hesitate for an instant was to be lost,) the "aliens" blanched?[20] And when at length the moment for the last decisive movement had arrived—when the valor so long wisely checked was at last let loose—tell me if Afric's sons, with less heroic valor than the whiteborn sons of your own glorious Republic, precipitated themselves upon, the relentless foe? The blood of Europe, America, and Africa flowed in the same stream on the same field. When the chill morning dawned, their dead lay cold and stark together. In the same deep pits their bodies were deposited. The greenness of spring is now breaking on their commingled dust. The dew falls from Heaven upon their union in the grave. Partakers in every peril, in the glory shall they not participate? And shall they be told as a requital, that they are to be estranged from the noble country for whose salvation their life blood was poured out? No, verily, they cannot; they will not be made the victims of such barbarity. As education does its elevating work the race will, in such degree, assist

---

successful in taking strategic ground and winning battles that laid the groundwork for a siege. The siege began on May 19 and lasted until July, with heavy casualties on both sides and considerable suffering among Vicksburg's residents. On July 4, Grant took the city and captured the Confederate defenders, including 2,166 officers, 27,230 enlisted soldiers, 172 cannon, and 60,000 rifles and muskets. See Hewitt, "Vicksburg, Siege of," 804.

20. Ulysses S. Grant (1822–1885) of Ohio received an appointment to the United States Military Academy at West Point and entered the U.S. army after graduating in 1843. Grant served in the U.S. war against Mexico under generals Zachary Taylor and Winfield Scott, rising to the rank of captain, but retired from the army in 1854 to farm and be close to his wife Julia and his two sons. He reentered service in 1861 and rose to prominence with daring but costly victories at Fort Donelson, Tennessee, in February 1862, and Shiloh, Tennessee, in April 1862. Grant was largely responsible for the success of the taking of Vicksburg in 1863, after which he became supreme commander in the West. He won the Battle of Chattanooga, Tennessee, in November 1863, after which President Lincoln placed him in overall command of the U.S. army in March 1864. He pursued Robert E. Lee's Army of Northern Virginia, eventually winning its surrender at Appomattox Courthouse, Virginia, in April 1865, which ended the cause of the Confederacy. Grant stayed in the army during Reconstruction, but resigned to run successfully for president as a Republican in 1868. The eighteenth President of the United States, Grant won reelection in 1872. He later toured the world, but suffered financial trouble after taking part in fraudulent investments in New York. He completed his memoirs, which restored his family to financial solvency, while dying of throat cancer. See Simon, "Grant, Ulysses S."

in building up a nation on this Western Continent, renowned for its intelligence, activity, and virtue, and generations yet unborn will yearly hold a festival in memory of freedom's natal day."[21]

21. These remarks were delivered on February 23, 1837, during a debate in the House of Commons on the Irish Municipal Bill. They were prompted by a remark made a few days before in the House of Lords by Lord Lyndhurst, who referred to the Irish as "aliens." Sheil then delivered a speech in Lyndhurst's presence objecting to the Lord's characterization of the Irish as aliens: "The Irish soldiers, with whom your armies are filled, were the inseparable auxiliaries to the glory with which his unparalleled successes have been crowned. Whose were the arms that drove your bayonets at Vimiera through the phalanxes that never reeled in the shock of war before." See Sheil, *Speeches of the Right Honourable Richard Lalor Sheil, M.P.,* lxxxix, 169–70 (quote).

CHAPTER 5

Remarks on some of the Southern States, and Emigration to them.

IT MAY NOT BE unacceptable to the reader, to give some slight picture of the peculiar physical features of the several States through which the author has travelled, with a view to assist the intending emigrant in his choice of a location, should the tidal movement once more set in in that direction. Much has been written, and said adverse to the Southern climate; but as a general rule there is much exaggeration upon this subject. It is not that the extreme heat is so much worse than the same extremity of heat here in Canada. The peculiarity of its oppressiveness arises from its long continuance, and not from its intensity. As a rule, the Southern States are healthy, and good water is generally procurable.

Persons intending to farm, must not expect to find a great deal of unimproved valuable land. The greater part of that which is capable of culture has long been under tillage. None but capitalists can expect to succeed in agriculture. Farmers are not often working men. The colored race have heretofore been the tillers of the soil. The state of society necessarily changes with the nature of the country, and the peculiarities of the races which inhabit it. Neither will the same mode of cropping be suited to a farm in Virginia or Georgia, that is successfully adopted in Canada. Cattle and sheep farming is extensively carried on, and from the shortness and general mildness of the winters, is a profitable branch of agriculture. But in the States south of Tennessee little grain is sown. Corn is a luxuriant crop, and is used much more for domestic purposes, than among the people inhabiting the more Northern part of the continent.

One of the finest, if not the finest, border State is Kentucky. Good turnpike roads intersect the State in every direction. Some districts are somewhat stony, yet in spite of this natural obstruction, much of the land has been under a high state of cultivation for a great number of years. Many of the settlers are wealthy. A large number of good families reside in the vicinity of Lexington. As a commercial emporium, the city of Louisville, Kentucky, takes high rank among the seats of Southern industry.

Tennessee, has thriven rapidly, and is well adapted for experiment by intending northern emigrants. In Murray County there is a good deal of rich land. There are many enterprizing settlers who have accumulated considerable wealth, [and] Dixon County is eminently adapted for settlement. A great deal of corn is raised, and about sufficient wheat for home consumption. The land in Memphis County is generally poor. There are large tracts of excellent timber. Railways intersect the best portions of this inland State.

The fine old State of Virginia has a reputation that it well deserves. Many of the old families of this section are descendants of illustrious Englishmen. Until the revolution of 1861, peace and plenty everywhere prevailed. Many persons would designate this as the "West End," or aristocratic quarter of the American continent.[1] Wealth and luxury have run riot in the "Old Dominion," The very names of the Counties indicate the thoroughly British sentiment that once prevailed among the denizens of this beautiful portion of the once happy and loyal colony. The statesmen that Virginia has produced have not been men belonging to a school of unthinking demogogues. They have possessed the vigour of chivalric manhood, combined with the deliberate coolness of a trans-Atlantic hero. Nurtured in ease and affluence, they have had leisure for reading and observation. The necessary result of such a training produces the same quality of men the wide world over—men essentially patriotic and unmistakably "Conservative."

Bitter towards their enemies, they are the most hospitable of friends. Profuse in their liberality, they are yet most tenacious of their rights. The wealth that many of them have inherited is held as a legacy in trust for future generations. Their most venomous foes cannot charge them with cowardice, nor their associates pronounce them as treacherous. They have little of the meanness peculiar to New England character. Faultless they are not, mistaken they sometimes may be, but, as a people, they possess traits of character that ennoble and dignify humanity.

Many parts of this fine old State are exceedingly fertile and productive. The picturesqueness of much of the scenery is unrivalled, In King and Queen County, there is a good deal of low swampy ground, yet often

---

1. According to the *Oxford English Dictionary,* one of the definitions of "West End" is "The fashionable or aristocratic quarter of a town or other place."

very rich and calculated to produce luxuriant crops of tabacco and rice.[2] In Jarvis County the land is generally poor.[3] Much of it remains covered with a stately growth of magnificent pine. New Kent lies high, the soil is good, producing corn in great abundance. There is considerable poor land in Charles City County, but a part of it is rich. Tobacco and corn are the staple products. Essex County is more famous for the beauty of its scenery, than its fertility. The notorious city of Petersburgh is surrounded by lovely alternations of hill and dale, ornamented with many a stately edifice, the home of the once thriving and contented planter.[4] The Western portions of Virginia, with valley, plain, and mountains, can hardly be surpassed for productiveness of soil and healthiness of climate.

North Carolina immediately south of Virginia, has an extensive sea board and in many parts is thickly populated. One of the richest counties is Halifax, producing large quantities of corn and cotton. The soil of Northampton County is generally light, especially on the lands overflowed occasionally by the Roanoke river. This section of Country is however, well formed, and amply repays the husbandman for his labor. In Wake County there are spots of rich land but interposed with large tracts of worthless soil. There are numerous fine homesteads inhabited by old families. There is much wealth in the different counties of N. C. Corn, wheat, oats, rye, and sweet potatoes, are all cultivated in this neighbourhood. The islands in the Roanoke river are famous for their fertility. The soil is very rich, and no pains are spared in its proper cultivation. The turpentine and rosin of commerce come largely from this State.

The central part of Georgia is well provided with Railway. Baldwin County is an old settled part of the Country. Around the important town of Milledgeville, the land is almost worn out. But as in the old country so in the new, agricultural improvements have taught systems of renewing the

2. King and Queen County, Virginia, certainly produced tobacco, and also produced small crops of rice as well. In the antebellum period, the planter Charles Hill of "Mantua" plantation attempted to grow rice on swampy ground that had yielded capacious crops of corn. Other residents reported buying rice. See Alfred Bagby, *King and Queen County, Virginia*, 74; and Bushman and Walker, *In Old Virginia*, 109, 223, 230.

3. James City County, Virginia.

4. Petersburg was notorious perhaps because of the nine-month siege in 1864–65 which culminated in the U.S. army's detonation of part of the Confederate army's defensive structure, resulting in a massive crater. Union forces attempts to assault the city from the crater resulted in 4,000 Union casualties, since the slope was too steep to ascend. Nevertheless, General Robert E. Lee's army left Petersburg in April 1865. See Bonekemper, *Grant and Lee*, 206.

energy of the soil. Plaster of Paris is successfully used as a manure.[5] There are many wealthy and distinguished families in all parts of this fine section of the Confederacy.

Much of the land in Alabama remains covered with heavy timber. In Dallas County the soil is inclined to sand, but produces valuable timber of all descriptions. Madison County is the richest in the State. Cotton is here produced in great abundance. Limestone County is also productive in cotton. A part of Wood County is poor, and the soil sandy.[6] The same may be said of Tuscaloosa County, but the heavy timber that remains, must long be a source of wealth to the owners of the soil.

Mississippi is exceedingly rich, in produce peculiar to its climate and soil. There is some corn raised here, but no grain. In Adams County the soil is rich, and cotton, the staple product. Orleans County at the mouth of the giant river of the Continent, is swampy, and in summer unhealthy for Europeans.[7] The land is rich and produces vegetables in abundance. At Baton Rouge and other parts, sugar is very extensively and successfully cultivated.

Arkansas offers great inducements for settlers who are prepared for roughing it. Pulaski County is hilly and broken, but back from the Mississippi River there is plenty of good land. This beautiful State is destined to be one of the most flourishing parts of the extreme Southern portion of North America. It has never had a large slave population, and may therefore be foremost in the van of liberty, and its companionship of blessings. At present, however, the humanity of hope is almost shadowed over by the tyranny of the "white race."

The Southern States are but in their infancy. They are now but undergoing a "second birth."[8] Peopled anew with a mixed and hardy race of European emigrants, and with the hardy enterprising settlers from Northern

---

5. Plaster of Paris, or gypsum, was used as manure in Virginia by 1784, and in the early nineteenth century Thomas Jefferson advocated its use. See Betts, *Thomas Jefferson's Farm Book*, 195.

6. "Wood" County is perhaps Walker or Wilcox County. The description of the soil generally conforms to either. See United States Department of Agriculture, "Soil Survey of Walker County, Alabama"; and United States Department of Agriculture, "Soil Survey of Wilcox County, Alabama."

7. Orleans County, Mississippi, borders the Mississippi River.

8. That is, the processes of reconstruction and emancipation. The statement echoes Abraham Lincoln's pronouncement that "this nation (under God) shall have a new birth of freedom." See Borrit, *The Gettysburg Gospel*, chap. 5.

States, they will become a self-reliant and prosperous people. The face of their country being no longer blackened with grim visaged slavery, they will henceforth in the United. States, take their proper place among the free nations of the earth.

Since writing the foregoing pages, a great reversion has taken place, both in the present and prospective condition of my colored brethren. The war, whose signet was impressed with oppression and blood, has ceased. Widow's tears, orphan's cries, desolated homes, and financial embarrassment, are heavy prices. Yet, the reward obtained is worth the sacrifice. The colored man has obtained his freedom. The bonds of human slavery have experienced such a disruption as human enactment can never again unite. The rivets that bound the African to his oppressor have been broken, and the affinity between the parts has become so utterly disturbed as to render combination forever impossible. The time has almost come, if not already, when slavery shall form more a matter of history than current existence. Its doom is sealed; its dying groans are heard; and soon the funeral knell shall sound its requiem over the everlasting and welcome departure of a monster, the traces of whose footsteps have too long left their foul impress upon a land otherwise lovely, noble and fair. This disgraceful stigma has now been nearly erased. At all events, the virulence of the poison has been diluted, and by degrees the most distant vestige of its fatality shall have been obliterated.

My dear Brethren, the rememberance of your oppressors, and the recollection of your oppression may cease to exist, but shall the memory of our champion ever stop to hold a high position among the tender and cherished feelings of your inmost soul. No. The memory of Abraham Lincoln shall retain a hallowed seat in our memories.[9] His statue shall occupy an imperishable standing in the niche of fame. Lincoln's name shall stand out in bold relief on the page of heroes. Revolutions may arise, dynasties start and sink to dust, the regular operation of nature may undergo a change, political plans may turn to chaos, still, still, shall we revere the memory of the man who counted not his life dear to redeem a race long oppressed and trodden.

9. Abraham Lincoln (1809–1865) of Illinois was a lawyer, a representative to Congress from Illinois from 1847 to 1849, and the sixteenth President of the United States, from March 3, 1861 to April 14, 1865. See Donald, *Lincoln.*

A murderer's bullet may have taken him from us ; the fatal weapon of an assassin may have been permitted to destroy the life that pertains to earth, and been the instrument of forwarding the perishable to the grave, and the immortal to a paradise of glory ; but no weapon, however powerful or dreadful in its effects, can ever wipe from our hearts the veneration we owe the great departed one. Time, in its steady course, shall only leave a deeper impress of his motto upon our nature, and tend to interweave the remembrance of his disinterested services with our own existence.

The night of the 14th of April, 1865, cast its shadow over a deed of darkness, in "Ford's Theatre," city of Washington, that bears no parallel for dastardly, treacherous, and satanic cruelty, either in ancient or modern times.

Brutus stabbing Caesar in the Roman Senate House, pales its guilt when placed in juxta position with "Booth's" act of cowardly assassination. It has been said, that, "the Martyr's blood is the seed of the Church."[10] This is true. The blood of a martyred Lincoln has already proved the seed of freedom. The fruits, 'tis true, have not yet been proved in all their harvest richness. But the time of reaping is not far distant, and the future ingathering shall speedily follow, our course of joy and gladness shall attune that as a ransomed people.

Elijah's ascent from Carmel was wonderful.[11] Another prophet's anxious eyes gazed with mingled feelings of awe and admiration upon the ascending path of the "Man of God," and as his eyes beheld the "Chariots of Israel and the horsemen thereof," patient expectation fixed him to the spot, whereon a prophet's mantle was to shroud his shoulders, and at the same time, impart an influence that should thereafter surprise the devotees of Baal and vindicate the absolute sovereignty of Elijah's God.[12] The mantle fell. The power was conferred. And, has not Lincoln's mantle fallen? Yes! and fallen too, not only in its shadow, but all its weight and glory have rested upon the shoulders of a man who entertains too deep a reverence for the departed, and too high a regard for human liberty, than to allow him to sanction the smallest deviation from those paths that bore his predscessor to the enjoyment of a martyr's unfading crown. Sainted Lincoln! thy spirit now lies in a region where all men of all colors serve a master who

10. "Semen est sanguis christianorum" (Tertullian, *Apology,* 50:13). See Pope Benedict XVI, *The Apostles,* 153n18.

11. See 1 Kings 18. Elijah established the divinity of the God of Israel through prayer and sacrifice.

12. See Second Book of Kings 2:12 for the "chariot." Elijah established the falsity of Baal's claim to divinity.

redeemed them, but the service they there render is their sweetest liberty. You have paved the way, by which an earthly foretaste of the same liberty may be enjoyed by the sable sons of Africa. Here the oppressors chains may gall the limbs of Ham's supposed descendants, then, where thou are now, the sound of chain has never echoed, save the melody of that chain of love and gratitude that ties the ransomed, to the arms of their great Redeemer. Our attachment to your memory would be sinful, did it forego our love to the Saviour, yet, as our best of earthly friends, we cannot do else than cherish a regard for you, so deep, that times corroding hand can never weaken. Rest in peace, thou martyred champion of human liberty! and may your noble and heroic spirit animate those you left behind, till every state and territory within the Union, and every soil that has been stained with the foot of slavery, shall listen to the song of freedom's enchanting voice!

My colored Brethren, hear with patience a word or two of counsel from one who loves you. While the rememberance of wrong long endured may sting your bosom, let not your sudden and unexpected emancipation have its lustre dimmed by violence or revenge. Leave the vindication of your rights in the hands of Him, who saith, "Vengeance is mine, I will repay."[13] In His hands your case is safe. Act as men, and though the taunt, the jeer, and scorn of the prejudiced may hurl their vindictive shafts against you, manfully exhibit yourselves, at least the white man's equal, by the exercise and cultivation of that Divine Spirit that led a betrayed Nazarine to say in the moment of his unjust suffering, "Father forgive them, they know not what they do."[14] To affluence and power, you cannot at once arise. This desirable position must be the work of time. However, show by your behaviour, as social, moral and political beings, that your innate nature entitles you to a position as high as any man whom a common God has yet created. If called upon to till the soil your sweat, and tears and blood have often watered, do it with the cheerfulness that freedom always bestows. If led to the pursuit of a mechanical employment, give unquestionable proof of your natural and acknowledged ingenuity. Supposing the battle of your future lives should lead you to the practice of a profession, allow your capability of becoming eminent to have its amplest developement. In whatever sphere of life you may hereafter move, lend every effort to establish your right to an equality of rank with your more highly favored

13. Paul's Epistle to the Romans 12:19.
14. This is a paraphrase of the Gospel of Luke 23:34. The exact quote is, "Father, forgive them; for they know not what they do."

brethren of the Anglo Saxon race. Indeed, I would give a wider latitude to my counsel, and impress upon your mind the necessity and importance of trying to acquire a superiority over every one of all and every colour. To use the words of Shylock, a Jew, as legitimately applicable to you and me: "If you tickle us do we not laugh? If you stab us do we not bleed?"[15] I purposely avoid the use of the entire quotation. Were I to endorse the whole sentiment of Shylock's language, I would be giving a contradiction to the spirit of an advice already rendered. No revenge! My object in the use of this quotation is simply to prove the fact that you and I are men, men made after the image of our Creator, according to His own unerring wisdom. Your color and mine differ from Europeans; our features differ, our tastes may vary, but, all these distinctive differences sink no deeper than the surface. Apply the standard of what a man should be, to the white and black, and the result of the application may prove the difference in mental capacity to be much less than is generally supposed. Aim at supremacy. At all events, assert, and keep your equality with all created sons of Adam, be their color, name or race what they may. My co-partners in former toil and suffering, you may for a time experience an inability to compete with your companions of another color, but let not this temporary inability for one moment thwart or weaken the energies of your spirit, or damp the ardour of your perseverance. No reasonable expectation would warrant the world in looking for immediate excellence upon your part. As reasonably, might we expect to see the strength of manhood in the infant of a day, as hope to find distinctive eminence in the character and attainments of race so long and cruelly oppressed, Who would calculate upon finding in the sprouting acorn, the stability and firmness of the aged mountain oak? And, who in justice, would seek to search for full, mature and attractive excellence in those, whose physical, intellectual and moral powers have hitherto been crushed and cramped and chained? Improve to the best advantage, the golden and opportune prospect a wise and kind Providence has opened to your view. Though mists may suspend their fleecy shadows upon the prospect, though clouds may spread their mantle, and seem to obscure the view, Aye, even, though darkness itself should spoil the eye from seeing far—still, beyond all there awaits for you and your posterity, yet unborn, a land of sunshine and gladness, where no mist or cloud or darkness shall

15. Shakespeare, *Merchant of Venice*, Act II, scene 1, lines 64–65: "If you prick us, do we not bleed? If you tickle us, do we not laugh?" Shylock continues, "If you poison us, do we not die? and if you wrong us, shall we not revenge?"

ever obscure the brightness of the landscape. Enter thou into the enjoyment of your "new born" liberty. With grateful hearts, taste its sweet with a firm, and unalterable determination to pursue the paths of virtue and of godliness, under the hope of one day experiencing the full fruition of that rest, in the possession of which, color, form or feature forms no essential element.

Colored Sons of Africa! I have already tendered my advice, so far as my judgment led me, touching your plans of personal procedure. But, while you and I have duties to discharge in relation to ourselves, as social, moral and political agents, we too, have duties bearing a close connection with our offspring. Bear with, me then, while I offer one or two observations in reference to the duties you owe the rising generation. Upon the character of your children, the hopes of your future position depend. On them the rank and position of unborn people rest. Whither as a race, we shall hold a commanding stand as intelligent and intellectual people among the future nations of the earth, or sink into eternal bankruptcy, solely poises upon the virtues or the vices of our children. I am a parent, therefore, do I feel the more deeply, the vast importance of this part of my subject. Although, you may be forced to endure the pinching bite of poverty, though you may be called upon to sustain the trying test of want and toil, bear on and well, rather than deprive your little ones, the children of your love and affection of the means of securing a thorough, liberal, and religious education. I implore you, that you would at every sacrifice, put the means of mental elevation within your children's reach. That our children have intellect of as high a figure as those of the white man, no unprejudiced and reasonable man can for one moment dispute. If this be questioned, all I can say is this, that the apparent latency of our mental powers, arises from the fact, that no favorable opportunities have been given for its mature development. But, now, since your liberty has been rendered you, spare no pains, consider no sacrifice too great, when the consideration of your children's moral and intellectual elevation is at stake. Train your children in the way they should go.[16] The trouble will repay you. Your eyes may have closed in the unbroken slumber of the grave, ere the fruits of your patient care shall delight them, by their appearance, but, generations shall arise and call you blessed.

I fear I have already wearied the patience of my readers, yet, I cannot conclude my narrative without adverting for a moment to the original basis

---

16. This is a paraphrase of the Book of Proverbs 22:6: "Train up a child in the way he should go."

of the United States' constitution. Upon this point, positively erroneous views have been lately advanced. Equal rights formed an essential element in the original constitution of the United States. Herein, no distinction was acknowledged between black and white. The same latitude of freedom was to form the inheritance of both. How far the terms of this agreement have been observed, I will leave the cry of the oppressed to answer. How truthfully the spirit of the constitution has been maintained, I will allow the voice of slavery long and patiently endured to tell. The terms have been violated, grossly violated; justice has been blinded, truth disregarded, oppression sanctioned, all for the love of gold. Southern planters held the belief that we are not men, but chattel property. Oh! what a stain upon humanity. Hath not God made of one blood all nations of the earth? And in the face of this Scripture truth, can any man, dare any man maintain the doctrine, that man should hold property in man? "Booth," whose name shall ever after stand for cowardice, maintained the unhallowed tenet, "that the Constitution of the States, never intended to acknowledge the black man's right to the immunities of a civilized people.["][17] But, who will respect the authority or opinion of a man whose hellish spirit prompted him to the commission of a cowardly assassination? If his faith warranted him in the enactment of such a tragedy, his views upon constitutional government must surely be received with the extremest caution. What! a murderer speak of human rights! Let no page record his name; except it be to stamp it with the infamy of never ending damnation. The name, aye, the very name of "Booth," spots the purity of any narrative, and shall, forever and forever, remain conspicuous upon the escutcheon of infamy and crime, and lies as a synonyme for Judas Iscariot.[18] Governor Wyre, who showed little less humanity than "Booth," gave public expression to the statement, "that such an inferiority obtained on the part of the colored

17. Goings here paraphrases John Wilkes Booth, who wrote a defense of his planned assassination of Abraham Lincoln: "This country was formed for the white, not for the black man. And, looking upon *African Slavery* from the same stand-point as the noble framers of our constitution, I for one, have ever considered it one of the greatest blessings (both for themselves and us) that God ever bestowed upon a favored nation" (John Wilkes Booth to John S. Clarke [November 1864], *New York Times*, April 21, 1865). Goings was perhaps reading the *New York Times*. See also Rhodehamel and Taper, *"Right or Wrong, God Judge Me,"* 147–53.

18. John Wilkes Booth (1838–1865) was a theater actor and the assassin of Abraham Lincoln. The author compares him to the biblical traitor Judas Iscariot.

man to the white, as forbade his claim to common respect."[19] Whence Mr. Wyre derived his authority for advancing such a monstrous doctrine as this, I know not; one thing I know, Heaven would refuse to admit it, the God, whose eyes and ears are open to the cries of the distressed of every age, has never lent his high sanction to such an unjust and preposterous principle.

Some have even dared to call in Scripture aid in support of slavery. Say they, the people of Israel themselves were slaves. Admit the fact. God did in the exercise of his unerring wisdom, permit his chosen ones to bear the yoke of bondage for a season. Heaven's righteous plan is not unfrequently traced in the furnace of affliction. Gold and silver are made more pure by fire. So, the pride of the sinner is humbled by the endurance of suffering. But, when once the wise purposes of an Allwise God, had been accomplished, the scheme of His people's redemption and escape was arranged. When the period of Israel's endurance had expired, the vaunted might of Egypt's king was powerless in its hold upon the enslaved seed of Abraham.[20] A Power mightier by far than President or earthly king, mapped the line of Israel's escape. The very laws of nature in gravitation were suspended, in order to allow Jehovah's Chosen to go free. Walls of water guarded their march. No such walls have ever since been seen; but so soon as the foot of the last slave trod the promised land, these strange embankments yielded to the Power that formed them, and the liquid particles of the Red Sea once more asserted their affinity and closed upon the pursuing hosts of an oppressive Monarch. So much for God's friendship for the slaves of ages past. And, will not He who is the "same yesterday, to-day, and forever," vindicate the rights of his people still.[21] He will, He has already done in his own good time, and by the use of such an instrumentality as

19. Henry A. Wise (1806–1876) was governor of Virginia from 1856 to 1860, and signed the death warrant of John Brown during his term, in 1859. He was also a general in the Confederate States army from 1861 until 1865. Before Emancipation, he held staunchly proslavery views. In an open letter in September 1854, Wise wrote that African Americans "are at present fit only for the patriarchal state of a Southern plantation. They are capable at present of a state only of pupilage. They can never amalgamate with the whites in this country" (*New York Times,* September 15, 1854).

20. The Israelites were enslaved under the Pharaoh of Egypt before Moses led them to freedom across the Red Sea, which God parted (from the Book of Exodus, the second book of the Hebrew Bible).

21. This is a paraphrase of Paul's Epistle to the Hebrews 13:8: "Jesus Christ the same yesterday, and to day, and for ever."

seemed to Him the wisest and the best. Let no one then, dare to be so impious, as to invoke the sanction of Divine authority for the continuance of such a cruel and soul degrading system! Let no proud planter of the South tell me that the God of freedom ever lent His countenance to oppression! Ye slave owners, assault not the High Majesty of Heaven, by saying that He ever lent his warrant to the prosecution of your cherished systems of wickedness. May the time soon come, when it can be said of black and white, "He is the freeman whom the truth makes free,"[22] when all, of every color shall have been brought to taste the sweets of that liberty "wherewith God makes his people free."[23]

22. Cowper, *The Task*, 144.

23. This is a paraphrase of Paul's Letter to the Galatians 5:1: "Stand fast therefore in the liberty wherewith Christ hath made us free." A similar phrase appears in Matthew Henry's commentary on Psalm 51, which precedes a reference to the above passage in Galatians: "What is this but the liberty wherewith Christ makes his people free" (Henry and Scott, *A Commentary upon the Holy Bible*, 221).

APPENDIX

S INCE WRITING the foregoing pages, some additional thoughts have suggested themselves to my mind, which I would venture to suggest, as well worthy the consideration of my colored brethren.[1] I know they will extend to me, that pardon which a disinterested motive should always demand. Should any one feel disposed to charge me with a dictatorial spirit, I would merely ask him to exercise the practice of that charity "that thinketh no evil."[2] The highest aim of my life on earth, would be to see my colored brethren happy. In the selection of a residence, many things should form a matter of consideration. Soil, climate and productions, ought to lend a fair influence in the choice of a permanent abode. All people are not equally adapted to every climate, nor are the soil and products, of every place alike suited to all constitutions. Now upon due consideration, I cannot see a more suitable locality for your settlement than Guatemala or Central America. Its latitude and longtitude adapt this place to your constitutional character. The productions of this colony are such as those, to which you have been accustomed. The civil laws of that settlement are so framed, as to secure the fullest enjoyment to men of every color. The advantages of civil life are many, whether confined to white or black. The place to which I kindly suggest to my emancipated brethren, the propriety of removing as a body would be the colony of "British Honduras" as I have already hinted, I know of none more constitutionally adapted to their present position, viewing it either in a political or physical aspect. The

1. The author here quotes from and paraphrases "Emigration and Colonization. Proposals for the Establishment of Colored People in British Honduras, Central America," which appeared in the May 23, 1863, edition of the *Christian Recorder.*

2. This is a paraphrase of Paul's First Letter to the Corinthians, 13:4–5: "Charity suffereth long, and is kind; charity envieth not; charity vaunteth not itself, is not puffed up, Doth not behave itself unseemly, seeketh not her own, is not easily provoked, thinketh no evil."

adaptation of the coast of this colony for trade and commerce is universally admitted. The length of its coast alone secures the ultimate attention
of commercial capitalists, while the facilities for internal communication
render it an enviable colony for settlement. The harbourage upon the coast
is capacious, deep, and large. The high average temperature of the colony
alone, constitutes it a most desirable place of refuge for the sable son of
Africa. The climate during both the summer and winter months is equable,
and therefore the more pleasant averaging in the former season 84 deg.
and in the latter 70 deg. The tenure by which the lands are held in "Fee
Simple" under the Land Titles Act of the colony, and having the high sanction of the Imperial Government, this tenure lends the holders of the soil
an undisputable title. The fact that the colony is free from financial embarrassment, makes taxation comparatively light. Indeed lands and houses
rest under no taxation at all. The various and valuable productions of the
soil, show its undoubted fertility. For your satisfaction, I would just mention some of the principle productions of the colony, all of which would be
useful for home consumption, and meet a ready demand upon the part of
other nations, viz.—cotton, sugar, (in this article the colony is more productive even than the state of Louisiana) tobacco is also largely grown;
other topical productions go to mark the richness of the soil, such as India
rubber, rich resinous pine trees, corn, rice, yams, sweet potatoes, arrow-
root, cassaia, plaintains, bananas, oranges, spices, oil and fruits of almost
every description. These are raised with very little labor, as they appear
to be more the spontaneous growth of the soil than the forced result of
toil. The soil is not the only source whence wealth may be realized. The
coast, the interior lakes, and inland rivers, teem with wholesome and pal-
atable fish. Also the turtle which is prized by epicures in every part of the
civilized world. Another additional reason why I would recommend the
place spoken of, as one very eligible, is the security afforded property. This
is no small consideration. The common law in England prevails in Central America, and while the Imperial Government must give its sanction
to all proposed enactments, which must emanate from the Local Legislature, a body whose election is vested in the people's hand. This secures
the amplest civil liberty. Access to religious and educational advantages is
full. The Christian religion is under different forms as in the United States
and here in Canada, and is the only one acknowledged. The different sectional denominations, are fully represented, by a staff of good and worthy
ministers, for whose ministrations the fullest church accommodation has
been provided. In the establishment of this colony, a due and deserved

regard has been paid to the interests of education. Large and substancial schoolhouses, have been erected in contiguons localities, in which the most approved systems of a free common school is administered. In this colony no inequality of respect between children of different color appears. In church and school, men, women, and children of every kind, are entitled to the same regard. All official positions, are equally open to all. The judge's seat, the magistrate's bench, the revenue office, are all filled in a large proportion, and efficiently filled, by gentlemen of color. In this colony, the valuable protection of British law is fully enjoyed. The exercises of its functions, is not dispensed with proud or partial feelings. Justice is equally meeted to black and white. Authentic reports testify, that mechanics wages are high, and that constant employment is secure. Ordinary laborers can easily command $12.00 per month, with board and lodging. Possession of land in this colony can be readily obtained. To prove this let me mention the fact that good land can be rented at 50c. per acre, or absolutely sold at rates proportionably low. Before concluding, there is one other idea that I would venture to suggest, and one too that must exercise an influence, upon the minds of my colored brethren. In the States wherever you now reside, avenues to office and influence are closed. Offices of emolument are filled, and filled by those who in many instances entertain anything but friendly feelings towards the emancipated slave. In British Honduras, offices of trust and profit are alike open to black and white, and not only so, but the people of color in the colony form the majority, and of necessity command the greatest influence. I would say then to my lately emancipated brethren, unite as one man in your resolve to emigrate to British Honduras. There you may, and can become a nation, then in the course of a very short time your moral and political influence, will undoubtedly spread its effect over other nations, and you soon shall rank, not in the lowest scale of God's intelligent and thinking beings. May the spirit of Divine wisdom guide you, and may the great deliverer of the oppressed, lead you in the path that conducts to freedom here, and carries the steps of the traveller, to a land where no oppressors voice ever echoes, and where no sound is heard but the sound of praise to him who redeemed us by his blood.

The Memphis Murders,—From the New York *Tribune*, Wednesday, July 4th, 1866.[3] Preceding the expected report of the Congressional committee,

---

3. The Memphis Race Riot of May 1–2, 1866, was one of the largest and most violent in American history. The riot began on the night of April 30 after a report circulated that black soldiers at Fort Pickering had killed white policemen after the police had

Col. Charles H Johnson, the Inspector General of Kentucky and Tennessee, has made a statement of his investigation of the Memphis riots, he
traces the remote cause, to a standing ill feeling between the low whites,
and blacks, (who are about equal in intelligence) which found an occasion
for strife, in the forcing of a number of negroes off the sidewalk, one of
whom stumbled over a policeman, whereupon the policemen drew their
revolvers and beat the negroes.[4] On the following day, about the time a
crowd of discharged colored soldiers had assembled, the police fired upon
some unoffending negroes, remote from the riotous quarter, and though
the colored victims of the original quarrel had returned to Fort Ficker-
ing, the police having reinforced themselves for indiscriminate slaughter,

---

attempted to arrest an African American solider. In response, the fort's commander,
General George Stoneman, confiscated the soldiers' weapons and ordered them confined to their barracks. That left nearby refugee camps of African Americans, black
settlers, and African American neighborhoods unguarded. Mobs of whites, including
policemen, assaulted the camps of the former slaves as well as blacks in African American neighborhoods. White resentment had simmered because many whites resented the
Confederate defeat, emancipation, and the new competition that had grown up among
African Americans for menial jobs. Businessmen and city officials looked down upon
the many indigent former slaves who inhabited the city. The incident at Fort Pickering
caused that resentment to boil over into a two-day riot that, according to a congressional
investigation, resulted in the burning of ninety-one homes, four churches, and eight
schools, and that injured seventy-five blacks and saw hundreds of African Americans
robbed and at least five women raped, as well as killing forty-six African Americans and
two whites. The riot led to congressional action, including the Civil Rights Act of 1866.
See Lovett, "Memphis Race Riot of 1866."

    4. Charles F. Johnson (1827–1867) of Philadelphia was a clerk, engraver, and investi-
gator before joining the 81st Pennsylvania Volunteer Infantry in September 1861. Johnson became colonel of the 81st after the Battle of Fair Oaks on June 1, 1862. During
the Battle of the Seven Days, on June 30, 1862, Johnson was shot four times below the
waist. Not expected to recover, he convalesced enough to return to his regiment during the battles of Second Bull Run, South Mountain, and Antietam. Troubled by his
wounds, he was given a medical discharge in November 1862 and went on to command
the 18th Regiment in the Invalid Corps and Veteran Reserve Corps from 1863 to 1865,
where he served as an investigator. He was transferred to the Freedmen's Bureau in April
1866, and in May of that year investigated and reported on the Memphis Race Riot with
Major T. W. Gilbraith. As inspector general of the bureau for the states of Kentucky
and Tennessee, Johnson interviewed African American victims and witnesses, and his
report detailed an accurate account of the causes and scope of the riot. He was thereafter
assigned as chief superintendent of the sub-district of Kentucky, where he died the following year. See Pelka and Johnson, *The Civil War Letters of Colonel Charles F. Johnson,
Invalid Corps*, introduction.

fired upon men, women, and children killing and wounding several.[5] Just at this time an official is said to have addressed the crowd of murderers: Boys, I want you to go ahead and kill every one of the nigger race, and burn up the cradle. After this advice, the negroes were hunted down day and night, by policemen, firemen, and others. They were shot, assaulted, and robbed, their houses searched, plundered, and burned. Meanwhile no resistance was offered by the negroes, who were shot down without mercy, women alike suffered with the men, and in several instances little children were killed. All crimes imaginable were committed, from simple larceny to murder. Several women and children were shot in bed, one woman, Rachel Johnson, was shot, and then thrown into the flames of a burning house and consumed, another was forced twice through the flames and finally escaped.[6] In some instances houses were fired, and armed men guarded them, to prevent the escape of the inmates inside. Loyalists, long residents of Memphis, who deprecated the riot, were called Yankees, and were cautioned to leave the town. Generals of the Freedman's and the army, found themselves powerless for interference. All that can be said of the mayor of the town, is that he was helplessly drunk. The fruits of the riots in figures are, as far as can be ascertained, thirty negroes killed, and sixty wounded, three negroe churches, eight school houses, and about fifty private dwellings were burned, and without counting the large sums of money, stolen by the police from discharged colored soldiers, and others, $125,000 worth of various property lost by the United States Government and the negroes. In all this cowardly, and atrocious massacre, and robbery, only two white men were killed, one of whom was killed by a white man through mistake, and the other according to the surgeon who attended him, shot himself by accident. Here we close a chapter which in a small space, has the horrors of St.

5. This is Fort Pickering, in Memphis, Tennessee.

6. The T. W. Gilbraith report reads, in part: "The city seemed to be under the control of a lawless mob during this and the two succeeding days (3rd & 4th). All crimes imaginable were committed from simple larceny to rape and murder. Several women and children were shot in bed. One woman (Rachel Johnson) was shot and then thrown into the flames of a burning house and consumed. Another was forced twice through the flames and finally escaped. In some instances houses were fired and armed men guarded them to prevent the escape of those inside. A number of men whose loyalty is undoubted, long residents of Memphis, who deprecated the riot during its progress, were denominated Yankees and Abolitionists, and were informed in language more emphatic than gentlemanly, that their presence here was unnecessary." See Johnson, "Report of an investigation of the cause, origin, and results of the late riots in the city of Memphis . . . ."

Bartholomew's day, and we leave it without comment.[7] Expatriated brethren, despised sons of Africa, does not your blood boil up with indignation,
at the wholesale massacre in the streets of Memphis, in the year of our
Lord one thousand eight hundred and sixty six. You are indeed freedmen,
endowed with civil rights, by Act of Congress, but remember, and learn a
lesson, from the Memphis bloody tragedy, that you are still, and for generations to come, will be at the mercy of the lowest ruffians among the white
population of the States. Politically, you may in the end gain a proper position as citizens by the right of universal suffrage, being extended to each
and every one without distinction of color. But my unfortunate brethren,
no act of Congress can pull down the social barrier erected by superstition
and prejudice; the foundation of which, seems, alas, too strong yet. By Act
of Congress, you may be entitled to stand eligible for any office, for a seat
in Congress if you please, but I don't think that I am much mistaken, if I
assert that the signs of the times do not justify any one of you to expect a
single vote outside of our own race. And as that respect and encouragement are wanting that a long suppressed people so greatly stand in need of,
in a time of its regeneration it is almost an impossibility with your slender
means, by your own energy and perseverance, to elevate yourselves on a
level with the better classes of the white population in that very country,
where our ancestors, nay, you yourselves and your children bore the curse
of slavery, and toiled for those who are now but your equals, with chains on
your necks. Oh, brethren if you hope ever to be placed on an equal footing
with the white lords of the States, I am ready to say that your hope is in
vain. Rather listen to the voice of the Lord our God which may happily be
applied to the cause of our down trodden race.[8]

North Carolina, Northampton Co. at the county seat a large tavern built
for the accommodation of people, also offices were built for the accommodation of judges, lawyers &c., a large pond of water where mortar was
taken out to make brick from the different ruins the hole became to hold
from three to four feet of water. Mr. Jones the proprietor of the tavern,
took sick after a term of years keeping this hotel. Before he was taken ill

---

7. The St. Bartholomew's Day Massacre began on the eve of the Feast of St. Bartholomew, August 24, 1572, in Paris, when Counter-Reformation Catholics killed thousands of French Huguenots. Perhaps three thousand died in Paris, and thousands more
perished in other areas of France in what was a turning point in the French Wars of
Religion. See Walker et al., *A History of the Christian Church*, 520–21.

8. The end of this paragraph marks a transition to the author's reflections on his life
in the South.

a Methodist preacher preached every Sabbath to the people who came to attend the court, he was regularly a Methodist any way. He seemed to be an excellent speaker, his congregation was very numerous. In the time he took ill, he lay for six months not expected to live from one hour to another, he had a servant that waited on him. He occasionally would be found walking out in the yard walking about where his master lying easy but still keeps a strict watch over his master; but, however, it seemed the master was watching him. At this time the master seemed to pray more fervently than at anytime previous, it seemed as if he was struck by the grace of God by his calamity fuller than ever, he had to be lifted in and out of bed and when he was struck forcibly by the grace of God he rose up out of his bed and he folded a sheet around him and he put as hard as he was able to go to this pond of water and there he baptized himself and there he proclaimed Christ and his crucifixion and said that he thought that he was a converted man before he was, but he was never converted until now, his servants and others put after him and went into the pond of water and brought him out, he then explained that God had spoken peace to his soul, and told him to go and sin no more and preach Christ and his baptism, and he was taken home, he recovered his good health and became a hearty hail man and gave up tavern keeping. He had twenty-five slaves large and small and set them all free, some left him and some remained with him. Mr. Jones was this sort of a man, he neither fed [n]or clothed his slaves, but he gave them every Saturday to do what they wished for themselves. He never had his field hands, previous to his conversion, to work for him on Saturdays, only the house servants. He then got baptized by a regular Baptist minister, then he went on riding a circuit; when I left North Carolina, he was riding a circuit still teaching the people to repent and be baptized. North Carolina, Northampton County, 2½ miles from where I belonged, a neighbor of Colonel Lawrence Smith his widow Mrs. Turner lived 2½ miles from that, she had a slave who was a preacher and allowed him to go out preaching, he was midling sort of a scholar; he finally thought that his fellow men should be free so he got them all persuaded to rise one future day, his name was that of Turner. There met him at the crossroads at Colonel Lawrence Smith's there they were to meet and kill all the whites for their freedom.[9]

---

9. Nat Turner's Rebellion, or Uprising, of August 22, 1831, killed more than fifty whites over two days before being violently suppressed. Whites panicked, and white violence against African Americans continued in Virginia and in North Carolina. In the wake of the uprising, the Halifax County, North Carolina, militia raced to Southampton

Many of them met, the foolish men did not arm themselves as men should have done to go into the field to fight but they happened on a Sunday where there was a Camp Meeting, 11 miles from there on Roanoak river and he did not go among the body of men to fight, but murdered many old men and women, and his army broke into collars as they marched along from one place to another got beastly drunk and when the whites came to get the news they surrounded all of his army, they shot down every colored man wherever they could see him. The loud cheers of white people they were more numerous in shooting and killing, more so than those who owned the slaves they proclaimed they were a fiend to the country and therefore they shewed neither mercy or feeling to anyone of color.[10] All the slave holders had to turn out as an army to prevent the shooting of those slaves they knew to be innocent and had nothing to do with the insurrection, they could not stop the people from shooting their slaves. The excitement was most desperate and they could not stop them, but had to confine the slaves and run them out of the country, many went to Alabama, Georgia, and Louisiana, I was not in Northampton County when this happened, but in Alabama.[11] My master's brother, he visited Alabama I was at one time going down the Mississippi River from Alabama. We changed boats

---

County, Virginia, to suppress the rebellion. In their absence, authorities in North Carolina rounded up and jailed black men in the county. By November 1831, twelve North Carolina blacks had been executed for participating in the insurrection after being convicted, and another fifteen were killed without trial. Perhaps hundreds were beaten and tortured, and local whites fixed decapitated heads on poles near Murfreesboro and other towns. See Grimsted, *American Mobbing, 1828–1861*, 138–39; and a petition "To the Honr. the Genr Assembly of the State of North Carolina," 22 December 1831, petition 11283106, Digital Library on American Slavery, University of North Carolina.

10. Nat Turner's Uprising was neither the start nor the finish of violence near the Virginia–North Carolina border in 1830–31. In 1830, following the dissemination of David Walker's *Appeal*, whites in Northampton County, North Carolina, were alarmed. Before a slave uprising that whites feared was planned for Christmas, rumors flew through the area that sixty slaves had armed themselves and that North Carolina citizens had killed them. The rumors were never substantiated, but the frenzy affected nearly every African American in the area, free and enslaved. See Grimsted, *American Mobbing, 1828–1861*, 138–39 Yellin, *Harriet Jacobs*, 36–37.

11. Slaveholders in the Deep South complained bitterly that they were sold rebellious slaves, probably with good reason. Selling enslaved people suspected of fomenting insurrection was a quick and profitable way to evade costly and disruptive investigations and prosecutions, but slave traders did their best to disguise such threats. See Gudmestad, *A Troublesome Commerce*, 42–45.

at Padukey,[12] it is where the three rivers empty together. The rivers were, viz., Cuntin,[13] Tennessee, Ohio. They empty together into the same basin. The Mississippi River helps to form the basin. All form themselves into the Mississippi. There we changed boats for New Orleans, viz., my Boss and self, as his servant.[14] There were a great number of passengers on the boat. In journeying on there were two young gentlemen, brothers; they made themselves very familiar and agreeable with me; they told me that they lived on the coast leading on to New Orleans; that they had been off to a school to graduate; in journeying on, when we came below Vicksburg, on the Mississippi River, we struck Levey at a considerable distance below Vicksburg. The Levey means the earth that is thrown upon the banks of the river for 260 miles. The river is much higher than the land, which caused the Levey to be built, to keep the river in its bounds. Though the river is higher by 3 or 4 feet than the surface, the boat stopped down a long way down on this side of the Levey. These gentlemen told me they be getting off as their home laid a little way from the river. Sure enough, when they got in sight of home they pointed out home. Their dwelling was a fine mansion. Saw a great many farms along the route, but as we approached these young gentlemen's farms, saw on the farms as we were approaching between 150 to 200 hands, working as hard as they were able to go ahead. I noticed some of the hands look up at the boat when she was landing, and just as soon as they raised up their heads to look, the overseer began, to cut and slash on all those who held up their heads to look at the boat, at the same time their friends at home seemed to know that they would be coming on the first boat. I saw an old lady, who I took probably to be their mother, who was, no doubt, a fine, young, portly looking young man who I took to be a brother, though the young man walked, very fast to reach the boat before she was shoved out. The mother moved slowly coming towards the boat as if she was glad to meet her sons. There was an old colored woman who seemed to step much quicker than the mistress. The young son that

12. Paducah, Kentucky.

13. Cumberland River.

14. Interestingly, he calls his owner Smith, "Boss." That is a variant of the Dutch word *Bos*, which white workers in the United States increasingly used to distinguish their work relationship from that of slaves. Slaves were compelled to refer to their owners as "Master," as Goings does in the first three chapters. Goings use of "Boss" could indicate that as Smith's personal servant and groom, he was on different terms than the field laborers whom Smith owned. See Roediger, *The Wages of Whiteness*, 54.

met the two brothers, he then started for the house, but they met the old colored woman before they reached the mother, but when the old woman ran towards them with so much anxiety as if she thought that they would shake hands with her, being so glad to see them, but they passed on by her, without paying any attention to her than if she had been an old dog. When the young gentlemen, passed by she stood half bent and seemed to gaze at them. She then followed them back towards the house. They met, as I supposed, the mother. They had a hearty shaking of hands. There was also two grown up young ladies, as I supposed, to be the sisters. After shaking hands they walked back to the mansion. It seemed to me that the old colored woman seemed to me to be much disappointed, as if they did not wish to seem to pay any respect to her in presence of those on the boat. At that time we were going out of sight. I could not help myself feeling sorry for the old woman. The small attention that they seemed to pay to her. I was disposed to think at least that this woman had been their nurse. Of course the old woman must have been very much mortified to meet her young masters who did not pay her any respect whatever.

I think it as well to say something about New Orleans, which city I have visited very frequently, I was occasionally out on the farms with my Boss, I then made some inquiries of the servants, about their manners and customs of their way of living, they told me that they worked night and day then, that the people are wearied out from constant work and hard laborious labor. They told me that they worked very hard during the planting of sugar cane, while the cane was getting its growth for ripening, that when the cane was ripe for cutting down, then the hardest work commenced, they would then commence to cut the cane low down to the root, then the horses and mules would be hauling as hard as they could drive them, the cane to the sugar mill. Then they commenced to cut down the cane, they then, draw off 50 of the ablest men off the farm, that 50 hands would work hard all that day first at the mill 12 o'clock at night they drew off 25 hands, they go home at 12 o'clock at night, sleep until morning as soon as they can just barely see to work. So by that the whole fifty every day is together at work at the mill, at night again they draw off the other 25 who had no sleep then when night shuts in they send the next 25 home to sleep, they only sleep, until 12 o'clock at night. In that way they change 25 hands every night in succession. The servants told me that there was little or no rest at the time they were grinding sugar-cane. The grinding season lasts 9 months, the mill is never stopped neither Sunday or any other day but running all the time. I had occasion to enquire of the servants how long people could live at that rate. Some said we don't live at all. They told me that it was death to those who worked at the mill, it was a rare thing if a man lived from more than 10 to 12 years of those who worked at the mill.[15] This work was so laborious, and so little rest, that men could not live, their diets was light, but it was so light that it never stayed with a man long, but yet they were not allowed strong food only occasionally, a little meat a bit of corn beef occasionally and salt fish, that was the way they fed their slaves. I suppose I may give to the reader the way that they plant the cane seed. That is they plant the rows five foot apart, the cane is cut with a joint at each end, the seed cane they put each cane three to four inches apart in the furrows, the furrows extend either a long or a short distances, there are three or four hands to each furrow in planting cane, then there is a horse or a mule, that is covering the cane with a plough, these hands are well up to planting and they have got to keep ahead of the plough, the whole field are employed in this way until all of the field is seeded. I don't think that the fields average more than 200 acres to each planters field. Then by the time they got over the planting well the stop from the field for a while for the crop to get its growth, I think it takes about six weeks for it to shoot up. Every hand goes to work, to haul all the hard crust from the young cane what they call pressing it down, and by the time they get through this 200 acres they commence back again to throw up high and light earth to the cane, and they continue on that for about three times working it. Then the crop grows spontaneously then they are mowing around cutting the grass down and by the time that is done the cane begins to ripen, their average crop generally from the mill is sixty hogsheads of sugar to the acre. The mills have large iron kettles in rows which hold from two hundred to three hundred gallons of juice from the cane, the rolling mills press the juice out which run from troughs into the kettles, the first and second crop of the cane makes the mill grind white fine sugar, called Mus Kovado,[16] which

15. This is an accurate assessment of the grim prospects for slaves put to work growing, cutting, and milling sugar. The overwhelmingly young, male workforce labored under similar conditions to those found in the Caribbean. "Strong food," or meat (flavored perhaps with pork fat and accompanied by whatever the slaves themselves could manage to grow in the gardens they kept on their own time), interrupted the monotony of the cornmeal porridge most owners fed their workers. Whether in Virginia, Alabama, or Louisiana, slaves were perpetually hungry and nearly always sick. See Follett, *The Sugar Masters*, 63–65; Lightner and Ragan, "Were African American Slaveholders Benevolent or Exploitative?"; and Coelho and McGuire, "Diets versus Disease."

16. Muscovado.

is equal to three crops off the same one stalk of cane, out of the one seed, that is to say suckers, that makes very good common class sugar, which, is very good but not equal to the other sugar. The last crop of the suckers is converted into molasses and dark sugar, the second crop is called syrup, from the first crop is the best sugar, from second class medium, from the third class molasses and syrup, there is a tassle on the top of the cane which is cut off at the last joint and thrown away.

My Boss knowing that a great many horses and mules were taken from Kentucky, also Missouri these were taken to New Orleans market, then they would be sold to the planters on the coast and for other purposes, for instance carriage horses, and drag horses, my master had occasion to enquire of the overseer the cause of so many horses being brought to that country. Hundreds of horses and mules were brought to New Orleans every fall. It seemed to me that the whole country would be overstocked with horses. The overseer very readily replied, that in fact sir, the horses have to go through so much fatigue that they can't live long, for we drive a horse here for all he can do with great speed, we cannot wait for a horse to take his time with moderate driving, for we can drive a horse so as to make him worth three horses with slow driving, he will more than earn the price of three horses, with moderate driving, so the horses very often drop down and die. The mules stand it better than the horses, but we may take all the hide off a mule and you cannot put him over his speed, one quick horse is worth two mules although the mules live the longest, the mule would live almost on anything what a horse would not eat, that's why the mule is more durable than the horse, though there is no driving a mule out of his own gait, he is so obstinate. I think to the best of my recollection that I have stated nothing more than what I have witnessed and came under my notice.

ADDRESSES DELIVERED BY BVT. COLONEL BEN. P. RUNKLE, U.S.A.,
CHIEF SUPT. OF THE, FREEDMEN'S AFFAIRS, STATE OF KENTUCKY,
AND BVT. LIEUT.-COL. I. S. CATLIN. U.S.A, TO THE FREEDMEN OF
LOUISVILLE. OCTOBER 1868.[17]

Freedmen of Kentucky:—I propose to speak to you earnestly and candidly, and it is well that you should know that I am no stranger to many of you, and in what character and capacity I am here to address you. I do not come

17. The text is almost certainly taken from Runkle and Catlin, *Addresses Delivered by Bvt. Colonel Ben. P. Runkle* . . . . Isaac S. Catlin (1835–1916) of New York was a lawyer

as a politician in the general and common meaning of the term, which is a man of artifice, shrewd and cunning, that he may get votes, that he may get office or popularity, that he may procure business, a man who appeals to the passions and prejudices of his fellow men with a word for your ears, and a hand for your pockets, or an eye to your votes, whenever the day shall come that you have votes. No, I have no need for your cash, I care not to be popular with you to have your good opinion, unless that opinion is founded

---

and a major in Oswego, New York, in 1860. Responding to President Lincoln's call for 75,000 troops in the aftermath of the fall of Fort Sumter, he enrolled the first regiment of United States volunteers and served as captain of the 3rd New York Infantry beginning in May 1861. He later was lieutenant colonel in the 109th New York beginning in August 1862, serving until June 1865 and rising to the rank of colonel. He was brevetted brigadier general of volunteers in March 1865, and also brevetted major general for valor at the siege of Petersburg, Virginia, where he lost his right leg and sustained other serious wounds in the explosion of the crater, for which he was later awarded the Congressional Medal of Honor. Because of the severity of his wounds, he enrolled in the U.S. army and served until May 1870, retiring at the rank of colonel. He then served as the Freedmen's Bureau Louisville Sub-district supervisor in 1867 and 1868, where he faced violent opposition to instituting schools for freedpeople in southern and western Kentucky. Catlin fought in behalf of African American civil rights, especially with respect to black codes. From 1877 to 1884, he was an assistant U.S. district attorney for Kings County, New York, and he ran for mayor of Brooklyn, unsuccessfully, in 1885. He was a Republican and an Episcopalian and is buried in Arlington National Cemetery. Benjamin P. Runkle (1836–1916) of Ohio served as captain of the 13th Ohio Volunteer Infantry beginning in April 1861 and was promoted to major that November. He was wounded at the Battle of Shiloh. He later served as colonel of the 45th Ohio Volunteer Infantry beginning in August 1862 in Kentucky. He was then a brigade commander in Kentucky and Tennessee. Mustered out in July of 1864, he served as lieutenant colonel of the Veteran Reserve Corps from August 1864 to October 1866, where he rose to the rank of major general of volunteers. Runkle served as a major in the 45th United States Infantry beginning in July 1866, and was brevetted lieutenant colonel in March 1867 for his service at Shiloh. He served in the Memphis Freedmen's Bureau beginning in 1866, enforcing labor rules designed to protect freedpeople against labor abuses. Sympathetic to the freedpeople's plight, he also attempted to use the army to protect African Americans from a rising tide of white violence and victimization at the hands of slaveholders-turned-employers. Runkles's military service ended in 1877 after he took a leave to edit the Urbana, Ohio, *Union* newspaper. He was a deacon in the Episcopal Church and taught military science at Kenyon College, Miami University, Peekskill Military Academy, the New Jersey Military Academy, and the Germantown, Ohio, Military Institute, and he helped to found the Sigma Chi fraternity in 1895. He is buried in Arlington National Cemetery. See the *National Cyclopaedia of American Biography*, 3:346; Schmidt, "'A Full-Fledged Government of Men,'" 234–35; Rhyne, "Rehearsal for Redemption," 230–44; and Howard, "The Struggle for Equal Education in Kentucky, 1866–1884."

on words of truth and candor, spoken, and deeds of justice and of duty done. As for your votes, while I hope that every true man may live to cast his vote for men who love justice, liberty and their country, I trust I shall never have need to ask you for them. But if to be a politician is to be a man who has an inborn fervent love for his government, who feels a deep interest in its preservation, in its peace and prosperity, and who glories in his country's domain, her resources, her strength, and her growing greatness, and more than all, in the determination of her loyal people. that justice and equal rights before the law shall be accorded to every man, however low his birth or humbleness of his position, who is the friend of every man that is ready to defend his country against all her oppressors, whether they be enemies abroad or traitors at home; if that is to be a politician, I trust I am one. I come, however, to speak to you as an officer of your government, and as your friend. We will consider for a moment the mighty work of the last seven years. The year 1861, found you four millions of bondsmen, from the blue grass hills of Kentucky to the rice swamps of the Savanah[18] and the everglades of Florida,—from the beautiful mountains in Virginia to the broad planes of Texas, four million toiled in the damps of morning, in the hot noon day and until the going down of the sun, waiting, yet scarce expecting the coining of a better day.[19] You waited not, perhaps, in content and in happiness, but that could not be, save in ignorance of a higher lot, but at least in patience and submission. True, a few now and then escaped through the aid of men who doubtless believed that they served God in aiding them—brave men who were not afraid to be called abolitionists, when, to be an abolitionist, was to be scoffed at, hooted at, and despised; but these few escaped to brave the rigors of a cold, inhospitable climate, many only to die. What will men do to achieve liberty? These men were but a few in number, and whether the efforts to aid them did not result in great disadvantage to those whom they left behind, may well be doubted, but whether this be so or not, it was a part of the plan worked out by an overruling Providence, and as such, has borne good fruit; it was agitation, and agitation is necessary to the political waters, it purifies, even as the storms that sweep over the face of the great deep purify the old ocean. At length, to those waiting in darkness, came the dawn of the grey morning dim with the mists of the early day, which will yet be succeeded by the sunrise of

18. Savannah, Georgia.

19. In 1860, census takers counted 3,953,760 slaves in the United States. See Rodriguez, *Slavery in the United States*, 2:113.

equal rights before the law and glorions noonday of citizenship. It matters not how you became slaves; you were born in bondage, and your ancestors were slaves before you. I have heard it said, and even now it is hissed in our ears, that Northern men landed many of the first slaves on American soil. Slave traders were fitted out in Boston harbor, and that slavery once existed in New England. It is true, men of Northern birth were engaged in the slave trade iniquity. Vessels to traffic in human flesh have been fitted out in Northern sea ports. Slaves have trodden on New England soil, but what of all that, terribly wicked men have lived in the North—in the Free States. We had Benedict Arnold, and ten thousand traitorous Tories in the days of the revolution, and we had Vallandingham, and an hundred thousand Copperheads in the days of the rebellion.[20] Benedict Arnold, and his followers have been Vallandingham's, and his followers shall be ground to powder by the weight of their own shame. If there were slaves in New England they shouldered their muskets, and side by side with their pale faced patriot masters, won their freedom by fighting in the ranks of the Continental army. As for the wicked Yankee slave-traders, Satan and his hosts of devils dwelt once in the region of the blest—they were hurled from the battlements of Heaven into everlasting darkness—so has New England banished the evils from her borders, and wiped the curse of slavery from her land, and that too when this great nation was in its infancy; and now

20. Benedict Arnold (1741–1801) of Connecticut was a general in the American War of Independence. He headed the capture of Fort Ticonderoga in 1775, avoided defeat at the hands of the British in smaller battles, and aided considerably in the successful battles of Saratoga, New York, in 1777. In 1780, he abandoned his American allegiance and fought for the British, earning himself a reputation as a traitor. Clement L. Vallandigham (1820–1871) of Ohio was a lawyer and a Democratic member of Congress from 1858 to 1863. He supported the Crittenden Compromise in 1861, then actively opposed military funding for the Civil War. He led the Copperhead faction of Democrats, who pressed for recognition of the Confederacy and an end to war. He denounced President Lincoln and the war effort, and after he ran afoul of General Ambrose E. Burnside's orders against seditious speech in Ohio, he was tried and convicted by a military tribunal for sedition and undermining the war effort. To quiet support for Vallandigham, Lincoln turned him over to the Confederate States, whereupon he traveled to Canada and then ran unsuccessfully for governor of Ohio in 1863. A political lightning rod, Vallandigham retained enough political popularity with antiwar Northerners that the Democratic Party permitted him to author part of its 1864 peace platform in support of George B. McClellan's candidacy for the presidency. After the war, Vallandigham ran unsuccessfully for the House of Representatives and the U.S. Senate, opposing Reconstruction. He later resumed his practice of law. See Wilson, *Benedict Arnold*, chap. 11 and passim; and Klement, *The Limits of Dissent*, chap. 6 and passim.

for every slave trader I can point you to an hundred Christian soldiers and statesmen. New England and the North may have done wrong, but fearfully has she atoned for it, 300,000 of her sons sleep beneath Southern soil at the prison at Andersonville, on the slopes of Fredericksburg.[21] There is many an empty seat by the Northern fireside, many a place at the Northern table vacant; scarce a family that does not mourn a father or a brother slain in an unrighteous war, a war made to destroy the Government and perpetuate the curse of slavery.

It is said that, those whom the Gods wish to destroy, they first make mad.[22] For thirty years demagogues and intriging politicians councilled together and plotted for the destruction of this government, for the overthrow of constitutional liberty, that they might erect upon its ruins a fabric with human slavery for its corner stone, and even in this in the acts of those men we recognize again the works of Providence. They inaugurated a revolution—they broke away the barriers and let loose a flood which was destined to overwhelm and destroy them.

Many were the men with pure motives and courageous hearts, who thought to stem the tide and to stop the mighty onward march of human events. The great Democratic party threw itself into the breach, and was swept away. Clay, Douglas, and Crittenden, good and great men, thought to control the course of the revolution and stay its progress, but despite the efforts of men and parties, like the resistless current of some majestic river,

21. Anderson Station, Sumter County, Georgia, was the site of an infamous Confederate prison for Union prisoners of war. Andersonville, eventually encompassing 26.5 acres of land, opened in February 1864. It housed 41,000 Federal soldiers—33,000 by the summer of 1864—until it was closed in April 1865. By that time, some 13,000 men had died there, of disease, exposure, and malnutrition, in squalid conditions. The Battle of Fredericksburg, Virginia, raged from December 11 to December 15, 1862, between the Confederate Army of Northern Virginia, commanded by General Robert E. Lee, and the Union Army of the Potomac, commanded by Ambrose E. Burnside. The fiercest fighting took place on December 13. In that major Confederate victory, the Union lost 12,653 killed, wounded, or missing, and the Confederacy lost 5,377 to casualties. The battle did little to turn the tide of the war, but on the eve of the Emancipation Proclamation, it signaled to both sides that the war would be long and extremely costly. See Marvel, *Andersonville*, 180, 224, and passim.

22. The phrase has been variously attributed: Euripides; Latin proverb; anonymous, Publius Syrus. See John Dryden's "The Hind and the Panther": "For those whom God to ruin has design'd / He fits for fate, and first destroys their mind" (*The Poetical Works of John Dryden*, 127).

the revolution rolled grandly on.[23] It was the work of the Maker of the universe—the omnipotent God. The pigmy efforts of man availed no more against it than the strength of a feeble bark against the rushing hurricane of the tropics, or the strength of a lone traveler against the burning, resistless sand storm of the desert. The Omnipotent had decreed that this people should be free, that through the length and breadth of this fair land liberty should reign supreme—it was and will be so. Secessionists and traitors were the instruments in his hands; yet none the less are traitors guilty, and treason a crime. At length, after thirty years plotting, after they thought everything was prepared, the government in the hands of its enemies, our little army and navy scattered far and wide, the Secessionists developed

23. Henry Clay (1777–1852) of Kentucky, known as the "Great Pacificator," was a U.S. congressman and senator, the Speaker of the House from 1811 to 1825, and secretary of state from 1825 to 1829. An early proponent of active government involvement in internal improvements, known as the American System, Clay was also the chief architect of the Compromise of 1820 and the founder of the American Whig Party in 1832–33. A nationalist and also a slaveholder, he ran for president unsuccessfully in 1832 and 1844, appealing to constituencies in the North, South, and West, and was the leader of the Whig Party in its heyday. Clay returned to political life in 1849 as a U.S. senator and lent his oratory and prestige to the Compromise of 1850, which sought to forestall disunion over the divisive issue of slavery expansion. Senator Stephen A. Douglas (1813–1861) of Illinois largely authored the Compromise legislation, backed by Northern Democrats and Southern Whigs. Douglas, called the "Little Giant" because of the contrast between his small physical stature and his towering political persona, was a U.S. senator from 1847 until his death in 1861. He was the principal supporter of the Kansas-Nebraska Act of 1854, which exacerbated political tensions over the expansion of slavery into the territories by letting settlers decide the issue. Douglas supported the U.S. Supreme Court's *Dred Scott* decision of 1857, and won reelection to the Senate against the Republican, Abraham Lincoln, in 1858. He was the presidential nominee of the Northern wing of a divided Democratic Party that nominated two presidential candidates in 1860; he lost to Abraham Lincoln. Following the election and the secession of South Carolina, in December 1860, U.S. Senator John J. Crittenden (1786–1863) of Kentucky authored a compromise that bore his name, which proposed to prevent other slave states from seceding. Despite support among Upper South unionists, president-elect Lincoln rejected the proposal, and so did Senate Republicans. Crittenden helped to keep his home state of Kentucky from following neighboring Virginia and Tennessee out of the Union in May 1861. Crittenden continued to seek compromises against the abolition of slavery and in behalf of a limited war for union, and he opposed the Emancipation Proclamation of 1863. See Howe, *What Hath God Wrought*, 151–56, 204–12, 240, 247–49, 384–85; Crofts, *Reluctant Confederates*, 77–81, 197–211; and Freehling, *The Road to Disunion*, vol. 2, *Secessionists Triumphant, 1854–1861*, 61–63, 103, 108, 309–11, 495–96, 514.

their plans, the slave holding States seceded from the Union, appealed to arms and again illustrated the strength of the truth of the sacred saying, "All they that take the sword shall perish with the sword;"[24] and these men counted upon aid from a certain portion of the people of the North, and they counted without their host. The echoes of the first gun at Sumter, rolling away over the hills of New England, and the valleys of the Ohio, had scarce died away, when a million loyal and true men sprang to arms to defend the heritage of their fathers, and an earnest, and terrible bloody war was upon us.[25] Oh, the agony of those four long years, when liberty trembled in the balance; when each household, each family trembled, when there was no peace, no rest in the houses nor in the hearts of man; it tested the courage, it proved the nerve and the endurance of the American people. But there is one fact, which, is acknowledged by the freed man's bitterest enemies, and that is the patience and the fortitude with which they bore their lot, and awaited the issue of the struggle. For a hundred years your masters said to you: "You are not men, toil for us, bleed for us, hunger and die for us," and you did it. And when after the immortal proclamation of the great hearted lover, Lincoln, had declared you free, and the question of its validity, its enforcement, hung on the fate of battle, and the strength of contending armies, what did these people do? Still patiently they bore their lot, labored upon the entrenchments that sheltered our foes, still worked and toiled, raising the food which sustained the rebel armies in the field, often left as the only protectors of the wives and children of their masters, they were true and faithful to their trust. How, in the face of all this devotion, could they so bitterly refuse to concede to a simple act of justice, proper protection, simple equality before the law. There is another fact, and that may account for it. When the Government, casting aside the last lingering remnants of prejudice, determined to use all the power it could command to crush the rebellion, it offered the musket to the black man. The musket without the promise of bounty and without the

---

24. Gospel of Matthew 26:52.

25. Fort Sumter, South Carolina, was the site of the first military confrontation between the Confederate States army and the United States. Confederate forces under the command of General Pierre G. T. Beauregard attacked the fort on April 12, 1861, and captured it for the Confederacy on April 14. In response to the Confederate military assault on a United States fort, President Lincoln, on April 15, summoned 75,000 volunteer soldiers to oppose the Confederacy. That was a major cause for the secession of the Upper South and the intensification of civil war. See McPherson, *Battle Cry of Freedom*, chap. 8; and Crofts, *Reluctant Confederates*, chap. 13.

reward. How they responded, let the names of 125,000 black men on the rolls of the national army answer.[26] How they used their arms, let Fort Wagoner and Fort Hudson respond.[27] Then amid the ringing of steel, the roar of cannon and musketry, was a people born from darkness to light, from bondage to freedom, and stood there shackleless and for ever free, waiting in the dim uncertain morning of the new day waiting counsel and advice, standing on the borders of the promised land, waiting to be taught the responsibility and duties of their new destiny as American citizens; and the hand that had burst the shackles, did not stop with the work of four years war, the result followed in the track of the army, and with it came books, school houses and teachers. A people were to be brought forth from the depths of ignorance, taught and made fit to receive and enjoy the rights and privileges of American citizens, and a great and efficient government, aided by the benevolent people of the north, came promptly to do the work. School houses sprung up like magic, but though often destroyed, phoenix like, others rose from the ashes; teachers were driven away, the gleaming of the bayonets is seen, the blue coats come, and with them the teachers return, and little colored children with their books go to and fro, an unaccustomed sight, men and women learn to read, the converts of the enemies of freedom; but the work goes on, the progress of civilization, the work of the Eternal can never be stopped by the curses of evil deeds of men. History does not record a greater work, no, none half so great; the fetters stricken from off four millions of people and protected, educated and guided in the way to heaven, fitted for citizens of a free nation, and that in the space of seven short years. You owe much to the government in this great work; you have had many friends, but one before and above all, the martyr President alone excepted, has been your friend who deserves to be remembered by you and your posterity for ever, whose name will be handed down to generations yet unborn. What the name of Cincinnatus was to the Romans, and the names of Washington and Lincoln to the Americans, will his name be to the colored freemen of this country.[28] The

---

26. Former slaves made up 141,000 of 179,000 African Americans who served in the United States Army and Navy during the Civil War. See Blight, *Frederick Douglass' Civil War*, 148, 163–65.

27. Fort Wagner, South Carolina, and Port Hudson, Louisiana. See Blight, *Frederick Douglass' Civil War*.

28. Lucius Quinctius Cincinnatus (519–ca. 430 BC), was a Roman political figure known for his reluctance to aggrandize political power. He became consul in 460, and was appointed dictator in 458. After defying the tribunes, he went into voluntary exile,

christian gentleman who left his study to grasp his sword and engage in the great struggle, became the christian soldier, yea more, the christian general, who never for an instant in the camp bivouc or the battle field forgot his duty as a christian to his God, who, when the contest ended would have preferred to go back to his chosen profession, only that an important work remained to be done, the protection, the education, the regeneration of a people. He took charge of your interests from that day to this, through all the turmoil and excitement of great political contests, he has not faltered in a hairs breadth in the face of prejudice and against all opposition, he has been true as steel, the mildest and most just of men, yet stern in the discharge of his duty, he has been the guardian of your peace, the protector of your interests, and the unswerving defender of your rights, and this, not only from a sense of duty as a military officer, but from a higher and nobler sense of justice as a christian man. Freed men of Kentucky! you little know what you owe to this man when we stood and plead your cause; when we earnestly asked of the great men of the nation that the burden might be removed, and this but a little time ago when we went to all statesmen and legislators, and left no means untried, no stone unturned, and all in vain; we at last came back to the place whence we started, and there found a man who had the nerve, the high moral courage to assume the responsibility to issue the order. I say nothing against other great men among whom were some of the truest patriots of the land. I do not know whether they would not or could not grant our prayer, I know that there

----

and in 450 ran unsuccessfully for the office of decimvir, opposing a proposal to open the consulship to plebeians. In 439, at age eighty, he was again appointed dictator, in order to oppose Spurius Maelius. George Washington (1732–1799), of Virginia, was a surveyor, soldier, planter, revolutionary, a general in the American War for Independence, and the first President of the United States, from 1789 to 1797. Washington was born into a planter family in eastern Virginia; he became a surveyor, and was commissioned a lieutenant colonel in the Virginia militia in 1754, fighting in the French and Indian War. He served in the Virginia House of Burgesses and was elected commander in chief of the Continental Army in July 1775. Washington led that ill-equipped army against the British in the War of American Independence, pursuing an audacious strategy of surprising the enemy and avoiding or withdrawing from battles that would destroy his forces. With the aid of the French, Washington prevailed over the British at the Battle of Yorktown, Virginia, in 1781, which ended the war. Contemporaries and biographers compared him to Cincinnatus for his reluctance to wield power. Washington retired to his Virginia plantation, but abandoned retirement to lend his prestige to the Constitutional Convention of 1787, which resulted in the creation of the United States republic. He served as president from 1789 to 1797, stepping down after a second term. See Smith, *A Dictionary of Greek and Roman Biography and Mythology*, 1:752; and Wills, *Cincinnatus*.

was great obstacles in the way, and I know that they did not grant it, and when I speak as I do, I only give poor credit to the man who richly deserves it. I tell you that when with his left hand, the other he lost in his country's service, he signed that order, he rendered you a service of inestimable value, but for that order supposing that half of the threats of your enemies had been carried into execution, blackened spots would mark the places where your little children to-day gather together to learn to read God's word and their country's history. You and your little children have not many such friends, and they should learn to bless the name of this great soldier this christian officer, Major General Howard.[29] But I did not come to speak of men, but of facts. The work is not yet done, you have entered the borders of the promised land, and many things remain to be accomplished. In the beginning of the existence of a people, leading men mould the character of that people, in the end the people mould the character of their leading men, so must it be with you. Your people must be taught, enlightened, elevated, certain rights you want, these rights you must fit yourselves for, and you must have them. You have a Douglas and a Langston; you are proud of these men, you have a right to be, they came up through privation and hardships, through scorn and oppression, they are worthy of your esteem, but I trust the day is not far distant when you will have a thousand such as Douglas and ten thousand Langstons.[30] Now how

29. General Oliver O. Howard (1830–1909) of Maine was a graduate of the United States Military Academy at West Point. He served as general and as brigade commander in the U.S. army during the Civil War, then headed up the Freedmen's Bureau, officially known as the U.S. Bureau of Refugees, Freedmen, and Abandoned Lands, from 1865 to 1872. See *Encyclopædia Britannica Online,* s.v. "Oliver O. Howard," http://www .britannica.com/EBchecked/topic/273459/Oliver-O-Howard.

30. Frederick Douglass (1818–1895), was an abolitionist and civil rights orator and editor. He was born a slave on the Eastern Shore of Maryland and escaped from Baltimore in 1838. In 1841, he became an agent for the Massachusetts Anti-Slavery Society and began a public-speaking career that spanned five decades. He published an autobiography in 1845, which prompted him to leave the United States on an eighteen-month speaking tour of Great Britain and Ireland. He returned in 1847 to found the *North Star* (later *Frederick Douglass' Paper*) and to agitate against slavery from Rochester, New York. He embraced political abolition after the passage of the Fugitive Slave Act of 1850 and urged the overthrow of slavery by violent means. Those means came in the Civil War and Douglass became a leading proponent and recruiter of African American soldiers. After Emancipation, he continued to press for civil rights for African Americans and women, and he served as U.S. minister to Haiti and as marshal of the District of Columbia. John Mercer Langston (1829–1897), a lawyer and civil rights activist, was born free in Virginia and then moved to Ohio. Langston earned two degrees at Oberlin

is this to be accomplished, how are you to gain the rights and privileges which you desire. What are these rights and privileges? You want the legal rights of American citizens, you want equality before the law, you do not want social equality. I shall not stop to discuss this; I know that you do not ask for or expect it, you have too much of it already. It would be the ruin and destruction of both races if an Almighty God had intended the races to be one, He, in His infinite wisdom, would have made them one. Man cannot set aside the decrees of the Almighty; we know this, you know it, your enemies know it; they have no more fear of negro equality than of Indian equality. It is the cry of unscrupulous demagogues appealing to the prejudices of the people; it is ridiculous, it is impossible, let it pass; but equality before the law is a very different thing. Life, liberty, the possession of property, and the pursuit of happiness should be guaranteed to every man who treads American soil, no matter what his color, cast or condition may be. Now what are the rights which you should have and yet have not, what do you want conceeded to you by the white? as freemen to possess property and pursue happiness. You want the right, as does every honest man, to labor for your daily bread, for such wages as you may agree upon, and to receive your pay when due, under the ancient maxim, "The laborer is worthy of his hire."[31] When your task is done, you do not want the contract repudiated and payment refused because you cannot prove by white witnesses, the terms of your contract; you want the right to till the soil throughout the length and breadth of this fair land, to plant and to sow, and when favored by Providence, your crops are ready for the harvest, you want to reap the reward of honest toil and not be driven from your fields and turned adrift, homeless and penniless by lawless bands of regulating villains.[32] You want the right to buy land, to pay for it, to build your little homes, to provide for your wives and children, by your own fire sides to rest

College and practiced law in Ohio. He was active in the Ohio Anti-Slavery Society and on the Underground Railroad. During the Civil War, he recruited African American soldiers for Massachusetts and Ohio infantry units. After Emancipation, he was dean of the Howard University Law School and president of the Virginia Normal and Collegiate Institute (later Virginia State University). He served as U.S. minister to Haiti and won a disputed congressional election as the first African American congressman from Virginia. See McFeely, *Frederick Douglass;* and Cheek and Cheek, *John Mercer Langston and the Fight for Black Freedom, 1829–1865.*

31. Gospel of Luke 10:7.

32. In many areas of the former Confederacy, beginning during Reconstruction, former slaves were required to agree to labor contracts, often with former owners on disadvantageous terms. See Blackmon, *Slavery by Another Name.*

after your daily labor, beneath your own roof, without the fear of having your houses broken into, your families insulted, and yourselves dragged forth to be beaten or murdered, on any pretence, whether it be that you served in the Union army or that the regulators are determined that you shall not live separate from your late masters, or that you have committed some offence against the laws of the land, if the latter be the accusation, be it true or not, you only ask a fair trial under the law, and will abide the result, you want the right to go through the land, to walk the streets, behaving yourselves respectfully and properly toward all, to go to places of amusement, theatres or circuses, subject to the rules governing such places, and all you ask is that the law of the land may protect you from the jeers, insults, or assaults of evil minded men whoever they may be. You want the right to open your school houses, and to send your children that they may begin to drink at the fountain of knowledge which has long been to you what the fountain of youth was to the Spanish adventurer, ardently hoped for, but scarce expected. This, that they may learn the maxims of truth, to love God and their fellow men, to be kind, honest, just and true to one another, and to all mankind; and you do not want this precious boon snatched from you by men who lighten the midnight heavens by your burning school houses, who mob and drive away your school teachers without reason or mercy. Last, but not least, you want the right to erect your churches, and to gather your people together to worship God after your own fashion, and according to the dictates of your own conscience, with none to molest or make you afraid. These are but simple rights, yet without them life is not worth having. They are but just and should not be denied to the poorest and lowest, in the country, and yet they are denied to you, so say the facts, and facts are stubborn things. Now, in order that you may secure these rights, that you may have this much of equality before the law, what should be done. I will tell you. I affirm that it is necessary that you should have the right to testify in all your cases before courts of justice. It is necessary, because with out it you have no adequate protection for your lives, your property, or the honor of your wives and daughters. No man can conceive a system more atrocious, more unjust, than the policy of this boasted State. A white man may murder, in cold blood, a negro, may rob him of his property, may outrage his sister, his wife or his daughter, and, unless a white man sees the act, the villain goes unpunished, at least, so far as the laws of Kentucky, a law paramount to her laws no civilized nation presents a parallel to this unjust system. A colored man makes a contract with a white man, there are no white witnesses present and the white man can defraud the poor laborer of his hard earned wages. Slavery was not so villainous, then they made no pretentions to honesty and just dealing. This is but to add deceit, fraud and treachery to wrong; and what valid reason is there for refusing this simple right. None; emphatically none. Can they not weigh a negro's testimony as well as a white man's, can not judges and juries take it for what it is worth, are there not hundreds, yea, thousands of white men whom no honest jury can believe under oath. Why is their testimony to be taken, and the testimony of an honest black man, whom every member of the community respects, and has confidence in, refused, simply because he is black and was a slave. A just and a generous people recognize no such distinction—an honest and upright people would not permit it. It is against the spirit of humanity, it is contrary to the immutable laws of justice; it cannot and will not last. I predict that the Bureau will remain, and the Civil Rights Bill will be enforced in Kentucky until this is changed.[33] In the next place you want, and you should have the right to sit upon juries in all cases where you are interested parties; this is not so important as the first but it is a right and should be conceded, bitter as is the prejudice against you, you require something to balance and offset that prejudice. Wenh a black man shall be tried by a mixed jury or a jury of his own race there will be no fear that if he is guilty he will escape and there will be some hope that if he is innocent his innocence will be vindicated, the penitentiary will not be crowded with men punished too severely for petty crimes as I am informed and fear it is now. The white man will learn that the black man has rights which he is bound to respect, and the result will be that each will treat the other with candor, fairness and justice; both will be gainers in the end. I venture to say, that the Bureau will remain and the civil rights bill be enforced till this also is done. And now the last and yet the first great right, the right which overshadows all others, which includes and guarantees all others the birthright of the native born, the gift of a free country to foreign born white men, the right of suffrage shall it be denied to American born black men, it is denied but it will not long be so,

33. The Civil Rights Act of 1866 was Congress's first federal measure to protect civil rights. Southern states had passed severe black codes restricting African Americans' rights. The Act, passed over President Andrew Johnson's veto, was designed to enforce the Thirteenth Amendment by granting all citizens the right to sue and testify in court, participate in legally binding contracts, and to buy, sell, and inherit property. In part, problems enforcing and legitimizing such civil rights legislation eventually led to the adoption of the Fourteenth Amendment in 1868 and the Fifteenth Amendment in 1870. See Foner, *Reconstruction*, 118.

Already the horrizon is red and brilliant with light of the rising sun of liberty, it is right you should vote, and why is it right? I assume that every man who pays taxes has an undeniable right to vote, for what principle did the founders of this Republic toil, suffer and bleed through a seven years war; in what principle was old Glory the banner of right and liberty born, what was the watch-word at Lexington, at Valley Forge, at York Town? No taxation without representation, no laws just or unjust which shall take away a man's property unless a man has a voice in electing the legislatures who make those laws. For this principle, our fathers fought; for this principle, naked and starving, they struggled, relying in the God of battles and the justice of their cause. There were black men in the Continental army, and it is recorded that through all that terrible struggle, the slaves in Virginia, in Carolina and throughout the colonies were true and faithful to their patriot masters' cause. In that principle the Continentals triumphed, it is one of the great corner stones of this Republic, it is one of the fundamental principles of the government; it should apply to all, save traitors, who have sought their country's ruin, both white and black. Yet what do we see here in Kentucky, we see this principle set aside and ignored, we see a people taxed on every dollar of their property, yea more, paying poll tax, and paying dollar for dollar, and head for head with the white man, and what do they receive in return, do they receive protection, away with such protection, when a black man cannot even tell his wrongs in a court of justice, when those dear to him are, so far as Kentucky law is concerned, at the mercy of every murdering villainous vagabond in the land, when their lives and property may be taken from them, and without white witnesses there is no redress, when their school houses are burned and their teachers mobbed, and they call this protection, protection, such protection as the robbing Barons of the feudal ages gave to their peasants, worse than the American master gave to his slave, and more, every black man is taxed over and above the white man's tax, two dollars, and for what, when the law was first enacted it was to support schools and to take care of colored paupers; and where did this money go, echo answers, where I know not, but where the teachers went I do know, to the Bureau which disbursed $35,000 a year, to do a work which was the duty of the State of Kentucky to do, and which the black man was taxed to do. Where do the paupers go, but first what has the last legislature done, repealed that section of the law which appropriated a portion of the fund for school purposes and it now all goes to the pauper fund. I repeat where do the paupers go? they go to the Bureau, to the maligned and slandered Bureau for fuel, for food, and clothing, to the hospital for medicine, and this work the State should do, and yet those people abuse the Bureau and when the foundling turns up, the off-spring perhaps of some rascally white man they take it to the Bureau, when they have a poor old decrept servant who has wasted the strength of his life toiling and working for them what do they do with him, come to the Bureau to have him taken to the hospital and then turn and abuse the Bureau again. All men do not do this, no, there is a leaven of just men in Kentucky who will see this wrong righted, who will see that there is no longer taxation without representation, contrary to the principle of free government. Again, I hold that every man who is liable to be called upon to bear arms in defence of his country, should have a voice in the government of that country, even in Rome under the king's sixteen hundred years ago, this principle was acknowledged, it is recorded, the patricians rich men supported alone the burden of war and consequently had the right of voting in the assemblies through the ranks of the army. A man obtained the right of suffrage and upon this principle, the principle that all men who sustained the government should have a voice in the government and that according to his fortune and his dignity a man should take his place in the army in the days when they fought hand to hand the richest in the front ranks. The founders of Rome built up a government at once the wonder and mistress of the world. In this boasted free land, what incentive can there be for a black man to bear arms in defence of his country when that country gives him no voice in its government and sent protection when this nation struggled for its life against the hosts of the rebellion, when it was absolutely necessary to strain every nerve and bend every energy to save the Republic did it stop to enquire whether the man who answered to the call and grasped the rifle was white or black? No! And when the ranks of the insurgents bore hard upon our bleeding and broken lines, when men fell thick and fast, when we saw Old Glory surrounded by the glittering bayonets coming to the rescue, did it matter to us whether the faces in that column were white or black? No! so they came under the same banner and fought with a loyal cheer it was all right; why should we who stood side by side in the same armies, who stood or fell as fortune willed, who were likely to fall before the foe on the same field and go side by side with the black man to the bar of the same just God, why should we object to vote with them at the same ballot box to support the same principles. I do not believe we would be called upon to answer whether we fought in a white or black regiment, but on what side we fought, on the side of God, liberty and humanity, or on the side of darkness, the devil, and slavery. Again, I repeat that every man who is liable to bear arms in defence of his country should have the right to vote, and as certain as the sun shines by day, so certain will that right be conceded. I have not told you all this to give you cause of complaint or stir you up to anger, but I have told you that you might plainly see the great prize for which you must struggle, that you might understand that the prize is well worthy the greatest exertion, and to warn you that without effort long and constant, you cannot succeed. Much has been done for you, all that can be, the rest depends upon yourselves alone. You must not expect Congress to reconstruct this State and give you these right; this cannot be done but from the people of Kentucky; as a free gift you must receive them, prove to these people that you are worthy and well qualified, educate public sentiment, by your daily walk and conversation, prove your fitness by your acts and the powerful voice of justice will plead and win your cause; your destiny is in your own hands, and now, in view of all this, what is your duty? To educate your children and yourselves; strain every nerve, leave nothing undone which shall tend to fit you for the duties and responsibilities of the undeveloped future. Cultivate and raise the standard of morals among your people and acquire property, get and keep the almighty dollar, and why do these things. Educate, because just as the precepts of faith, the teachings of Christianity, the Word of God raises your souls above the interests of this world, so will the pursuit of education inspire you with a love of the beautiful and the just, and a hatred of whatever is wrong, it will teach you to cast your votes intelligently for the right. As it is spoken in the Sacred Scriptures, "Happy is the man that findeth wisdom and the man that getteth understanding, for the mercandise of it is better than the merchandise of silver and the gain thereof than fine gold. She is more precious than rubies and all the things thou can'st desire, are not to be compared unto her. Length off days is in her right hand, and in her left hand riches and honor; her ways are ways of pleasantness, and all her paths are peace."[34] In the pages of history you will read of the deeds of great men, statesmen and warriors, and learn to emulate their example, you will see that nations and people before you have come up through hardships and oppressions to liberty, through wrong to justice, through stripes and slavery to freedom and legal rights. It was not the sword, the battle axe, or cannon, not armies or navies that brought the Anglo Saxon, the German, and the Gaelic races from ignorance and barbarism into light and civilization. It was the pen and the printing press, and the diffusion of knowledge

34. Book of Proverbs 3:13–17.

among the masses of the people. You will learn the principles of the Government under which you live, learn to love and cherish the memory of its founders and defenders, you will disarm your enemies, they can then no longer say the colored man is unfit to vote, he is ignorant, he is degraded, you will no longer need white people to preach to you, and you will be able to read the word of God for yourselves and understand the teachings of your divine Master, you will learn to forgive your enemies, and to be patient under oppression. I would not have you stop with the attainments of a common education. I would have you go into the higher branches and give the lie again to the assertion that there is a point and that soon reached, beyond which the mind of a black man cannot rise; in the end, your leaders will be ranked among the educated men of the nation, and you will be known as a happy and prosperous people, but first you must encourage religion and good morals, and occupy your minds with the thoughts of good deeds, to remember that there is an over-rulling Providence, let your hearts be penetrated with honesty and fidelity, so that good faith shall reign among you more than the fear of laws and punishments, true religion will soften your manners and elevate your minds, good morals will nourish and strengthen the better impulses of your natures, more than this they will make you respected and strengthen you where you are now weak. One of the greatest misfortunes that has befallen your people is the opening of dram shops and the facilities for obtaining liquor. When I saw the black man free, working for his daily bread, I rejoiced, but when I saw him wasting his wages for drink which ruins both body and soul, I thought that with the good comes evil. My friends, shun the dram-shop as you would the cup of death. Again, I trust the practice of taking up[35] will disappear from amongst you; there are many other people who behave very badly, yet they throw around their conduct a mantle of concealment, this will profit them nothing in the next world. I ask you to destroy the evil, root and branch, let the the sentiment of justice enter your conscience, let virtue the highest expression of duty become the general rule of your public and private life; there was once a nation, but partially civilized, the morals of the people were so pure that for two hundred and thirty years no husband was known to repudiate his wife, nor any woman to separate from her husband, and building upon such principles, that nation came to rule the world. Show your enemies that you can cease to do evil without law, and learn to do good without statutes. Lastly, acquire property and preserve it, it will give

---

35. "Taking up" is an archaic expression for adultery.

you importance, standing, and consideration, to have a home, however lowly, a home of his own, let him gather around his hearthstone his wife and little ones and with no fear of oppressive landlords, thank God that his lot is cast in a fee land and be happy. Gather, I say, your wife and little ones around your herthstone, their love will shed a sun-gleam of happiness upon your existence, and with them you will enjoy serene content; there is no happiness save in contentment, no contentment save in doing right. Work, labor is not a hardship, it is a privilege: what you did for your masters before, do now for yourselves, you made them rich, is there anything to prevent you from becoming rich; if any of you are to receive bounty money for serving your country, save it, buy a home with it, do not waste it as many have done, make it the foundation upon which to build your fortune, do not sell your bounty. You were ready to shoulder the musket and encounter hardships, to face danger and death for your government, are you not willing to trust her good faith until she is ready to pay you. Believe no man when he says you will never get it, if he was not sure of his money he would not touch it. When colored Tom Jones gets $1,000 he becomes Thomas, when he gets $5,000 he becomes Mr. Jones, and when he gets $20,000 he becomes Thomas Jones, Esq., such is the consideration money gives a man. Education, cultivation of morals, and the acquirement of property will enable you to vindicate your right and will certainly secure the privileges you desire and fit you to enjoy them. History furnishes an hundred examples from which you may draw lessons of trust and confidence, trust in God and confidence in yourselves. More than two hundred years ago a little band of brave, true-hearted men coming in a feeble bark over the winter waves of a stormy ocean, landed where grim and grey the rocks of new England lay frowning along the sea, fleeing from tyranny and oppression in a foreign land, sought a home, rest and peace amid the wilderness of an unknown land. Scarce had they sheltered themselves from the fierce storms that swept through the then trackless forests, than with united efforts they reared a rude structure of logs, which served alike for church and school, the humble spire of which pointing to a cold new England sky symbolized as well their faith in their destiny as their trust in God who had brought them safely through the perils of the great deep and would yet bless their efforts until those wild inhospitable shores should bloom and blossom like a rose. And when these people first stood beneath the roof of that humble edifice, they doubtless felt deeply grateful for this great blessing. In that little house those stern men laid the foundation of that indomitable and unconquerable spirit which triumphing over all obstacles founded the edifice of American free institutions, there they began to educate their children, to teach them those truths first proclaimed by the Saviour sixteen hundred years before; to instill into them that spirit of truth, that hatred of wrong and love of the good which has enabled their posterity to stretch their power over vast mountain chains; mighty rivers and boundless plains, and build up a giantic republic, whose flag floats in the breeze that dashes the spray of the Pacific on the golden sands of the California coast, which has planted its emblems of beauty and power over the orange groves of Florida and on the ice ribbed rocks of the artic zone. If, then, that people in the midst of a boundless wilderness, separated from civilization by a dreary waste of waters had reason for faith and hope, how much more have you? Your path is lightened by the sun of liberty, you live amid the glorious civilization of the nineteenth century, a powerful government is pledged to protect you, twenty millions of loyal people are your friends. True, you are not pilgrim fathers, you are not descendants of the proud anglo-saxon race, but you may become none the less fathers of a happy and intelligent people. I am not one of those who believe that the intelligence of any race, or the capacity of acquiring knowledge, depends upon the color of their skin, for the reason that the annals of nations tell a different story. It is recorded that the great pyramid, covering acres of ground and yet but the tombstone of a king who reigned in the morning of the world, the eternal pyramid, since the building of which the very heavens have changed which looked on in grim silence when the pole star first cast its light on Egypt, and which yet stands so firm that to this day the variation of the mariner's compass is determined by the position of its sides, this wonder of the world was built four thousand years ago by dark skinned men. The statutes of Egyptian kings, of one of which is told that when it was touched by the rays of the rising sun it gave forth strange strains of music, and the Obelisks carved with wondrous skill from single blocks of stone and raised by seemingly superhuman power, and covered with curious hieroglyphics telling that they had been erected to commemorate the deeds of men whom kings delighted to honor; the vast temples supported on countless ranges of statutes, the catacombs, tombs of the dead, containing the corpses of generation upon generation, and labyrinths with their hundreds of vaults and chambers, into which, whoever entered without a guide never came forth, but, wandering on in silence and alone found in that vast solitude a living tomb, all these were the works of the dark skinned sons of Egypt. When Vasco Degama, the Portuguese mariner, sailed around the Cape of Good Hope in 1497, circumnavigating Africa, when he inaugurated a commercial revolution whereby Venice, the gem of the Adriatic, lost her supremacy, prosperity took wing and fled from the Italian cities, the commercial sceptre of Egypt was broken, and European Jews lost their hold on the monoply of European commerce, whereby commercial prosperity dawned for the first time upon Europe, and the British Isles took the first steps towards becoming mistress of the seas, this great navigator only sailed over the same track followed by the dark skinned sailors of Pharaoh Necho the Egyptian king, two thousand years before.[36] When Napoleon, III., opened the Suez canal and connected the Mediterranean with the Red Sea amid the flourish of trumpets and the rejoicing of Europe over a great triumph of engineering skill, he only accomplished what had been done twice before by the colored kings of Egypt, when they constructed the great canal from the Nile to the Red Sea twenty-one hundred years ago.[37] To this people are we indebted for the first gems of the art of writing. And when the historian (or the recorder of fables he should be called,) states that brass was first made at the burning of Corinth, and that glass was first discovered when shipwrecked mariners propped their kettles, boiling on the sand with pieces of nitre, they only robbed the people of Egypt of the credit of having first made these discoveries.[38] I cannot see

36. Vasco de Gama (ca. 1469–1524) was a Portuguese explorer famous for rounding the horn of Africa and mapping an ocean passage from western Europe to India in 1497– 99, afterward establishing routes of trade, conquests, and political alliances between Portugal and East African and Indian rulers. Pharaoh Necho, or Necho II, was King of Egypt, 610–595 BC. He is mentioned in 2 Kings 23:29, Jeremiah 46:2, and 2 Chronicles 35:20 and 36:4, and is noted for pursuing an ambitious canal project linking Lake Timsah to the Gulf of Suez, which he did not complete. Necho II assaulted and subdued Syria and Palestine, but was forced to return to Egypt, where his armies were destroyed by Nebuchadnezzar II. See Hartig, "Vasco de Gama"; and Budge, *A History of Egypt from the End of the Neolithic Period to the Death of Cleopatra VII, B.C. 30*, 6:220–24.

37. Napoleon III (1808–1873) was born Charles-Louis-Napoléon Bonaparte. He was president of the Second French Republic, 1848–52, and emperor of France, 1852–70. After two decades of relative stability, he led France into the Franco-Prussian War in 1870–71, was captured at the Battle of Sedan in 1870, deposed, and went into exile in England. Napoleon III sponsored the construction of the Suez Canal, completed by the French Suez Canal Company in 1869, which connects the Red Sea with the eastern Mediterranean Sea. That 101-mile canal shortened shipping routes from Europe and the Mediterranean to Asia. Until completion of the canal, ships had to travel around the horn of Africa in the South Atlantic and Indian Oceans. See Goyau, "Napoleon III."

38. The Roman historian and naturalist Pliny the Elder (23–79 AD) contends that brass was invented in Corinth in 146 BC, when the city was sacked and burned (*Natural History*, 34.3), and that shipwrecked Phoenician sailors discovered glass when they used blocks of natron instead of stones to support cooking pans and the soda ash vitri-

that the color of a man should prevent him from becoming a true and intelligent citizen, fit to appreciate the privileges and enjoy the rights of free government. I do not believe that Hannibal, who led the Carthagenian armies across the rivers and plains of Spain, over the frozen and almost impassable Alphs, hurling back the legions of Rome upon the gates of the eternal city, and making the mistress of the world tremble for her fate, would have been any less great or greater had he been a blue eyed, light haired, fair skinned Saxon.[39] Mental power does not depend upon the color of the skin but upon the brain. It is true that you are descended from these people no more than I. yet while it proves that nations like men, are born, live, die, and pass away, it also proves that the color of skin has nothing to do with the progress of a people in the march of intelligence and civilization. I have not told you these things as an idle story, but that you may have hope. The past, with its evils, has gone by; the future is yours, and if you but do your duty the wings of old time shall come laden with flowers; the issue cannot be doubtful; this nation has by the aid of the God of battles, solved the problem of American slavery with the sword, and by the help of the same Omnipotent arm, we will solve the question of the education and elevation of this people. With school houses and books, with the pen, the printing press and the diffusion of knowledge among the masses of the people, and before these agencies prejudices shall go down in the dust, even as the armed columns of the rebellion went down before the bayonets of the loyal legions of this land.

ADDRESS OF LIEUT,-COL. I. S. CATHIN.[40]

Freedmen,—What a world of music there is in that one word to you who have just come up out of your bondage; dearer and sweeter to you is it than

---

fied into glass (*Natural History,* 36.65). See Bostock and Riley, *The Natural History of Pliny,* 6:150–53, 379.

39. Hannibal (247–183 BC), a Carthaginian military leader, is remembered as a brilliant strategist and one of the finest generals of Western classical antiquity. At the outbreak of the second Punic War, "Hannibal's War," in 218, he marched scores of elephants over the Pyrenees and the Alps, along with 50,000 soldiers and 9,000 horsemen, to attack the Roman Republic, winning victories at Trebia in late 218, at Lake Trasimene in 217, and at Cannae in 216. He was defeated at the Battle of Zama, in North Africa, in 202, and returned to Carthage before living in exile. He advised the Seleucid monarch and afterwards traveled to Armenia and Bithynia in 187–183, where he masterminded a naval victory against Eumenes of Pergamum, only to be betrayed to the Romans by Prusias of Bithynia, at which time he committed suicide. See Lancel, *Hannibal.*

40. See note 17 above.

silver and gold or precious stones; dearer than anything save your manhood and womanhood, for you are not only freedmen and freedwomen, but men and women clothed with important civil rights, charged with the responsibilities to some extent of citizens, citizens, not only of Kentucky; but American; free to breathe the pure air of heaven wherever you please—equal in the sight of Him who made all men of one flesh—free to earn your bread by the sweat of your brows—equal before the law to demand protection of person and property—free to praise God and denounce the devil—equal to demand security in the sacred relations of husband and wife, of parent and child. Yes, free and equal with the inalienable rights of life, liberty and the pursuit of happiness. A few years have wrought a vast revolution in your condition. A short time since you were abject slaves; and you had no rights. It was said that white men bound to respect but you were used as beasts of burden and treated with no higher consideration than other beasts of burden. The tenderest ties were sundered in a moment, never more to be united. Your lives were at the mercy of your masters, the virtues of your wives and daughters, your mothers and sisters, was but the sport and pastime of your masters. In fine, a more utterly debased and down trodden race never walked upon God's green earth. This outrage against you, this outrage against humanity, this outrage against a Republican form of government, this practice existing in the face of the declaration of independence, at last stirred up conflicting elements that shook the nation from centre to circumference with the fires and convulsions of civil war. From this sea of fire and blood you came up into the glorious sunlight of freedom: God opened up a pathway through the red sea of rebellion, and you was lead safely out on dry land, while the dark waters covered the mighty host who were moving against you to forge the chains of slavery forever upon you. Now you are free men and free women: your bodies are your own, your labor is your own, and what is dearer yet, your wives and children are your own. You are permitted to assemble here in great numbers to listen to the advice and counsel of one who has had much experience and taken much interest in freedmen's affairs. It would seem almost impertinent in me to attempt to say anything in the presence of one so much abler than myself, but as an officer of the Bureau, charged with the immediate supervision of your interests in this district, I do not feel like letting this opportunity pass by unimproved. I have been on duty here for nearly sixteen months, during which time I have endeavored to administer my official duties with strict reference to your best interests. I have not been as faithful as I ought to have been, but taking all in all, I feel that I have done in the main what will be considered in the future, if not to-day, for your highest good. It is not he who devotes all his time in telling you that you are as good or as intelligent as the white man, who is your true friend: it is not he who endeavors to keep alive the prejudice that now exists against you, that is your best adviser: it is not he who would attempt to array you in hostility to your former master that is consulting your immediate or future welfare. No, he is your enemy, and if you watch him carefully you will find that he is only acting and working for some base and selfish purpose. He who is your friend will not flatter you, but will, is far as he is able, give you a true exposition of your real situation and condition. You must remember that though you are free you are still in your infancy as freedmen and freedwomen. For years you were kept in utter ignorance and darkness, and, therefore, it will take years of patient suffering, and toil and study, before you can hope to fully attain that position in the community for which you have commenced so earnestly to strive. Though you have rights that must and shall be protected as far its possible, yet you must remember that you are living among those who believed, and now believe, that slavery was and is your normal condition; and that it was not only a political but moral sin to take you away from their households and fields. These people have been taught from infancy to look upon you as their property and their inferiors, and that you were suited to no other condition than bondage. These views so universally entertained, though erroneous and mischievous, must be recognized as existing facts: and I, for one, feel inclined under the circumstances, to treat them with some degree of charity. At any rate, these people are now in power in the State: you are at their mercy in spite of the general government. It is in the power of the people of the State, in their legislature and court to discriminate unjustly against you and in many respects to render your condition more oppressive and hateful even than when you were their chattels. One great and important question for you, then, is how can the prejudice and hate of your former masters be removed? To answer this question intelligently, let us enquire what are the causes for this prejudice? As I have said before, you were once their property, and when you were set at liberty almost every man in the State considered that he was robbed of his property, influenced by this loss the people of the State almost irresistibly, though very unwisely and unjustly, concentrated their spite and prejudice against you as the cause of all their trouble. They, therefore, oppose you in everything. Hence the reason of their hostile attitude toward you. While this state of things exists, I care not how strong the arm of the general government may be over you, it cannot successfully protect you till these erroneous ideas are removed, and the people allow you, at least, to go along unobstructed and unopposed in your own efforts to become what God intended you to be. Now, I say again, that while I recognise the importance, humanity and justice of the acts of the national legislature in providing for your protection in consequence of the hostile attitude of the State authorities, still I also deem it of the utmost importance that the time shall quickly come when the people of Kentucky will look upon you as their fellow citizens, and will willingly and cheerfully aid you in all your efforts to ameliorate your condition as men and women. Upon your own conduct, upon your own efforts, upon the attitude which you yourselves assume, very greatly depend the conduct and attitude of the people who are in power toward you. You are no longer slaves, but as free as they. Show them and prove to them that you recognise the important fact that you live in their midst and are still largely dependent upon them for your happiness and prosperity. They assert that you cannot take care of and provide for yourselves. Demonstrate to them by a frugal and economical industry that the men and women, upon whose unremunerated labor they are so greatly indebted for their own wealth and prosperity, can also take care of themselves and accumulate fortunes. They say you will lie. Show them by a strict adherence to the truth that it would be well for them and society if they would imitate you. They say you are ignorant. Answer them yes, it is true, and point sadly back to your years of servitude, during which even the simple lessons, which Jesus taught for all men, irrespective of race or color, were kept away from you, and the light of revelation itself was shut out from your vision, and then ask them who were to blame. Then point to your schools scattered all over the South, and say, give us a chance. If you will pursue such a course it will not be long before the people of Kentucky will not only cease from the unholy crusade which they have carried on against you since you became free by the fundamental law of the land, but will, themselves provide for your protection and advancement. I do not ask for you the right to vote at this time in the State of Kentucky, for it would only delay you in obtaining that right. I do not ask for you the privileges of sitting as jurors, as judges or legislators for the same reason. You are willing to forego these high and important privileges, until brighter days dawn upon you. You desire the privilege of laboring, where and for whom you please, and for the largest wages you can get. You desire the undisturbed right to acquire property; and you want the grand old maxim that your house is your castle, recognised as applying to you. You want to be safe from midnight attacks of desperate men, organized to murder you and burn down your houses over your heads. You want to be and feel as safe and as secure in your life and liberty as your more fortunate white neighbors. You demand the right to protect your person and property. You cannot do this by the laws of the State until her legislators give you the right to testify in her courts. Now if a white man comes into your house and inflicts an outrage upon you or any member of your family, you have no remedy in the State courts.—If a white man enters a congregation of colored persons and deliberately kills one of them he cannot even be apprehended before an officer of the State courts, unless satisfactory white evidence can be obtained. You demand that this unnatural, inhuman and unjust bann upon you shall be removed. Above all, greater than all, beyond all you ask the privilege of educating yourselves and your children. This is a God given right that no man or State can deprive you of without doing violence to the laws and plans of the great head of intelligence who implanted within your bosoms as well as in mine an immortality. You have already demonstrated that you can learn, and have advanced in learning to a remarkable degree under the most unfavorable circumstances. You now demand of the people of the State not only protection of your schools from violence but provisions for their aid and encouragement by beneficent and humane legislation. Intelligence, whether found under the dark brow of the African, or in the delicate, pale forehead of the Anglo Saxon, will vanquish mountains of prejudice; it is a force and power by which anything human can be accomplished, and which naught on earth can withstand; it is God like. Kings and queens descend from their glittering thrones and bow down to pay it homage. By it rank and knightly titles are rent asunder, like glittering cobwebs formed in a summer's night. You demand them; I demand in your name civilization all over the world, God, on His eternal throne, demands that you shall be permitted to develope every noble faculty and quality of your being, and that from this time henceforward no man or State shall place obstructions in the pathway by which this consummation, so devoutly to be wished, shall be effected. When the country shall be wholly restored; when the thirty seven stars shall glitter again upon the old banner; when the clouds that have lowered above and threatened us give away once more to the full light of peace, prosperity and union, then the hate, and bitterness, and prejudice of to-day will be no more, and the men who now persecute you, and even demand your reenslavement, will say to you, freedmen and freedwomen, you were once our slaves; long and faithfully you labored for us in our households and fields; by the sweat of your brows we ate our bread and gained our wealth; in our infancy you tenderly fondled us and watched our shortest footsteps; from childhood to manhood and old age you were ever near us, to administer to our wants all this you did, not only without remuneration but often with kicks and curses. Our relations are now changed. You are no longer our slaves, but our fellow citizens. Though we may not ask you to our firesides and social circles, yet, all your rights of person and property shall be protected. Live, be prosperous be happy, build for yourselves school houses, and churches all over the State, and become scholars and christians. You are entitled to these rights both by the laws of an impartial God, and by virtue of your services for the union during the late rebellion. You were not in at the beginning of the fray, but when the war grew fiercest and the nation began to groan with the labor of the long continued contest, and mourning and sorrow were draping the land, you stepped into the rescue and you dealt quick, thick, heavy blows upon your enemies and the enemies of the Union. I have seen you in the fight, I have fought on the same field; we stood together when the pillars of the Republic were shaking and the structure of Republican government was threatened with destruction; we stood together when the peoples of the earth were looking towards us with sad and down cast eyes fearful of the fate of the only nation on the earth where the theory of government was nearly perfect in liberty; we stood together clad in the same glorious blue, under the same beautiful stars, and the same glorious stripes, symbolizing union and liberty, and shoulder to shoulder and side by side we carried the flag sometimes to to defeat, but still carried it on and on with the same faith and the same hope until we were marching and singing glorious old songs of triumph under the shadows of the, nation's capital, from whose high dome looked the beautiful goddess of liberty. When it was proclaimed that not an armed foe was in the field and that the union of the States and universal liberty were one and indivisible. Let us stand together till the victory of arms is crowned by that far more glorious and eternal victory, the victory of ideas; till every creature made in God's own image, who obeys the law, shall have its full protection, till the prejudice of caste and color shall give way to a more enlightened and universal civilization. But while millions are proclaiming your cause. you must not falter, you have just begun to stand alone; have just begun the battle of life alone, and no race of men ever lived in any land from whom such heroism and endurance are expected. Be not satisfied with mere freedom, but become men and women in the highest and noblest acceptation of the term. Are you equal to the work, my friends, of causing yourselves to be equal with the white man? Have you fairly weighed the mighty task which freedom and citizenship have imposed upon you? Remember that there are men conspiring to wrench from you the boon which the nation's throes and labors of a civil war gave you. Will you not grow weak as those without hope? Will you not grow mad with despair? Oh no! my friends, bear stiffly up, suffer and grow strong. Remember that behind the clouds the Sun is shining and soon streaks of light will appear upon the horizon, and then it will not be long before the full flood light of a cloudless sky will illumine your pathway. Let me cell on you to-night to press onward toward the prize of the high calling. You have no time for folly, you have not a day to waste in idleness and sin. Every morning and evening you will be called upon to give an account of your stewardship. The eyes of the world are upon you, and your conduct is constantly undergoing a searching scrutiny. In the name of the government that gave you liberty, I demand from you untiring efforts in fitting yourselves morally and intellectually for the discharge of the grave and important trusts committed to your keeping.

A SERMON TO SERVANTS.

While travelling through Tennessee, I heard a sermon which is worth reporting. The preacher was a clergyman who had just purchased a plantation with slaves upon it. This was the first Sunday of his occupancy, and he proposed to inaugurate his new "settlement" by instructing his people as to their duties. The audience composed of his slaves, stood before him. He sat on the tongue of a cart. After a hymn had been sung, he held forth from the text, "Servants obey your master's according to the flesh."[41] "My colored friends," he began, "we have not long sustained to each other the relation of master and servant, and I feel called on to speak to you on the subject of your duties to me, your master. In the first place, it is your duty to rise promptly in the morning at the blowing of the horn. Too much sleep is not good for either body or mind. All through this blessed book," he holding up by mistake the hymn book, "if you could read you would find exhortations on the subject of over-sleeping and warnings against it. 'A little more sleep,

---

41. This is a paraphrase of Paul's Letter to the Ephesians 6:5: "Servants, be obedient to them that are your masters according to the flesh, with fear and trembling, in singleness of your heart, as unto Christ."

a little more slumber, a little more folding of the hands together,"[42] is the language of your hearts. Now this is nothing more nor less than a temptation of that old wicked spirit, the Devil. If you yield to this temptation your souls will surely be lost. You will burn in hell. Just think for a moment of the greatness of your sin. I, your kind master, who has the bronchitis, and knows not what it is to have a well day, gets up early on a cold morning, and stands undressed at the open door or window, liable to take his death by cold, and blows his horn. He returns to his bed believing that his servants will obey his summons. Think of your sin when he awakes two hours after to find you in bed. When you over sleep it is not your time but mine you are squandering. You have no time; you are my property. I earned you riding on horseback in the blazing midsummer sun, and in the snow and sleet, preaching until I have worn myself out in the service of God. You will not long have me for a master"— [Here the preacher was almost choked by his emotion.])[43] "If you are unfaithful to me now you will, when you hear the clods rattling on my coffin," [at this point the speaker drew out a handkerchief, blew his nose, and wiped his eyes. Having recovered his composure by this diversion, he added in low tremulous tones][44] "you will be stung by the worm of remorse." This pathetic sentence brought tears to the eyes of many of his impulsive hearers. Having disposed of this point the preacher proceeded to enlarge upon the other duties of slaves. His hearers were threatened, in case of their violation, with everlasting destruction. He then proceeded by the law of association to set forth a somewhat original theology, in something like these terms:—It is your duty to improve the time which I will give you wisely. I'll give you every Saturday night after your day's work is done, and all the little jobs, such as feeding, milking, bringing the water, and chopping the wood for Sunday. I can give you no other night for there is a great many things to be done at night. There is the cotton to be baled, corn to be shucked, wood to be chopped, apples and peaches to he brought from the orchard, and cut for drying; the peas and beans to be threshed out and spinning to be done. All these things must be done at night, besides many which I have not mentioned. We can't spend daylight

42. This is a paraphrase of the Book of Proverbs 6:10: "Yet a little sleep, a little slumber, a little folding of the hands to sleep," and 24:33: "Yet a little sleep, a little slumber, a little folding of the hands to sleep."

43. Goings's brackets.

44. Ibid.

on such trifles, because if we did the cotton would rot in the boll. But the nights are getting long and if you will, you can accomplish a great deal. I can give you but Saturday night. If I gave you any other night you would sit up too late and then sleep over my work next day. You will need to put up beds and get some bed clothing for the winter. To accomplish this, you, men, can make bread trays—there's plenty of cypress on the plantation, or you can braid foot mats, or you can make brooms, tables and chests to sell. Or you can have coal kilns, and any Saturday night for a small share in the profits, I would let you take my waggon and horses and haul it to some blacksmith. Or you can have a patch and raise some sweet potatoes or water melons. I'll go shares with any of you in this matter. I'll furnish the land and you do the work on Saturday nights when there is moon. There's a thousand ways in which you can make all the pocket money you need. But mind, I'll have no raising of fowls and pigs for sale. They would get their living from my corn; besides, you would claim all the eggs on the plantation as laid by your hens and would sell three times as many pigs and chickens as you raised. There's to be no selling of apples and peaches; you are not to go into my orchards at all. But there are always berries and nuts in the woods which you can gather and take to the village Saturday night or Sunday. A little later and persimmons will be ripe, you can gather them and make beer of them and have it all winter to sell. There are partridge eggs, you can get 5c. per dozen for all you find. You can have your traps for birds, and coons, and possoms. Any of you, men or boys, by going into the village Sunday morning, can make half a dollar in no time by blacking the boots and brushing the coats for young men. Or you can make your dime or quarter by taking care of the horses of planters' sons while they are in church. If I was a nigger I could get rich; and the preacher smiled at his facetiousness. "As for the women, you can make money in almost all the ways I have mentioned; and besides this you can knit socks to sell. You can wash and sew for the negroes around here who have'nt =anybody to do these things for them. You can make soap and sell it. You must have an ashhopper. I will allow you half the ashes you burn in your houses and all the grease from the tops of the pots where you boil your bacon, and all the bones from the meat you eat. You can have all the goose quills the geese lose. You must have kettles and pot hooks, and skillits, and lids for the purpose of baking. You can't always bake in ashes and broil your meat on the coals as you have done. There's too much waste in it. You'll have to have tin buckets to carry your dinners to the field in, and tin cups to drink your buttermilk from. I can't have you using my vessels much longer. Then you want water buckets and plates, cups and saucers, knives and forks, and spoons. You see I am ambitious for you. In getting these things the expense will be devided among you, whereas if I got them all it would come hard on me. You must have stockings and shoes. I don't want you to be hobbling around this winter with frost bitten feet and chilblains. One pair will last the winter. You can go barefooted till late and turn your feet out to grass early."—Here he smiled at his own wit. "I have some pride for my servants; I want them to appear as well as other folks' negroes. Mr. Shoemaker braggs about his negroes, and I want to be able to bragg about mine. Now you can go to your cabins. I wish you to spend your Sunday quietly, for it is God's holy day. Think seriously over what I have said to you and make out your plans. If any of you wish to take a quiet walk in the woods to pick berries or nuts there is no harm in it. If you will come to me after we have sung another hymn, I will give you passes, provided you promise not to stand around the streets engaged in loud talking and laughing with other negroes. You must come directly back. I can see no harm in your going there quietly, and attending to your business, and returning quietly home. Everybody isn't required by God to keep the Sabbath in the same way. You are simply not to do the same things on Sunday as during the week; the idea is relaxation from the work of the week.

THE END.

Editors' Appendices

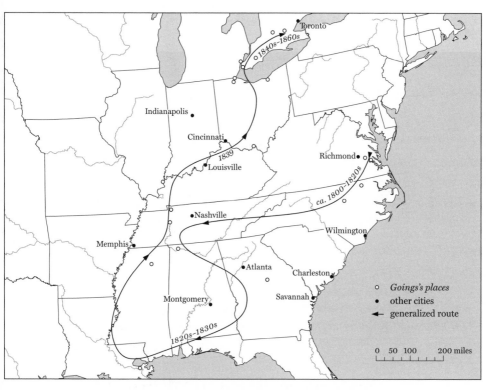

Map 1. Henry Goings's travels

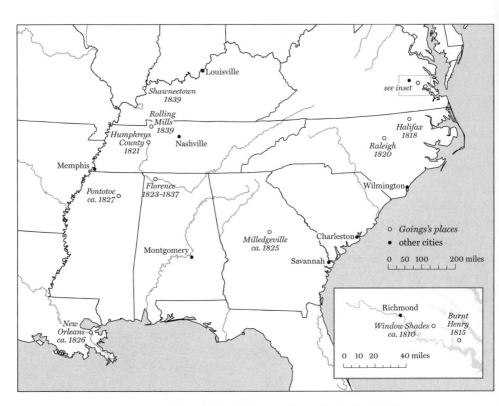

MAP 2. Goings's birthplace and travels in the South

MAP 3. Places Goings lived or visited in the North

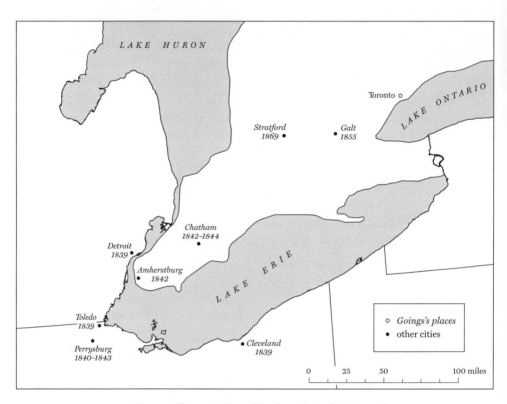

MAP 4. Places Goings lived or visited in Canada

Appendix B

Interviews with "Henry Gowens" and "Mrs. Henry Gowens"

(From Benjamin Drew, *A North-Side View of Slavery,* in *The Refugee, or,
the Narratives of Fugitive Slaves in Canada Related by Themselves; with
an Account of the History and Condition of the Colored Population of
Upper Canada* [Boston: John P. Jewett and Co., 1856], 138–46)

Henry Gowens.

I have had a wide experience of the evils of slavery, in my own person, and have an
extensive knowledge of the horrors of slavery, in all their length and breadth, having
witnessed them in Old Virginia, North Carolina, New Virginia, Tennessee, Alabama,
and Mississippi. I belonged in the State of Virginia, and am, I suppose, about forty years
old. Were I to write out all my experiences and what I have observed, (and I intend to do
this, having commenced already) it would make quite a large volume. In Humphreys Co.
on the Tennessee River, were one hundred and ten slaves; I witnessed their treatment
with a heartache. In Alabama, I know how two plantations, of one hundred and fifty, and
one hundred and thirty each, were managed, who were whipped and slashed under the
kindest overseers they had,—and when they had a hard overseer, there was no peace at
all. It was whip, whip, continually, old and young; nobody got too old to be clear of the
lash. It seemed as if the whipping had to be done, whether the work was done or not.
My own master was kind at first, but as he grew older, he grew more and more severe,
getting overseers who were harder and harder.

About the first of Gen. Jackson's Presidency, my master employed an overseer, named
Kimball, over one hundred and thirty slaves, in Lauderdale Co., Alabama. This Kimball
was one of the most cruel men I ever saw. When he commenced, all the field hands were
called together on Sunday morning, up to the great house, and then Mr. Kimball, a well
dressed gentleman in appearance, and a fine looking man, walked out in company with
my master. The master said, "These are my hands, that I now give up to you; take charge
of them and manage them to the best of your judgment." He gave the names of the foremen of the gangs, and pointed them out to Mr. K.: then the names of the men who had
charge of the women in ploughing; then the name of the man who had charge of the
women in grubbing: and so he went through all the different portions of work that were
done on the plantation.

Then Mr. Kimball spoke to Donnison, one of the principal men, a field hand, and
to each one severally, so that all could understand what his charges were. He told them
what his rules were, and what should be law: "I give you a horn, Donnison, to blow two
hours before day: and recollect, every one of you, every man, every woman, and every
boy and girl who is able to work, is to be up within the hour after the horn blows: at the
end of that hour, every one is to be found starting out of their doors, making ready for
the field. If you have any morning bits," (these they are to provide for themselves in the
best way they can, otherwise, they have nothing to eat until 12 o'clock; the calculation
being, for the slaves, two meals a day,) "you can take them with you: but no time will be

allowed to eat them until twelve. This is my law, and I give it not thinking that you will forget it. If you forget it, I will not, but will remember it by throwing the lash well on your hide." A most horrible man! "You recollect I don't whip any of you with a chemise on, nor with a jacket on your backs. I get at the naked skin. If I find any of you lagging back after the last horn blows, I shall whip you up to the spot where the work is to be done." My master gave Donnison a first-rate English watch to keep his time and blow the horn by. After Kimball had given his charge, my master spoke to all the people again: he said, "I want every one of you to remember that you are not to come to me with any complaints against the overseer, for I have nothing to do with you. If you have any complaints even among yourselves, you must go to the overseer; nor are you to go to your mistress at any time with any complaints against the overseer. If I know one of you to do it, either man or woman, I will give a note to the overseer, and he shall not hit on you less than a hundred lashes on your bare back."

On Monday morning, all were up to the mark. Tuesday morning, I was awakened by the noise of the lash, with cries and groans. From this time the lash was going every morning, and in the course of the day. I was a house-servant, and so was exempt from Kimball's orders, but my heart ached to see the suffering and punishment that our people had to undergo. Things went on so the whole year. The people were afraid to go to the master or mistress under the sufferings they endured from the torment and sting of the lash. In the course of about six months from the time Kimball took charge, some two or three ran away, he was so severe. That was a new thing to my master. He sent word by slaves that if they saw the runaways, to tell them if they would come home and go to work, they should not be whipped. Then they would come in. This running off happened occasionally all through the remaining part of the year.

In the picking cotton season, Mr. K. would punish the women in the severest manner, because they did not pick cotton fast enough. He would thrust their heads into a cotton basket. What I say now would scarcely be believed only among those who are in that neighborhood, because it looks too cruel for any one to do or to believe, if they had no experience of such things or had not seen the like,—they would not dare lift up their heads, as perhaps he would punish them twice as much. Then he would throw their clothes up over their heads and the basket, and flog them as hard as he could with a rugged lash, cutting their flesh terribly, till the blood ran to their heels. Sometimes they would from the torment lift their heads, when he would perhaps give them a third more than he otherwise would; and this without reference to any particular condition they might be in at the time. The men he would generally place across a log, tie their hands together, and their feet together, and put a rail through under the log with the ends between their feet and hands; and in this condition, which is itself painful, he would apply the lash. Sometimes, to cramp down the mind of the husband, he would compel him to assist in the punishment of his wife. Who will tell of the good of slavery? I would rather be a brute in the field, than to endure what my people have to endure, what they have endured in many parts of the slave-holding States.

There was one religious old woman, Aunt Dinah,—very pious: all believed she was, even my master. She used to take care of the infants at the quarters while the mothers were out at work. At noon, the mothers would come home to nurse their children, unless they were too far off—then the infants were carried to them. Aunt Dinah, knowing how cruelly the women were treated, at last, when the master was absent, picked up courage to go to the mistress and complain of the dealings of the overseer. My mistress belonged to the Presbyterian Church; Aunt Dinah to the Baptist. The mistress then began to my master about the cruelty on the place, without disclosing how she got her information. I do not think the master would have interfered, were it not that the mistress also told him of the overseer's intimacy with some of the female slaves. She being a well-bred lady, the master had to take some notice of the management. He told the overseer to change his mode of punishing the women; to slip their clothes down from their shoulders, and punish them on their backs. No interference was ever made except in this one instance.

The overseer had one child by a slave woman. I left the child there a slave. At the expiration of a year Kimball left. Three months after, or thereabouts, he was hanged in Raleigh, N. C., for the murder of his step-father. The slaves were rejoiced at his being hung, and thought he ought to have been hung before he came there to be overseer.

I effected my escape about sixteen years ago. I was questioned twice about papers, but got through it without much difficulty. I escaped from Alabama. I shall give the particulars more in detail when I publish the whole history of my life to the people of the United States and Canada.

The colored people can do as well in Canada as they could in the United States under any circumstances. Even in the free States they are accounted as nothing, or next to nothing. But in Canada, all are really free and equal. Color is not recognized in the laws of the land. During all the time I have lived in Canada, no white person has suffered any inconvenience, or had cause to complain, because I was placed on an equality with him. They come here destitute of any advantages—but they are getting along in a respectable, upright way, and there is plenty of work for them. If the colored people had come into Canada with a knowledge of reading, writing, and arithmetic, there would now be no difference between them and white people, in respect to property or business. They would have been just as skilful, just as far advanced in art and science as the whites. But they have to contend with the ignorance which slavery has brought upon them. Still they are doing well,—no one could expect them to do any better.

Every thinking, every candid man that knows me, knows that I would not utter any thing that is not true.

How much longer, in the name of God, shall my people remain in their state of degradation under the American republic?

MRS. HENRY GOWENS.

My name in the South was Martha Martin. When I came to the North I took the name of Martha Bentley—Bentley being my mother's name before she was married. My father was my master, Mr.—, who died in 1843. He lived in Georgia, but removed with one set of farm hands to Mississippi. He had one other child by my mother, but it died young. He liberated all the children he had by my mother, and one other slave woman, with one exception—that was a daughter whom he had educated and put to the milliner's trade. After she had learned the trade, he went to the place where she was, with money to establish her in business. But he found she had two children by a white man. This so enraged him, that he carried her and her two children back to his farm, and put her to work in the field, and there, he said, she was to die. The father of the two children came on, and offered two thousand dollars for the woman and the children, as he wished to marry her. But her father would neither let him have her nor his children. Afterwards he offered three thousand dollars,—then five other grown-up slaves, for Minerva and the two children; but my master told him he would not, but if he ever set foot on the farm again, he would blow his brains out. So, I suppose, they are slaves yet, and will be: for their mistress never was disposed to sell; she would rather keep them and punish them, on account of his having so many wives. But he had told her beforehand, and said she need not find fault with it: all his wives were equally well used. Keep on the right side of him, and he was very kind: every slave would be well treated. He did not mind if they stole from him, but if they stole from another man, he would whip them. He was Scotch Irish.

My mother had been set free on the eastern shore of Maryland, in this way. My mother's mistress promised my mother's mother (who was at the time free) that on her death she would set my mother free. When she died, she left her to wait on her niece until the niece died, she being very low,—then her free papers were to be given her. That was in the white woman's will. The niece died in two or three weeks, and then they talked of selling my mother to the traders, because they had got so little work out of her. Then they all—the whole family—ran away into New Jersey. My master bought them running, and kidnapped my mother and her cousin's family, although he knew the circumstances, and that they were entitled to their freedom.

When I was twelve years old, my father took me to Cincinnati. He charged me to marry neither a white man nor a black man: if I should, he would take me back south, and put me on the farm. There he paid one year's tuition in advance, and money for shoes,—we had clothes enough. Two others went with me,—one a half brother, the other a half sister. But I was cheated out of my education: for the guardian in Cincinnati kept the money, but did not send me to school, excepting one year: whereas I was to have gone three. When my father heard of this, he started on to see to it, but fell sick and died before he got there. He was a large, heavy man, and had been liable to sudden fits of illness. When these came on, he would be frightened very much, and would send for some of the pious slaves to come in and pray for him. He was a very wealthy man, and always said he would leave me in comfortable circumstances. But the money which he sent us at different times was kept from us, and it may be that he died without a will.

I remained in the northern States a few years, and then came to Canada. I have five smart children, and send all to school but the two youngest. I mean they shall have a good education; what little knowledge I have, has just made me hungry for more.

My mother was in expectation of being set free, but did not get her free papers. She was religiously inclined, and being afraid of sinning, and thinking she might be left a slave after all, she married a colored man against my father's consent. For this reason, she remains a slave to this day, as I suppose, but I have not heard from her for thirteen years.

I remember enough of slavery and have heard and seen enough of it to know that it is unfavorable to virtue. I have known many owners to have two or three colored women for wives, and when they got a white wife, keep all. If the slave woman would not comply she would be whipped, or else sold to the lowest, meanest fellow he could find. Some of the masters have their slave children's hair shaved off, so that people need not notice that they favor them. I have known cases of this kind close by me in Mississippi.

Appendix C

Letter to the Editor, by Henry Goins

(Published in the *Courier and Western District Advertiser* [Amhersburg, Canada West], November 3, 1849)

To the Editor of the 'Chatham Chronicle.'

Sir,—I have seen in your paper a memorial from the Western District Council to the Governor General. To this memorial, outrageous enough in itself, you have prefixed some remarks still more offensive. It is said that the Council unanimously adopted the prayer to the executive government to disallow the proceeding of the Elgin Association, and to take active measures in respect to the colored race, to prevent their obtaining that standing in society which their proportionate wealth, intelligence, and mental capacity, may hereafter, if not now, entitle them to expect and demand.[1]

1. The Elgin Association, 1849–73, was an African American settlement in Buxton, Ontario, founded by Presbyterian minister William King after King manumitted slaves he had owned in Louisiana and moved them north to Ohio. King believed that emancipation was incomplete without material assistance to former slaves, and he became the managing director of the settlement corporation. Named after Lord Elgin, the governor general of Canada, the association sold stock to buy farmland and fund the settlement's schools, chapels, and the missionary work that centered on the Buxton Mission. By March 1848, 335 stockholders had supplied enough funds to launch the settlement, purchasing 4,300 acres of land in 1849 and another 3,000 acres in 1853. The Elgin Association resold land to black farmers on terms that former slaves could afford, and Buxton was close to transportation routes to market. Opposition to the settlement delayed its incorporation until September 1850. In March 1849, some local white residents of Raleigh Township vehemently opposed the settlement and petitioned the district council and legislative assembly, arguing that the resettlement of black Americans would have deleterious effects on the local community. Using anti-black and xenophobic appeals, opponents also petitioned the Presbyterian Synod in Toronto, and a protest group of some three hundred whites met in Chatham, Ontario, in August 1849 to oppose plans to sell land to people of African descent. Their resolutions against black settlement inspired more-unified support among proponents of the settlement, including politicians, and had the unintended effect of publicizing the settlement to African Americans abroad. In October, the Western District Council protested the settlement to the Canadian Parliament and drafted a petition to Lord Elgin himself, opposing black settlement by denigrating the abilities of people of African descent. The *Chatham Chronicle* endorsed the petition and reprinted it. Goings rebuts those charges in this article. Lord Elgin supported King and the settlement, though protests continued as black settlement got underway. See Hepburn, *Crossing the Border*, chap. 3.

What would be more oppressive and tyrannical than a policy founded upon principles such as those recommended in this publication?—The idea of levying a poll tax upon a poor wretch escaping from the deep damnation of slavery! What could be more monstrous?—And then the thought of requiring security that the colored man will not become a *burden upon the Parish* while no question is asked of the whites though coming from the same place, and, it may be, much more apt to become a burden than their suspected vilifiers, and as the petitioners express it, *hated* brethren the negroes.

That such language should be used, and such principles advocated by a grave body like the District Council is too much to be believed by one who has not seen the document in question. It is even intimated that the colored people should not be allowed to vote at Township meetings. Taxation, without representation, is a thing which a free country where liberal laws are in operation, is not to be endured, and he is either a coward or a fool that submits to it. I ask the memorialists themselves how they would like to live in a country where they were precluded from the privilege of voting for officers who were to have the control of affairs that concerns their interests materially, and the power of levying assessments on their property. I do not wish to trouble you at great length Mr. Editor, but beg that you will give the above a place in your columns.

I do not think the petitions will have any effect, or that the government will refuse to grant deeds for lands bought and paid for by our people. I have written this merely to show that, although we have received injuries without number, we yet have some sensibility left, and can perceive, and deeply feel a home thrust, like that aimed at us and our children, by the memorialists.

Yours truly,
Henry Goins

Appendix D

"Farm for Sale" Notice
Showing Henry Goings as Sales Agent

(From *Voice of the Fugitive*, December 16, 1852)

VALUABLE FARM FOR SALE

Lot No. 3 in the Township of Raleigh containing 100 acres, 10 of which are under cultivation with a good rail fence: a new frame house, a good log barn and shed: a thriving young orchard of 60 trees, some bearing fruit: one mile from Buxton: 15 miles from Chatham and 50 miles from Detroit. There is also 15 acres fall wheat on the above lot, and 25 acres of clover, which can be mowed the ensuing season. The property is well watered.

Besides the above, the subscriber offers for sale other landed property which can be had cheap for cash, and part credit, by application to

HENRY GOINGS, Agent
Chatham, C.W. Dec. 7, 1852

Bibliography

PRIMARY SOURCES

Archival materials

Boylan, Lucas, and A. H. Boylan, "A roster of the names and dates of commissions of the several major-generals, in command of the Militia of North-Carolina, as enrolled on the first of January, A.D. 1813." Raleigh, N.C.: Printed by Lucas and A. H. Boylan, 1813. Available online from *Early American Imprints, Series II: Shaw-Shoemaker, 1801–1819* (no. 29383).

Drake, Benjamin Michael, Papers. J. B. Cain Archives of Mississippi Methodism, Millsaps College, Jackson, Mississippi.

Gandrud, Pauline Jones. *Alabama Records*. Vol. 199, *Lauderdale Co.* (originally published April 1961). Alabama Department of Archives and History (ADAH), Montgomery. Microfilm.

Gandrud, Pauline Myra Jones (and Kathleen Paul Jones), comps. *Alabama Records*. 245 vols. Easley, S.C.: Southern Historical Press, 1981 (reprint of works originally published in typescript, 1932–79).

James City County Personal Property Tax List, 1782–1799: Virginia personal property tax list 1782–1799. Salt Lake City, Utah: The Genealogical Society, 1955. Available on microfilm, no. 7247, at Alderman Library, University of Virginia.

Jones, Kathleen, and Pauline Jones Gandrud. *Alabama Records*. Vol. 123, *Lauderdale County* (originally published July 1951). Alabama Department of Archives and History (ADAH), Montgomery. Microfilm.

———. *Alabama Records*. Vol. 213, *Lauderdale County* (originally published July 1964). Alabama Department of Archives and History (ADAH), Montgomery. Microfilm.

———. *Alabama Records*. Vol. 217, *Lauderdale County* (originally published May 1965). Alabama Department of Archives and History (ADAH), Montgomery. Microfilm.

———. *Alabama Records*. Vol. 221, *Lauderdale County* (originally published March 1966). Alabama Department of Archives and History (ADAH), Montgomery. Microfilm.

Lauderdale County Marriage Books. Alabama Department of Archives and History (ADAH), Montgomery. Microfilm.

"To the Honr. the Genr Assembly of the State of North Carolina," 22 December 1831. Petition 11283106. Digital Library on American Slavery, University of North Carolina at Greensboro, http://library.uncg.edu/slavery/.

Vanleer Papers. Chester County Historical Society, West Chester, Pa. Available online at http://www.vanleerplus.org/vanleerpapers.htm.

Will of James Jackson. Lauderdale County, Alabama, Will Book (microfilm, LGM box location: 00196, reel 26), Alabama Department of Archives and History (ADAH), Montgomery.

Will of Joseph L. D. Smith. Lauderdale County Will Records, 1835–58, Vol. A (microfilm, LGM box location: 00196, reel 26), Alabama Department of Archives and History (ADAH), Montgomery.

Washington Family Papers, 1796–1959. Tennessee State Library and Archives, Nashville, http://www.tennessee.gov/tsla/history/manuscripts/findingaids/68-029+.pdf.

Census, Court, and Government Records

All U.S. and Canadian census documents were accessed at http://www.ancestry.com.

1810 U.S. Census
1820 U.S. Census
1830 U.S. Census
1840 U.S. Census
1850 U.S. Census
1851 Personal Census of Canada West
1860 U.S. Census
1860 U.S. Census, Slave Schedule
1861 Personal Census of Canada West
1870 U.S. Census
1880 U.S. Census
1890 U.S. Census
1900 U.S. Census
1910 U.S. Census
1920 U.S. Census

Buzzard Roost, "National Register of Historic Places" (no. 76000157). National Park Service, Department of the Interior, Washington, D.C.

Historical Census Browser, University of Virginia, Geospatial and Statistical Data Center, http://mapserver.lib.virginia.edu/.

Johnson, Charles F. "Report of an investigation of the cause, origin, and results of the late riots in the city of Memphis made by Col. Charles F. Johnson, Inspector General States of Ky. And Tennessee and Major T. W. Gilbreth, A. D. C. To Maj. Genl. Howard, Commissioner Bureau R. F. & A. Lands." The Freedmen's Bureau Online, http://freedmensbureau.com/tennessee/outrages/memphisriot.htm.

National Register of Historic Places—Nomination Form for "Windsor Castle," Toano, Virginia, 1987, National Park Service, Department of the Interior, Washington, D.C., http://www.dhr.virginia.gov/registers/Counties/JamesCity/047-0021_Windsor_Castle_1987_Final_Nomination.pdf.

State v. Kimbrough, 13 N.C. 431 (N.C. 1830). Available online at www.LexisNexis.com.

United States. Department of Agriculture. "Soil Survey of Walker County, Alabama." Washington, D.C.: USDA, 1992. Available online at http://soildatamart.nrcs.usda .gov/Manuscripts/AL127/0/walker.pdf.

———. "Soil Survey of Wilcox County, Alabama." Washington, D.C.: USDA, 1999). Available online at http://soils.usda.gov/survey/online_surveys/alabama/wilcox/ al_wilcox.pdf.

National Park Service. *U.S. Civil War Soldiers, 1861–1865.* Provo, Utah: Ancestry.com Operations, 2007, www.ancestry.com (under search terms M589 roll 33, plaque C-101).

Newspapers

Chatham Chronicle (Canada West)
Chatham Journal (Canada West)
Christian Recorder (Philadelphia, Pa.)
Courier and Western District Advertiser (Amherstburg, Canada West)
Herald and Perth County Advertiser (Canada West)
New York Times

Raleigh (N.C.) Register
Raleigh (N.C.) Star
Ohio Statesman (Columbus, Ohio)
Voice of the Fugitive (Canada West)

Maps

Asher and Adams, "Illinois," 1874. David Rumsey Historical Map Collection, Cartography Associates, http://www.davidrumsey.com/insightredirector/insightredirector. asp?cid=8&iia=0&ig=David%20Rumsey%20Collection&isl=0&gwisp=0%7CList% 5FNo%7CList%20No%7C1%7C0041.021%7C2&gwia=3&gc=0.

Abbot, Henry L. "Williamsburg to White House," 1862. David Rumsey Historical Map Collection, Cartography Associates, http://www.davidrumsey.com/ luna/servlet/detail/RUMSEY~8~1~1422~170067:Campaign-Map,-Army-Of-The-Potomac—?sort=Pub_List_No_InitialSort%2CPub_Date%2CPub_ List_No%2CSeries_No&qvq=q:Williamsburg%2Bto%2BWhite%2BHouse; sort:Pub_List_No_InitialSort%2CPub_Date%2CPub_List_No%2CSeries_ No;lc:RUMSEY~8~1&mi=1&trs=2.

"Map of Cincinnati and Suburbs and Covington & Newport," 1880. David Rumsey Historical Map Collection, Cartography Associates, http://www.davidrumsey.com/ luna/servlet/detail/RUMSEY~8~1~23953~870016?id=1-1-23953-870016&name= Cincinnati+&+suburbs.

"Outline plan of Portsmouth, Ohio. (with) Sciotoville, Haverhill, Ohio," 1877. David Rumsey Map Collection, Cartography Associates, http://www.davidrumsey.com/ detail?id=1-1-3586-380107&name=Outline+plan+of+Portsmouth++Ohio+++with+ +Sciotoville++Haverhill++Ohio+.

Published Primary Sources

Ball, Charles. *Slavery in the United States: A Narrative of the Life and Adventures of Charles Ball, a Black Man, Who Lived Forty Years in Maryland, South Carolina and Georgia, as a Slave Under Various Masters, and was One Year in the Navy with Commodore Barney, During the Late War.* New York: John S. Taylor, 1837.

Bayley, Solomon. *Narrative of Some Remarkable Incidents in the Life of Solomon Bayley, Formerly a Slave in the State of Delaware, North America; Written by Himself, and Published for His Benefit; to Which Are Prefixed, a Few Remarks by Robert Hurnard.* 2nd ed. London, 1825.

Benedict XVI, Pope. *The Apostles: The Origin of the Church and Their Co-Workers.* Huntington, Ind.: Our Sunday Visitor, 2007.

Betts, Edwin Morris, ed. *Thomas Jefferson's Farm Book.* Redmond, Wash.: Thomas Jefferson Memorial Foundation and American Philosophical Society, 1999.

Bibb, Henry. *Narrative of the Life and Adventures of Henry Bibb, an American Slave, Written by Himself.* New York: 1849. Available online at http://docsouth.unc.edu/ neh/bibb/bibb.html.

Blackmon, Jean E. *James City County, Va. Land Tax Records, 1782–1813.* Athens, Ga.: Iberian Publishing Co., 1991.

Boritt, Gabor. *The Gettysburg Gospel: The Lincoln Speech that Nobody Knows.* New York: Simon and Schuster, 2006.

Bradley, Stephen E., Jr. *The Deeds of Halifax County, North Carolina, 1758–1771.* South Boston, Va.: S. E. Bradley, 1989.

———. *Halifax County, North Carolina, Voters and Scholars, 1839–1862*. South Boston, Va.: S. E. Bradley, 1989.

Brown, William Wells. *Narrative of William W. Brown, a Fugitive Slave. Written by Himself.* Boston: Antislavery Office, 1847.

Campbell, Teresa Brewer, et al. *Lauderdale County, Alabama: Annotated Index to Chancery Court Records, Equity Record Book C, 1827–1830*. Florence, Ala.: Natchez Trace Genealogical Society, 1985.

Chamberlayne, C. G., ed. *Vestry Book of Blisland (Blissland) Parish, New Kent and James City Counties, Virginia, 1721–1786*. Richmond: Division of Purchase and Printing, 1935.

Chapin, William. *A Complete Reference Gazetteer of the United States of North America*. New York: Chapin and J. B. Taylor, 1839.

Cowart, Margaret Matthews. *Old Land Records of Lauderdale County, Alabama*. Huntsville, Ala.: The author, 1996.

Douglass, Frederick. *My Bondage and My Freedom*. New York: Miller, Orton, and Mulligan, 1855.

———. *Narrative of the Life of Frederick Douglass, An American Slave, Written by Himself.* Boston: Anti-Slavery Office, 1845. Available online at http://docsouth.unc .edu/neh/douglass/douglass.html.

Drew, Benjamin. *A North-Side View of Slavery: The Refugee, or, The Narratives of Fugitive Slaves in Canada*. Boston: Published by John P. Jewett and Co., 1856.

Evans, Tad. *Milledgeville, Georgia, Newspaper Clippings (Southern Recorder)*. 12 vols. Savannah, Ga.: The author, 1995.

Fisher, Richard Swainson, M.D. *A New and Complete Statistical Gazetteer of the United States of America, founded on and compiled from Official Federal and State Returns, and the Seventh National Census*. New York: J. H. Colton, 1859.

Gammon, David B. *Halifax County, North Carolina, Tax Lists*. Vol. 1, *1782 & 1783*. Raleigh, N.C.: David Gammon, 1985.

———. *Records of Estates, Halifax County, North Carolina*. North Carolina(?): The author, 1985.

Gammon, David B., and William L. Murphy Jr. *Marriage Records: Halifax County, North Carolina, 1758–1872*. North Carolina(?): The authors, 1983.

Gandrud, Pauline Jones. *Alabama Records*. Vol. 12, *Newspapers, "Huntsville Democrat," 1833–1840*. Greenville, S.C., 1980.

———. *Alabama Records*. Vol. 43, *Lauderdale County*. Easley, S.C.: Southern Historical Press, 1980.

———. *Alabama Records*. Vol. 104, *Lauderdale County*. Columbus, Mo., 1980.

Gibson, Campbell. "Population of the 100 Largest Cities and Other Urban Places in the United States, 1790–1990." Population Division Working Paper, no. 27. U.S. Bureau of the Census, Washington, D.C., 1998.

Gibson, John. *Gibson's Guide and Directory of the State of Louisiana, and the cities of New Orleans & Lafayette*. New Orleans: John Gibson, 1838.

Grand Rapids City and Kent County Directory, Vol. XIV. Compiled by R. L. Polk and Co. Grand Rapids: M. A. True Printing and Engraving Co., 1886.

Grand Rapids City and Kent County Directory, Vol. XVIII. Grand Rapids, Mich.: R. L. Polk and Co., 1890.

Green, Jacob D. *Narrative of the Life of J. D. Green, a Runaway Slave, from Kentucky,*

Containing an Account of His Three Escapes, in 1839, 1846, and 1848. Huddersfield: Henry Fielding, 1864.

Hageness, MariLee Beatty. *Alabama Genealogical Sources, Series, Abstract of Equity Record Book C (1808–1830), Lauderdale County, Alabama.* Anniston, Ala.: MLH Research, 1998.

Harris, Malcolm Hart. *Old New Kent County.* Vol. 1. West Point, Va.: The author, 1977.

Hartz, Fred R., and Emilie K. Hartz. *Genealogical Abstracts from the Georgia Journal (Milledgeville) Newspaper.* 5 vols. Vidalia, Ga.: Gwendolyn Press, 1990.

Heard, William H. *From Slavery to the Bishopric in the A.M.E. Church. An Autobiography.* Philadelphia: A.M.E. Book Concern, 1928. Available online at http://docsouth.unc.edu/neh/heard/heard.html.

Helper, Hinton Rowan. *The Impending Crisis of the South: How to Meet It.* New York: Burdick Brothers, 1857.

Henson, Josiah. *An Autobiography of Rev. Josiah Henson ("Uncle Tom") from 1789–1881.* Edited by John Lobb. London, Ont.: Schuyler, Smith and Co., 1881.

———. *The Life of Josiah Henson, Formerly a Slave, Now an Inhabitant of Canada, as Narrated by Himself.* Boston: Arthur D. Phelps, 1849.

Hofmann, Margaret M. *Genealogical Abstracts of Wills, 1758 through 1824, Halifax County, North Carolina.* Weldon, N.C.: Roanoke News Publishers, 1970.

Hosmer, Hezekiah L. *Adela: The Octoroon.* Columbus, Ohio: Follet and Foster, 1860.

Hutchings, Vicky L. *Humphreys County, TN Deeds, Books A–D, July 1810–June 1832.* [1 vol.?]. Signal Mountain, Tenn.: Mountain Press, 2003.

Jacobs, Harriet. *Incidents in the Life of a Slave Girl. Written by Herself.* Edited by Lydia Maria Child. Boston: The author, 1861.

Jefferson, Thomas. *Notes on the State of Virginia.* Edited by William Peden. Chapel Hill: University of North Carolina Press for the Institute of Early American History and Culture, 1955.

Kimball & James' Business Directory for the Mississippi Valley: 1844. Edited by John F. Kimball. Cincinnati: Kendall and Barnard, 1844.

Knorr, Catherine L. *Marriages of Greensville County, Virginia, 1781–1825.* Pine Bluff, Ark.: The author, 1955.

Louisiana State Museum. "Antebellum Louisiana: Politics, Education, and Entertainment." The Cabildo website, http://lsm.crt.state.la.us/cabildo/cab7.htm.

Lucas, Silas Emmett, Jr., ed. *Obituaries from Early Tennessee Newspapers, 1794–1851.* Easley, S.C.: Southern Historical Press, 1979.

Mallory, William. *Old Plantation Days.* Hamilton, Ont.: The Author, 1901–2(?).

Meaders, Daniel, ed. *Advertisements for Runaway Slaves in Virginia, 1801–1820.* New York: Garland, 1997.

Mitchell, W. M. *The Underground Railroad from Slavery to Freedom.* London: William Tweedie, 1860.

Neal, Lois Smathers, comp. *Abstracts of Vital Records from Raleigh, North Carolina, Newspapers.* 2 vols. Spartanburg, S.C.: Reprint Company, 1979.

Olmstead, Frederick Law. *A Journey in the Seaboard Slave States: With Remarks on Their Economy.* New York: Dix and Edwards; London: Sampson Low, Son and Co., 1856. Available online at http://docsouth.unc.edu/nc/olmsted/olmsted.html.

Robertson, John William. *Book of the Bible against Slavery.* Halifax, Nova Scotia, 1854.

Royall, Anne. *Letters from Alabama on Various subjects: to which is Added, an Appendix, containing Remarks on Sundry Members of the 20th & 21st Congress, and other High Characters, &c. &c. at the Seat of Government. In One Volume.* Washington, D.C.: The author, 1830.

Runkle, Benjamin Piatt, and Isaac Swartwood Catlin. *Addresses Delivered by Bvt. Colonel Ben. P. Runkle, U.S.A., Chief Supt. of the, Freedmen's Affairs, State of Kentucky, and Bvt. Lieut.-Col. I. S. Catlin. U.S.A, to the Freedmen of Louisville. October 1868.* Louisville, Ky.: Calvert, Tippett and Co., Printers, 1868.

Sheil, Richard Lalor. *Speeches of the Right Honourable Richard Lalor Sheil, M.P.: With a Memoir, &c.* Edited by Thomas MacNevin. London, 1847.

Smallwood, Thomas. *A Narrative of Thomas Smallwood, Coloured Man: Giving an Account of His Birth—The Period He Was Held in Slavery—His Release—And Removal to Canada, etc. Together with an Account of the Underground Railroad. Written by Himself.* Toronto: The Author, 1851. Available online at http://docsouth .unc.edu/neh/smallwood/smallwood.html.

Smith, William Henry. *Smith's Canadian Gazetteer; Comprising Statistical and General Information Respecting all Parts of the Upper Province, or Canada West.* Toronto: H. and W. Roswell, 1846.

Stewart, Mrs. Frank Ross. *Lauderdale County, Alabama, Marriage Records, 1820–1840.* Centre, Ala.: Stewart University Press, 1983.

Sutherland, James. *Counties of Perth and Waterloo Gazetteer and General Business Directory, for 1870 and 1871.* Hunter, Ontario, 1870.

Torrens, W. T. McCullagh. *Memoirs of the Right Honourable Richard Lalor Sheil.* London: Published for H. Coburn by His Successors Hurst and Blackett, 1855.

Vogt, John, and T. William Kethley Jr. *Greensville County Marriages, 1781–1853.* Athens, Ga.: Iberian Publishing Co., 1985.

Walker, David. *David Walker's Appeal, in Four Articles, together with a Preamble, To the Coloured Citizens of the World, but in particular, and very expressly, to those of the United States of America.* With an introduction by Sean Wilentz. New York: Hill and Wang, 1995. First published 1829.

Whitley, Edythe Rucker. *Tennessee Genealogical Abstracts: Records of Early Settlers from State and County Archives.* Baltimore: Genealogical Publishing Co., 1981.

SECONDARY SOURCES

Abdi, Ali A. "Reflections on the Long Struggle for Inclusion: The Experiences of People of African Origin." In *The African Diaspora in Canada: Negotiating Identity and Belonging,* edited by Wisdom J. Tetty and Korbla P. Puplampu, 49–60. Calgary: University of Calgary Press, 2005.

Abernethy, Thomas Perkins. *The Formative Period in Alabama, 1815–1828.* University: University of Alabama Press, 1965.

Andrews, William L. *To Tell a Free Story: The First Century of Afro-American Autobiography.* Urbana: University of Illinois Press, 1988.

Ayers, Edward L. *In the Presence of Mine Enemies: War in the Heart of America, 1859–1863.* New York: W. W. Norton, 2003.

———. *What Caused the Civil War? Reflections on the South and Southern History.* New York: W. W. Norton, 2005.

Bagby, Alfred. *King and Queen County, Virginia.* New York and Washington: Neale Publishing Co., 1908.

Baker, Lea Flowers. "Fulton, William Savin." In *The Encyclopedia of Arkansas History and Culture,* www.encyclopediaofarkansas.net/encyclopedia/entry-detail .aspx?entryID=2653.

Baptist, Edward E. "'Stol' and Fetched Here': Enslaved Migration, Ex-Slave Narratives, and Vernacular History." In *New Studies in the History of American Slavery,* edited by Edward E. Baptist and Stephanie M. H. Camp, 243–74. Athens: University of Georgia Press, 2006.

Bauer, K. Jack. *Zachary Taylor: Soldier, Planter, Statesman of the Old Southwest.* Baton Rouge: Louisiana State University Press, 1985.

Berlin, Ira. *Generations of Captivity: A History of African-American Slaves.* Cambridge, Mass.: Harvard University Press, 2003.

———. *The Making of African America: The Four Great Migrations.* New York: Viking, 2010.

———. *Many Thousands Gone: The First Two Centuries of Slavery in North America.* Cambridge, Mass.: Harvard University Press, 1997.

Berlin, Ira, and Philip Morgan, eds. *Cultivation and Culture: Labor and the Shaping of Slave Life in the Americas.* Charlottesville: University Press of Virginia, 1993.

Biographical Directory of the United States Congress, 1774–Present. Available online at http://bioguide.congress.gov/biosearch/biosearch.asp.

Black, Frederick R. "Bibliographical Essay: Benjamin Drew's Refugee and the Black Family." *Journal of Negro History* 57, no. 3 (July 1972): 284–89.

Blackett, R. J. M. "Dispossessing Massa: Fugitive Slaves and the Politics of Slavery after 1850." *American Nineteenth Century History* 10, no. 2 (June 2009): 119–36.

Blackmon, Douglas A. *Slavery by Another Name: The Re-Enslavement of Black Americans from the Civil War to World War II.* New York: Doubleday, 2008.

Blight, David W. *Frederick Douglass' Civil War: Keeping Faith in Jubilee.* Baton Rouge: Louisiana State University Press, 1989.

Bonekemper, Edward. *Grant and Lee: Victorious American and Vanquished Virginian.* Westport, Conn.: Greenwood, 2008.

Bordewich, Fergus M. *Bound for Canaan: The Underground Railroad and the War for the Soul of America.* New York: Harper Collins, 2006.

Bostock, John, and Henry Thomas Riley, eds. *The Natural History of Pliny.* Vol. 6. London: Henry G. Bohn, 1857.

Bristol, Douglas W., Jr. *Knights of the Razor: Black Barbers in Slavery and Freedom.* Baltimore: Johns Hopkins University Press, 2009.

Bruce, Dwight H. *Onondaga's Centennial: Gleanings of a Century.* [Boston]: Boston History Company, 1896.

Budge, E. A. Wallis. *A History of Egypt from the End of the Neolithic Period to the Death of Cleopatra VII, B.C. 30.* Vol. 6, *Egypt under the Priest-Kings, Tanites, and Nubians.* New York: Oxford University Press, 1902.

Bushman, Claudia L., and John Walker. *In Old Virginia: Slavery, Farming, and Society in the Journal of John Walker.* Baltimore: Johns Hopkins University Press, 2002.

Camp, Stephanie M. H. *Closer to Freedom: Enslaved Women and Everyday Resistance in the Plantation South.* Chapel Hill, N.C.: University of North Carolina Press, 2003.

Carretta, Vincent, and Philip Gould, eds. *Genius in Bondage: Literature of the Early Black Atlantic.* Lexington: University of Kentucky Press, 2001.

Cashin, Joan. *A Family Venture: Men and Women on the Southern Frontier.* New York: Oxford University Press, 1991.

Cayton, Andrew R. L., and Peter S. Onuf. *The Midwest and the Nation: Rethinking the History of an American Region.* Bloomington: Indiana University Press, 1990.

Cheek, Aimee Lee, and William Cheek. *John Mercer Langdon and the Fight for Black Freedom, 1829-1865.* Urbana: University of Illinois Press, 1989.

Cimbala, Paul A. "Reconstruction's Allies: The Relationship of the Freedmen's Bureau and the Georgia Freedmen." In *The Freedmen's Bureau and Reconstruction,* edited by Paul Cimbala and Randall Miller, 315–42 (New York: Fordham University Press, 1999).

Clarke, George Elliot. *Odysseys Home: Mapping African-Canadian Literature.* Toronto: University of Toronto Press, 2002.

Clarke, George Elliott. "'This is No Hearsay': Reading the Canadian Slave Narratives." *Papers of the Bibliographical Society of Canada / Cahiers de la Société bibliographique du Canada* 43, no. 1 (March 2005): 7–32.

Clinton, Catherine. *Harriet Tubman: The Road to Freedom.* Boston: Back Bay Books, 2004.

Coelho, Philip R. P., and Robert A. McGuire. "Diets versus Disease: The Anthropometrics of Slave Children." *Journal of Economic History* 60, no. 1 (March 2000): 232–46.

Collins, Gilbert. *Guidebook to the Historic Sites of the War of 1812.* Toronto: Dundurn Press, 1998.

Cook, Anna Maria Green. *History of Baldwin County, Georgia.* Spartanburg, S.C.: Reprint Company Publishers, 1978.

Cooper, Afua. "The Fluid Frontier: Blacks and the Detroit River Region, 1789–1854, A Focus on Henry Bibb." *Canadian Review of American Studies* 30, no. 2 (March 2000): 129–49.

Cowper, William. *The Task.* London: John Sharpe, 1817. First published 1785.

Crofts, Daniel W. *Reluctant Confederates: Upper South Unionists in the Secession Crisis.* Chapel Hill: University of North Carolina Press, 1989.

Dalleo, Peter T. "'Persecuted but not forsaken; cut down, but not destroyed': Solomon and Thamar Bayley, Delawarean Emigrants to Liberia." *Delaware History* 31, no. 3 (Spring/Summer 2006): 137–68.

Daniel, Pete. "The Metamorphosis of Slavery, 1865–1900." *Journal of American History* 66, no. 1 (June 1979): 88–97.

Davis, James E. *Frontier Illinois.* Bloomington: Indiana University Press, 1998.

Deyle, Steven. *Carry Me Back: The Antebellum Slave Trade in American Life.* New York: Oxford University Press, 2005.

Donald, David Herbert. *Lincoln.* New York: Simon and Schuster, 1995.

Drake, Richard B. "Freedmen's Aid Societies and Sectional Compromise." *Journal of Southern History* 29, no. 2 (May 1963): 175–86.

Dryden, John. *The Poetical Works of John Dryden.* Edited by John Dryden, Joseph Warton, and John Warton. London, 1851.

Eltis, David. *Economic Growth and the Ending of the Transatlantic Slave Trade.* New York: Oxford University Press, 1987.

Ely, Melvin Patrick. *Israel on the Appomattox: A Southern Experiment in Black Freedom from the 1790s through the Civil War.* New York: Knopf, 2004.

Engerman, Stanley, and Robert E. Gallman, eds. *The Cambridge Economic History of the United States.* Vol. 2, *The Long Nineteenth Century.* Cambridge: Cambridge University Press, 2000.

Eudell, Demetrius Lynn. *The Political Languages of Emancipation in the British Caribbean and the U.S. South.* Chapel Hill: University of North Carolina Press, 2002.

Flaherty, Matthew. "Richard Lalor Sheil." In vol. 13 of *The Catholic Encyclopedia.* New York: Robert Appleton Company, 1912. Available online at http://www.newadvent .org/cathen/13754b.htm.

Fleming, Patricia, Yvan Lamonde, and Dwight H. Bruce, eds. *History of the Book in Canada.* 3 vols. Toronto: University of Toronto Press, 2004.

Follett, Richard. *The Sugar Masters: Planters and Slaves in Louisiana's Cane World, 1820–1860.* Baton Rouge: Louisiana State University Press, 2007.

Foner, Eric. *Reconstruction: America's Unfinished Revolution, 1863–1877.* New York: Harper and Row, 1988.

Franklin, John Hope, and Loren Schweninger. *Runaway Slaves: Rebels on the Plantation.* New York: Oxford University Press, 2000.

Frazier, Harriet C. *Runaway and Freed Missouri Slaves and Those Who Helped Them, 1763–1865.* Jefferson, N.C.: McFarland Press, 2004.

Freehling, William W. *The Road to Disunion.* 2 vols. New York: Oxford University Press, 1990–2007.

Gallatin County, Illinois, Slave and Emancipation Records, 1839–1849. Translated by John W. Allen, edited by Jon Musgrave. Marion, Ill.: IllinoisHistory.com, 2004.

Garrett, Jill K. *A History of Florence, Alabama.* Columbia, Tenn.: The author, 1968.

———. *A History of Humphreys County, Tennessee.* Tennessee(?): Jill Knight Garrett, 1963.

Garrison, Tim Alan. "Worcester v. Georgia." In *The New Georgia Encyclopedia,* http:// www.georgiaencyclopedia.org/nge/Article.jsp?id=h2720.

Gates, Henry Louis, Jr. *The Signifying Monkey: A Theory of African-American Literary Criticism.* New York: Oxford University Press, 1988.

Gilroy, Paul. *The Black Atlantic: Modernity and Double Consciousness.* Cambridge, Mass.: Harvard University Press, 1993.

Gosse, Van. "'As a Nation the English Are Our Friends': The Emergence of African American Politics in the British Atlantic World, 1772–1861." *American Historical Review* 113, no. 4 (October 2008): 1003–1028.

Goyau, Georges. "Napoleon III." In vol. 10 of *The Catholic Encyclopedia.* New York: Robert Appleton Company, 1911. Available online at http://www.newadvent.org/ cathen/10699a.htm.

Gray, Lewis Cecil. *History of Agriculture in the Southern United States to 1860.* 2 vols. Washington, D.C.: Carnegie Institute, 1933.

Gray, Susan E. *The Yankee West: Community Life on the Michigan Frontier.* Chapel Hill: University of North Carolina Press, 1996.

Grimsted, David. *American Mobbing, 1828–1861: Toward Civil War.* New York: Oxford University Press, 1998.

Gudmestad, Robert Harold. *A Troublesome Commerce: The Transformation of the Interstate Slave Trade.* Baton Rouge: Louisiana State University Press, 2003.

Hairr, John. *North Carolina Rivers: Fact, Legends, and Lore.* Charleston, S.C.: History Press, 2007.

Harrell, Willie J., Jr. "'Thanks be to God that I am Elected to Canada': The Formulation of the Black Canadian Jeremiad, 1830–61." *Journal of Canadian Studies* 42, no. 3 (Fall 2003): 55–79.

Hartig, O. "Vasco de Gama." In vol. 6 of *The Catholic Encyclopedia.* New York: Robert Appleton Co., 1909. Available online at http://www.newadvent.org/cathen/06374a .htm.

Hawkins, Susan. "Forts Henry, Heiman, and Donelson: The African-American Experience." M.A. thesis, Murray State University, 2004.

Heglar, Charles J. *Rethinking the Slave Narrative: Slave Marriage and the Narratives of Henry Bibb and William and Ellen Craft.* Westport, Conn.: Greenwood Press, 2001.

Hembree, Michael F. "The Question of 'Begging': Fugitive Slave Relief in Canada, 1830–1865." *Civil War History* 31, no. 4 (December 1991): 314–27.

Henry, Matthew, and Thomas Scott. *A Commentary upon the Holy Bible: Job to Solomon's Song.* London: Religious Tract Society, 1835.

Hepburn, Sharon A. Roger. *Crossing the Border: A Free Black Community in Canada.* Urbana: University of Illinois Press, 2007.

Hewitt, Lawrence Lee. "Vicksburg, Siege of." In *The Oxford Companion to United States History,* ed. Paul S. Boyer, 804. New York: Oxford University Press, 2001.

Hill, Daniel G. *The Freedom-seekers: Blacks in Early Canada.* Agincourt, Ont.: Book Society of Canada, 1981.

Hill, Samuel S. *Religion in the Southern States: A Historical Study.* Macon, Ga.: Mercer University Press, 1983.

Hine, Darlene Clark. *Black Women and the Re-construction of American History.* Bloomington: Indiana University Press, 1997.

Hinks, Peter B. *To Awaken My Afflicted Brethren: David Walker and the Problem of Antebellum Slave Resistance.* University Park: Pennsylvania University Press, 1997.

History of Hancock County, Ohio. Chicago: Warner, Beers, and Co., 1886.

Horton, James Oliver, and Lois E. Horton. *In Hope of Liberty: Culture, Community, and Protest among Northern Free Blacks, 1700–1860.* New York: Oxford University Press, 1997.

Howard, Victor B. "The Struggle for Equal Education in Kentucky, 1866–1884." *Journal of Negro Education* 46, no. 3 (Summer 1977): 305–28.

Howe, Daniel Walker. *What Hath God Wrought: The Transformation of America, 1815–1848.* New York: Oxford University Press, 2007.

Hurt, R. Douglas. *The Ohio Frontier.* Bloomington: Indiana University Press, 1996.

Jeffrey, Julie Roy. *Abolitionists Remember: Antislavery Autobiographies and the Unfinished Work of Emancipation.* Chapel Hill: University of North Carolina Press, 2008.

Johnson, Walter. *Soul by Soul: Life Inside the Antebellum Slave Market.* Cambridge, Mass.: Harvard University Press, 1999.

Johnston, William. *History of the County of Perth from 1825 to 1902.* Stratford, Ont.: Printed by W. M. O'Beirne, 1903.

Jones, Louis, and Darryl G. Shreve, eds. "Detroit African-American History Project." Wayne State University, http://www.daahp.wayne.edu/1800_1849.html.

Kang, Nancy. "'As If I Had Entered A Paradise': Fugitive Slave Narratives and Cross-Border Literary History." *African American Review* 39, no. 3 (Fall 2005): 431–57.

Kaye, Anthony E. *Joining Places: Slave Neighborhoods in the Old South*. Chapel Hill: University of North Carolina Press, 2007.

Kett, Joseph F. *The Pursuit of Knowledge under Difficulties: From Self-Improvement to Adult Education in America, 1750–1990*. Stanford, Calif.: Stanford University Press, 1994.

Keyssar, Alexander. *The Right to Vote: The Contested History of Democracy in the United States*. New York: Basic Books, 2001.

Kirby, Jack Temple. *Mockingbird Song: Ecological Landscapes of the South*. Chapel Hill: University of North Carolina Press, 2008.

Klein, Herbert S. *A Population History of the United States*. New York: Cambridge University Press, 2004.

Klement, Frank L. *The Limits of Dissent: Clement L. Vallandigham and the Civil War*. New York: Fordham University Press, 1998.

Landon, Fred. "Fugitive Slaves in Ontario: A Digest of Two Papers by Fred Landon Read before the Middlesex Historical Society, 1989–1919." *Quarterly Bulletin of the Historical Society of Northwestern Ohio* 8, no. 2 (April 1936): 1–6.

Lakwete, Angela. *Inventing the Cotton Gin: Machine and Myth in Antebellum America*. Baltimore: Johns Hopkins University Press, 2003.

Lancel, Serge. *Hannibal*. Translated by Antonia Nevill. Oxford: Blackwell, 1998.

Leeson, M. A. *Commemorative Historical and Biographical Record of Wood County, Ohio*. Chicago: J. H. Beers and Co., 1897.

Levine, Robert S. *Martin Delany, Frederick Douglass, and the Politics of Representative Identity*. Chapel Hill: University of North Carolina Press, 1997.

Lightner, David L., and Alexander M. Ragan. "Were African American Slaveholders Benevolent or Exploitative? A Quantitative Approach." *Journal of Southern History* 71, no. 3 (August 2005): 535–58.

Lovett, Bobby L. "Memphis Race Riot of 1866." In *Tennessee Encyclopedia of History and Culture*. Available at http://tennesseeencyclopedia.net/images.php?rec=&page=17&start=320 (quick browse under letter "M").

Lytle, William M., and Forrest R. Holdcamper. *Merchant Steam Vessels of the United States, 1807–1868*. Mystic, Conn.: The Steamship Historical Society of America, 1952.

Marsh, Jan. "From Slave Cabin to Windsor Castle: Josiah Henson and 'Uncle Tom' in Britain." *Nineteenth Century Studies*, no. 16 (2002): 37–50.

Martin, Bonnie M. "'To Have and To Hold' Human Collateral: Mortgaging Slaves to Build Virginia and South Carolina." PhD diss., Southern Methodist University, 2006.

Marvel, William. *Andersonville: The Last Depot*. Chapel Hill: University of North Carolina Press, 1994.

McCartney, Martha W. *James City County: Keystone of the Commonwealth*. James City County, Va.: James City County Board of Supervisors, 1997.

McDonald, William Lindsey. *A Walk through the Past: The People and Places of Florence and Lauderdale County, Alabama*. 1997; reprint, Killen, Ala.: Bluewater Publications, 2003.

McFeely, William S. *Frederick Douglass*. New York: W. W. Norton, 1991.

McMichael, Lois. *History of Butts County Georgia, 1825–1976*. Atlanta: Cherokee Publishing Company, 1978.

McPherson, James. *Battle Cry of Freedom: The Civil War Era*. New York: Oxford University Press, 1988.

Middleton, Stephen. *The Black Laws: Race and the Legal Process in Early Ohio*. Athens: Ohio University Press, 2005.

Miles, Tiya. *Ties That Bind: The Story of an Afro-Cherokee Family in Slavery and Freedom*. Berkeley: University of California Press, 2005.

Miller, James David. *South by Southwest: Planter Emigration and Identity in the Slave South*. Charlottesville: University of Virginia Press, 2002.

Miller, Larry L. *Tennessee Place Names*. Bloomington: Indiana University Press, 2001.

Mull, Carol E. *The Underground Railroad in Michigan*. Jefferson, N.C.: McFarland and Co., 2010.

National Cyclopaedia of American Biography. Vol. 3. New York: James T. White and Co., 1893.

Nelson, Harold L. "Military Roads for War and Peace, 1791–1836." *Military Affairs* 19, no. 1 (Spring 1955): 1–14.

Nelson, Scott Reynolds, and Carol Sheriff. *A People at War: Civilians and Soldiers in America's Civil War, 1854–1877*. New York: Oxford University Press, 2007.

Neville, Burt. *Directory of Tennessee River Steamboats (1821–1928), with Illustrations*. Selma, Ala.: Coffee Printing Co., 1963.

O'Donovan, Susan Eva. *Becoming Free in the Cotton South*. Cambridge, Mass.: Harvard University Press, 2007.

Olbey, Christian. "Unfolded Hands: Class Suicide and the Insurgent Intellectual Praxis of Mary Ann Shadd." *Canadian Review of American Studies* 30, no. 2 (March 2000): 151–75.

Ontario Genealogical Society. *Wesleyan Methodist Baptismal Register, Perth County, 1844–1898: A Transcription*. Toronto: Perth County Branch, Ontario Genealogical Society, 2001.

Ormsby, William G. "Hincks, Sir Francis." In *Dictionary of Canadian Biography Online*, http://www.biographi.ca/009004-119.01-e.php?BioId=39705.

Overton, Ed. "Farming Grew from Fallow to Fruit." In "James City County, 350th Anniversary," newspaper supplement to *The (Williamsburg) Virginia Gazette*, August 24, 1984.

Paulding, James K., Washington Irving, and William Irving. *Salmagundi: Or, the Whim-whams and Opinions of Launcelot Langstaff, Esq., and Others*. London: T. Davidson, 1824.

Pelka, Fred, and Charles F. Johnson. *The Civil War Letters of Colonel Charles F. Johnson, Invalid Corps*. Amherst: University of Massachusetts Press, 2004.

Penningroth, Dylan C. *The Claims of Kinfolk: African American Property and Community in the Nineteenth-Century South*. Chapel Hill: University of North Carolina Press, 2003.

Perdue, Theda. "Cherokee Planters: The Development of Plantation Slavery before Removal." In *The Cherokee Indian Nation: A Troubled History*, edited by Duane H. King, 110–28. Knoxville: University of Tennessee Press, 1979.

Perdue, Theda, and Michael D. Green. *The Cherokee Nation and the Trail of Tears*. New York: Viking Press, 2007.

Peterson, Norma Lois. *The Presidencies of William Henry Harrison and John Tyler*. Lawrence: University Press of Kansas, 1989.

Pope, Alexander. *An Essay on Man and Other Poems*. London: John Sharpe, 1829. First published 1734.

Powell, William S., ed. *Dictionary of North Carolina Biography*. 6 vols. Chapel Hill: University of North Carolina Press, 1996.

Rael, Patrick. *Black Identity and Black Protest in the Antebellum North*. Chapel Hill: University of North Carolina Press, 2002.

Rhodehamel, John, and Louise Taper, eds. *"Right or Wrong, God Judge Me": The Writings of John Wilkes Booth*. Urbana: University of Illinois Press, 1997.

Rhodes, Jane. *Mary Ann Shadd Cary: The Black Press and Protest in the Nineteenth Century*. Bloomington: Indiana University Press, 1998.

Rhyne, James Michael. "Rehearsal for Redemption: The Politics of Post-Emancipation Violence in Kentucky's Bluegrass Region." PhD diss., University of Cincinnati, 2006.

Ripley, C. Peter, Mary Alice Herrle, and Paul A. Cimbala, eds. *The Black Abolitionist Papers*. Vol. 2, *Canada, 1830–1865*. Chapel Hill: University of North Carolina Press, 1986.

Robb, Phyllis. *The Robbs of Mitchell, Ontario, Canada and Derrynoose Parish, Armagh County, Northern Ireland*. Fort Wayne, Ind.: Robb, 1998.

Rodriguez, Junius P., ed. *Slavery in the United States: A Social, Political, and Historical Encyclopedia*. 2 vols. Westport, Conn.: ABC–CLIO, 2007.

Roediger, David. *The Wages of Whiteness: Race and the Making of the American Working Class*. London: Verso, 1991.

Rohrbach, Augusta. *Truth Stranger than Fiction: Race, Realism, and the U.S. Literary Marketplace*. New York: Palgrave, 2002.

Roth, Sarah N. "'How a Slave was Made a Man': Negotiating Black Violence and Masculinity in Antebellum Slave Narratives." *Slavery and Abolition* 28, no. 2 (August 2007): 255–75.

Rothman, Adam. *Slave Country: American Expansion and the Origin of the Deep South*. Cambridge, Mass.: Harvard University Press, 2005.

Rousseau, Peter L. "Jacksonian Monetary Policy, Specie Flows, and the Panic of 1837." *Journal of Economic History* 62, no. 2 (June 2002): 457–88.

Russell, John H. *The Free Negro in Virginia, 1619–1865*. 1913; reprint, New York: Cosimo, 2009.

Saillant, John. "Aspirant Citizenship." In *Beyond Douglass: New Perspectives on Early African-American Literature*, edited by Michael J. Dexter and Ed White, 123–40. Lewisburg, Pa.: Bucknell University Press, 2008.

Schiller, Ben. "Learning Their Letters: Critical Literacy, Epistolary Culture, and Slavery in the Antebellum South." *Southern Quarterly* 45, no. 3 (Spring 2008): 11–29.

Schmidt, James D. "'A Full-Fledged Government of Men': Freedmen's Bureau Labor Policy in South Carolina, 1865–1868." In *The Freedmen's Bureau and Reconstruction: Reconsiderations*, edited by Paul Alan Cimbala and Randall M. Miller, 234–35. New York: Fordham University Press, 1999.

Schoen, Brian. *The Fragile Fabric of Union: Cotton, Federal Politics, and the Global Origins of the Civil War*. Baltimore: Johns Hopkins University Press, 2009.

Schwarz, Philip J. "Emancipators, Protectors, and Anomalies: Free Black Slaveowners in Virginia." *Virginia Magazine of History and Biography* 95, no. 3 (July 1987): 317–38.

Scott, Rebecca. *Slave Emancipation in Cuba: The Transition to Free Labor, 1860–1899*. Pittsburgh: University of Pittsburgh Press, 2000.

Sears, Stephen W. *Gettysburg*. New York: Mariner, 2004.

Shakespeare, William. *The Merchant of Venice*. Edited by Barbara A. Mowat and Paul Werstein. New York: Simon and Schuster, 2009.

———. *Richard III*. Edited by Jonathan Bate and Eric Rasmussen. New York: Modern Library, 2008.

Simon, John Y. "Grant, Ulysses S." In *The Oxford Companion to United States History*, edited by Paul S. Boyer, 318–19. New York: Oxford University Press, 2001.

Simpson, Brooks. *America's Civil War*. New York: Harlan Davidson, 1996.

Sisco, Lisa A. "'Writing in the Spaces Left': Literacy as a Process of Becoming in the Narratives of Frederick Douglass." *American Transcendental Quarterly* 9, no. 3 (September 1995): 195–227.

Smith, Hugh McCormick. *The Fishes of North Carolina*. 2 vols. Raleigh, N.C.: E. M. Uzzell and Co., State Printers and Binders, 1907.

Smith, Sir William, ed. *A Dictionary of Greek and Roman Biography and Mythology*. Vol. 1. London: John Murray, 1880.

Stanley, Amy Dru. *From Bondage to Contract: Wage Labor, Marriage, and the Market in the Age of Slave Emancipation*. New York: Cambridge University Press, 1998.

Steckel, Richard H. "Stature and the Standard of Living." *Journal of Economic Literature* 33, no. 4 (December 1995): 1903–40.

Stock, Melissa. "William McIntosh." In *New Georgia Encyclopedia*, http://www.georgia encyclopedia.org.

Stoll, Mark R., and Donald E. Davis. *Southern United States: An Environmental History*. Santa Barbara, Calif.: ABC-CLIO, 2006.

Sublette, Ned. *The World That Made New Orleans: From Spanish Silver to Congo Square*. Chicago: Lawrence Hill Books, 2008.

Symonds, Craig L., and William J. Clipson. *The Naval Institute Historical Atlas of the U.S. Navy*. Annapolis, Md.: Naval Institute Press, 1995.

Tadman, Michael. *Speculators and Slaves: Masters, Traders, and Slaves in the Old South*. Madison: University of Wisconsin Press, 1989.

Troutman, Phillip D. "Slave Trade and Sentiment." PhD diss., University of Virginia, 2000.

United States. Immigration Commission. *Statistical Review of Migration, 1820–1910; Distribution of Immigrants, 1850–1900*. Reports of the Immigration Commission, vol. 3. Washington, D.C.: Government Printing Office, 1911. Available online at http://www.latinamericanstudies.org/immigration/immigration_1820-1903.pdf.

Vorenberg, Michael. *Final Freedom: The Civil War, the Abolition of Slavery, and the Thirteenth Amendment*. New York: Cambridge University Press, 2001.

Walker, Williston, and Richard A. Norris, David W. Lotz, and Robert T. Handy. *A History of the Christian Church*. 4th ed. New York: Scribner, 1985.

Walton, Jonathan William. "Blacks in Buxton and Chatham, Ontario, 1830–1890: Did the 49th Parallel Make a Difference?" PhD diss., Princeton University, 1979.

Washington, John. *John Washington's Civil War: A Slave Narrative*. Edited by Crandall Shifflett. Baton Rouge: Louisiana State University Press, 2008.

Wayne, Michael. "The Black Population of Canada West on the Eve of the American Civil War: A Reassessment Based on the Manuscript Census of 1861." In *A Nation of Immigrants: Women, Workers, and Communities in Canadian History, 1840s–1960s*, edited by Paula Draper with Franca Lacovetta and Robert Ventresca, 58–81. Toronto: University of Toronto Press, 1998.

Williams, Andrea. *Self-Taught: African American Education in Slavery and Freedom.* Chapel Hill: University of North Carolina Press, 2005.

Wills, Gary. *Cincinnatus: George Washington and the Enlightenment.* New York: Doubleday, 1984.

Wilson, Barry K. *Benedict Arnold: A Traitor in Our Midst.* Montreal, Quebec: McGill–Queen's University Press, 2001.

Wilson, Robert J., III. "Milledgeville." In *New Georgia Encyclopedia,* http://www .georgiaencyclopedia.org/nge/Article.jsp?id=h-769.

Winks, Robin W. *The Blacks in Canada, A History.* 2nd ed. Montreal: McGill–Queen's University Press, 1997.

Wortman, Richard. *Scenarios of Power: From Alexander II to the Abdication of Nicholas II.* Princeton, N.J.: Princeton University Press, 2000.

Yarborough, Fay A. "Power, Perception, and Interracial Sex: Former Slaves Recall a Multiracial South." *Journal of Southern History* 71, no. 3 (August 2005): 559–88.

Yellin, Jean Fagan. *Harriet Jacobs: A Life.* New York: Basic Civitas Books, 2004.

Index

abolitionists: Bentley's interview with, 129–30; efforts of, 92, 99–100; Freedmen's Societies established by, 61; Goings's independence from, xv; Goings's interview with, 127–29; as orators, xvi, xviii–xix; white Southerners' excoriation of, xxvii, 10, 27

Adams, Joseph, xxxiii

Adams County, Mississippi, 70

African American political consciousness, xx–xxi, xxiii, 61–62, 90–116

African emigration, idea of, 63

Alabama, Goings's advice on emigrating to, 70

Allen, Elizabeth, 6n8

American Colonization Society, 34n88

American Missionary Association, 61n11

American Theater (New Orleans), 34, 34n89

Amherstburg, Ontario, xxx, 41, 41n13, 46n27, 48

Andersonville prison, Virginia, 94

Andrews, William L., xix

Appomattox Courthouse, Virginia, 65n20

Arkansas, 18; Goings's advice on emigrating to, 70

Baldwin County, Georgia, 69

Ball, Charles, xviii, xxvii

Barbados, 62–63

Barksdale, Alexander, 26n66, 28–29, 29n71, 32

Baton Rouge, Mississippi, 70

Bayley, Solomon, xviii

Beckwith, Rebecca M., 24n61

Bentley, Martha (second wife), xiv,

xviii, xxxi–xxxii, 55; interview with Drew, 129–30

Berry's Ferry, Kentucky, 42n15

Bibb, Henry, xvi, xxx–xxxi, 47n31; *Narrative of the Life and Adventures of Henry Bibb*, xviii

biblical allusions by Goings, xxiv, 57, 59, 72, 73, 75, 77–78

black codes, xxix

Bogsdale. *See* Barksdale, Alexander

Bolivar, Tennessee, 40

Booth, John Wilkes, 76nn17–18

British Honduras, 79–81

British West Indies, emancipation of slaves in, xxi, 62–63

Brothers (steamboat), 48–49n4

Brown, Colwin, xxxiii

Brown, John, xxxi, 77n19

Brown, William Wells, xvi, xviii, xxi–xxii

Bunker Hill (steamboat), 45n26, 45–46

Burgess, Thomas, 10, 10n21

Burnside, Ambrose E., 93n20, 94n21

Burnt Henry, Virginia. *See* Burnt Ordinary, Virginia (now Toano)

Burnt Ordinary, Virginia (now Toano), xxv, 3nn1–2, 3–4, 5n7, 5–6

Bush, William, 5n5, 7n13, 7–8, 8n14

Buxton, Ontario, xxx

Buzzard Roost Hotel, Alabama, 39, 39n4

Calumet, Michigan, xxxiii

Canada, African American expatriates in, xxx–xxxiii, 41, 41n11, 42, 46nn27–28, 48, 55n15, 62, 67, 129

Caruthers, James, 24n61

Cary, Mary Ann Shadd, xxxi

Catlin, Isaac S., xxiii, xxiv, 90–91n87, 110–16
Central America, xxii, 79–81
Charles City County, Virginia, 69
Charlotte, Tennessee, 16, 16n38, 40
Chatham, Ontario, xvii, xxx–xxxi, xxxii, 54–55
Chatham Chronicle, xv, 131–32
Cherokee Indians, 20–21
Chickahominy River, Virginia, 3n2
Chickasaw Indians, 24n62, 29n72
Choctaw Indians, 29n72, 35n90
Christianity, slavery and, 58–59, 60, 77–78, 84–85
Christian Recorder, xxiv
Cincinnati, Ohio, 44, 44n19, 55
Cincinnatus, Lucius Quinctius, 97–98n28
civil rights, 100–105, 113–16, 131–32
Civil Rights Act (1866), 82n3, 102, 102n33
Civil War, xx–xxi, 3n2, 59–61, 64–65, 95–97
Clary (freedman), 6n8
Clay, Henry, 94, 95n23
Cleveland, Ohio, 45
Coffee, John, 22n57, 29n72, 35n90
Coffinberry, William, 52n11, 52–53
Colbert, George and Levi, 24n62
Colbert's Reserve Plantation, Alabama, 24, 24n61
Confederate States of America, 59–61, 65n20, 95–96
cotton plantations, 17, 17n40, 23–28, 29–32, 127–29
Cowper, Thomas, xxiv, 78n22
Crittenden, John J., 57n4, 94, 95n23
Crittenden Compromise (1860), 57n4, 93n20
Cuba, abolition of slavery in, 57–58n6

Dallas County, Alabama, 70
Dancey, William, 14n35, 14–15
Davis, John, xxviii, 26n67, 129
Dawn Settlement, xxx
de Gama, Vasco, 108–9, 109n36
Delany, Martin R., xxi–xxii; *Blake; or, the Huts of America*, xxxi

Dennis, Bucky, 7
Dennis, Matthew, 7n13
Dennis, William M., 8n14
Detroit, Michigan, xxix, 45–46, 46n27, 49, 54
Dinah, Aunt, 128–29
Dixon County, Tennessee, 68
Donerson (or Donnison), 25, 127–28
Douglas, Stephen A., 94, 95n23
Douglass, Frederick: accomplishments of, 99; acquisition of literacy, 8n15; background, xxiv–xxv; on betrayal of fugitives, 49n5; life of, 99n30; *My Bondage and My Freedom*, xix; political considerations of, xxi–xxii; on Southerners' views toward abolitionists, xxvii
Drake, Benjamin M., 34n88
Drew, Benjamin, xviii–xix, xxviii, xxxii, 127–30
Drew, William, 9, 9n20
Durnford, Andre, 34n86

Eaton, William, 13n33
Edmonds, Howell, 16–19
Egypt, 108–10
Elgin Association, xv, 131n1, 131–32
Elgin Settlement, xxx
emancipation of slaves, 56–59, 62–63, 70–71, 96
Emancipation Proclamation (1863), 57n5
emigration, compulsory, 63
emigration to Central America, 79–81
Erie, Pennsylvania, 47

Farragut, David, 64n19
Fields, John G., 51n7, 51–53, 54
fishing, 13, 13nn31–32
Florence, Alabama, xiv, xxix, 14n35, 18n45, 18–19, 23–28, 29, 37, 45, 49, 86–87
Forks of Cypress Plantation, 19, 19n47, 35n90
Fort Hudson, Louisiana, 97
Fort Malden, 48n1
Fort Sumter, South Carolina, 96n25
Fort Wagoner, South Carolina, 97

Fort Wayne, Indiana, 46–47
Freedmen's Aid Societies, 61
Freedmen's Bureau, xxiii, 103–4; Catlin's address to, 90–91n87, 110–16; Howard as head of, 99n29; Runkle's address to, 90–110
Fugitive Slave Act (1850), xxx–xxxi, 53, 53n13
Fulton, William Savin, 18n43

Georgia, Goings's advice on emigrating to, 69–70
Gilbraith, Major T. W., 82n4, 83n6
Going, Nancy, 38n1
Goings, Agnes "Minnie" (daughter-in-law), xxxiii
Goings, Catharine J. (daughter), xxxii, xxxiii
Goings, Harriet (daughter), xxxii, xxxiii
Goings, Henry: advice on emigration to Southern states, 67–78; autobiography's authenticity, xxvii–xxviii; autobiography's importance, xiii; as Baptist, xxx; as barber, xiii, xv, xxix, xxxii, 45, 46; biblical and literary allusions, xxiv; birth and early life, 3–4; birth name, xiv, 4; brother of, 55; in Canada, 48; children, xxxii, 55, 130; as cook, xxix, xxxiii, 45; court appearance, 51–53; deception and arrest, xvii, 49–51; escape, xiv, 38–47, 129; essays, xx–xxiv; as everyman, xv–xvi; farm sale notice, xxxii, 133; father of, 4; first wife of, xiv, xviii, xxx, 34–37, 49–50, 55; flight after capture, 53–55; free paper of, 38–39, 40; as groom and manservant, xvii–xviii, 6, 11–12, 18, 23, 27–28; horse of, 11, 39–44; horse-handling skills, xxvi; intellectual progress, xxiv; intended audience of African Americans, xviii–xix; interview with Drew, xviii–xix, xxviii, 127–29; journey to Tennessee, 15–16; later life, xxxii–xxxiii; lawyer's bill, 55; letter to editor of *Chatham Chronicle*, xv, 131–32; life in freedom, xiv–xvi, xxix–xxxiii;

literacy and self-education, xv, xxiv–xxv, xxvii, 7–8; manumission denied to, 35–37; market value placed on, xxvi, 6, 7, 9–10, 22; marriage of, 35; message and voice of, xvi–xvii; moral uplift views, xxiii, 73–77; mother of, 4, 5, 6, 9; narrative strategy, xviii, xix–xx; observations on slavery and the Civil War, 56–66, 87–90, 127–29; owners of, xiv, xxvi, 3–5; purposes for writing autobiography, xxxiii; as real estate agent, xv, xxxii; sale of home, 55, 55n15; sale of horse, 43–44; second wife of, xiv, xviii, xxxi–xxxii, 55; sister of, xix, xxvi, 5, 6, 8–9, 10, 55; slavery as depicted by, xvii; spellings of, xxv; steamboat travel, xxviii, 22–23, 44–46, 47, 48; as steward, xv, xxx, xxxii, 48, 49n4; travels of, xiv, *123–26* (maps); as waiter, xv, xxvi, xxix, 6–7, 25, 46; writing and observational skills, xiii–xiv. *See also specific locations and topics*
Goings, Henry (original man), 38–39
Goings, James T. (son), xxxii, xxxiii
Goings, Maria (daughter), xxxii
Goings, Samuel (son), xxii, xxxii
Goings, Samuel H. (son), xxxiii
Golconda, Illinois, 42n15
Grand Rapids, Michigan, xxxiii
Grant, Ulysses S., 64–65nn18–20
Green, Jacob D.: *Narrative of the Life of J. D. Green*, xix
Guatemala, 79

Halifax, North Carolina, xxv, 6–11
Halifax County, North Carolina, 69, 85–86n9
Hanna, Sarah, 23n59
Hannah, Mary. *See* Smith, Mary Hannah
Hannibal, 110, 110n39
Harrison, William Henry, 47n32
Heard, William H., 4n3
Henson, Josiah, xvi, xix, xxx
Hill, George, 27n69, 27–28
Hincks, Sir Francis, 62n15, 62–63

Hives, Mr., 10–11
Hogg (lawyer), 7–8
Hogg, Peter, 7n12
Hollister, B. F., 51n8
Hollister, John, 51n8
Hollister, William, 51
Hosmer, Hezekiah L., 52n10, 52–53
Howard, Oliver O., 99, 99n29
Huic Plantation, Virginia, 5n5
Hunt family, 21n52

Illinois, laws as free state, 42
Indiana, laws as free state, 46n30
Indian Removal Act, 20n49
Indian Springs Hotel, Georgia, 22,
    22n56
Irish politics, xxiv, 64–66
Irving, Washington, 63–64n16

Jackson, Andrew, 18, 20n49, 22n57,
    35n90
Jackson, James, 19, 19n46, 22n57,
    23n59, 25, 31n79, 35n90
Jackson's Military Road, 18, 18n44
Jacobs, Harriet: background, xxiv–xxv;
    Incidents in the Life of a Slave Girl,
    xix
James City County, Virginia, xxv,
    5–6n8, 69
Jarvis County, Virginia. *See* James City
    County, Virginia
Jefferson, Thomas, xxiv, xxvi
Jim Crow laws, xxix
Johnson, Andrew, 102n33
Johnson, Charles H., 82, 82n4
Johnson, Rachel, 83
Jones, Mary, 6n8
Jordan, Abner, 21n53, 21–22
Jordan, Benjamin, 21–22, 21–22n55
Jordan, Hezekiah, 21–22, 21–22n55
Jordan, Mary, 21n51

Kemble. *See* Kimbrough, Elijah W.
Kent (steamboat), 48, 48n3
Kent County, Ontario, xxx
Kentucky, Goings's advice on emigrat-
    ing to, 67–68
Key, James, 27n68

kidnappers of runaway slaves, xxix,
    46n28, 49–51, 53n12, 54
Kimball. *See* Kimbrough, Elijah W.
Kimbrough, Elijah W., xxviii, 24–27,
    26–27n67, 127–29
King, William, 131n1
King and Queen County, Virginia,
    68–69, 69n2
Kirkman, Jackson, 31n79
Kirkman, Thomas, 23n59, 29n72,
    31n79, 31–32, 38–39
Kirkman, Thomas, Jr., 31n79

Langford, Joseph, 50n6, 50–51, 54,
    54n14
Langston, John Mercer, 99–100n30
Lee, Robert E., 59, 65n20, 94n21
Lexington (steamboat), 44n20, 44–45
Lexington, Kentucky, 68
Limestone County, Alabama, 70
Lincoln, Abraham, xxi, 57n6, 97; assas-
    sination of, xxii, 72–73, 76; Booth
    on planned assassination of, 76n17;
    as Commander-in-Chief, 65n20,
    91n17, 96n25; Douglas and, 95n23;
    emancipation of slaves by, 57n5,
    96; "Gettysburg Address," 70n8;
    life of, 71n9; tribute to, 71–73;
    Vallandigham's denunciation of,
    93n20
literacy of slaves, xxvi–xxvii, 7–8, 35
London (steamboat), 41n13, 48,
    48nn2–3
Louisville, Kentucky, 44, 44n23, 68

Mack (freedman), 6n8
Madison County, Alabama, 70
Mason, Daniel, 14n34, 16n39
Mason, David, 10n24, 10–11, 11n25
Mason, Henry D., 24n61
Massachusetts Anti-Slavery Society,
    99n30
McCulloch, Elizabeth, 31n79
McDonald, William, 31, 31n80
McIntosh, William, 22, 22nn56–57
McKinley, John, 28, 28n70
McMicking, Major, 44
McPherson, John, 9, 9n18

Memphis, Tennessee, race riot, xxiii,
81–82n3, 81–84
Memphis County, Tennessee, 68
Michigan, laws as free state, 46n27
Milledgeville, Georgia, xiv, 19n48,
19–22, 69
Mississippi, Goings's advice on emi-
grating to, 70
Missouri Compromise (1820), 57n4
Mitchell, William M., xxx
Monroe, Michigan, 54
moral uplift, xxiii, 73–77, 105–16
Morris, Mary, 5n6, 5–6
mortgaging of slaves, 8n16, 8–9
Moscogee-Creek Indians, 19n48
Murray County, Tennessee, 68
Muscle Shoals, Alabama, 18n45
Muskogee Indians, 22n57

Nashville, Tennessee, 15–16
Nat Turner rebellion, xxvii, 85–86n9
New Design Plantation, Virginia, 5n5
New Kent County, Virginia, 55, 69
Newman, William P., xxxi
New Orleans, Louisiana, xiv, 32n82,
32–34, 33–34nn84–85, 34n87, 87,
88–90
New York Times, xxiv
New York Tribune, xxiv
Northampton County, North Carolina,
69, 84–86
North Carolina, Goings's advice on
emigrating to, 69
North Star, 99n30
Nowland, Matilda Frances, 18n42
Nowland, Rebecca, 18n42

Ohio, laws as free state, 45n25, 46n29,
51–53
Ohio Anti-Slavery Society, 100n30
Ohio River, 42–43
Old Northwest, xxix–xxx
Olmstead, Anthony, 24
Olmstead, Frederick Law, 4n3
Orleans County, Mississippi, 70
Osage (steamboat), xxviii, 23
overseers, xviii, xxviii, 16–19, 23–24,
127–29

Panic of 1837, 61n13
Perrysburg, Ohio, xxix–xxx, 47, 47n31,
50–55
Petersburg, Virginia, 6, 69, 69n4
Piggott, Francis, 5n5
Piggott, Hannah, 5n5
Piggott, John, 5n5
Piggott, Nathaniel, 5n5, 7n13
Piggott, Pearson, 5n5, 5–11
Piggott, William, 5n5
Plaster of Paris, 70
Pontotoc County, Mississippi, xiv,
28–29n71, 28–32
Pope, Alexander, xxiv
Portsmouth, Ohio, xxix, 44, 44n21, 45
Powell, Daniel, 7
Powell, Elizabeth, 7n11
Powell, Martha, 7n11
Powell family, 9, 9n17
Pricket, Pearson. *See* Piggott, Pearson
Provincial Freeman, The, xxxi
Puerto Rico, abolition of slavery in,
57n6
Pulaski County, Arkansas, 70
Purdy, Robin, xxviii, 36

Raleigh, North Carolina, 11–13, 26, 129
Randolph, John, 58, 58n7
Reconstruction, xxii–xxiii, 70–71,
100n32
Refugees' Home Colony, xvi
Richardson, Littleton, 38n1
Robinson, Christopher, 6n8
Rolling Mills, Tennessee, 40, 40n9
Royall, Anne, 18–19n45, 27–28n69,
43n18
runaway slaves, xxix, 6n9, 31–32,
39nn5–6, 41, 49n5. *See also* Goings,
Henry
Runkle, Benjamin P., xxiii, xxiv,
90–91n87, 90–110
Russia's abolition of serfdom, 57n6

Scott, Winfield, 65n20
Scruggs, Mary S., 26n66
Shakespeare, William, xxiv, 74
Shawneetown, Illinois, xxix, 42n16,
42–44

Sheil, Richard Lalor, xxiv, 64n17, 64–66

Sherman, William Tecumseh, 64n18

slaveholder's sermon, xxiii–xxiv, 116–19

slave narratives: abolitionists and, xv, xvi, xviii–xix; Goings's autobiography contrasted with, xv–xvi, xviii–xix

slavery as institution: abolition of, 57–58n6, 71, 93–97; African Americans as slaveholders, 33–34, 34n86; Civil War and, xxi; in colonial Louisiana, 33n84; in Deep South, 16–19, 86n11; flogging and other punishments of slaves, 26, 27–28, 31–32, 127–29; Goings's observations on, xvii–xviii, 56–59, 87–90, 127–29; illegitimate children of white owners, 12n28; informers, 44–45, 49n5, 49–51; literacy and, xxvi–xxvii, 7–8, 35; livestock analogy, 4n3; marriage and, 15, 35; migration's destruction of families, 15; mortgaging of slaves, 8n16; Native Americans as slaveholders, 20n50; new suit of clothes's significance, 11n26; overseers, xviii, xxviii, 16–19, 23–24, 127–29; sale of rebellious slaves, 86n11; Scripture used in support of, 77–78; slaves' birthdays, 4; slaves' homes, 11n*

Smith, Constable, 50–51

Smith, Henry D., xxviii, 10–11, 13, 13n33, 21n51, 24, 36n94

Smith, James McCune, xxiii

Smith, Jane, 10n23, 11n25, 36nn92–93

Smith, Joseph Lawrence Dawson: acquisition of Mississippi land, 28–32; Alabama land holdings, 23n59; ambition of, xiv; called "Boss" by Goings, 87n14; death and will, xxviii–xxix, 29nn72–73, 35–37, 36n94, 36nn91–92; family of, 11–13, 21n51; move to Alabama, 17–19, 23–24; move to Tennessee, 14–17; places visited with Goings, xxiii, xxvi; purchase of Goings, 10–11

Smith, Lawrence, 85

Smith, Mary Hannah, xxix, 10n23, 26, 26n65, 31n79, 35–36, 128–29

Southampton County, Virginia, 85–86n9

Southern Confederacy. *See* Confederate States of America

Southern states, Goings's advice to Canadians on emigrating to, 67–78

Spink, John C., 52, 52n9

steamboats, xxviii, 22–23, 44–46, 47, 48

Stoneman, George, 82n3

Stowe, Harriet Beecher: *Uncle Tom's Cabin*, xxx

Stratford, Ontario, xxxii

suffrage, black, 102–5

sugar cane plantations, 88–90

Sweet Water Plantation, Alabama, 24n61

Taylor, Henley, 7n13

Taylor, Zachary, 41, 41n12, 65n20

Tecumseh, 48n1

Tennessee, Goings's advice on emigrating to, 68

Tertullian, xxiv, 72n10

Thomas, George, 64n18

Toano, Virginia. *See* Burnt Ordinary, Virginia (now Toano)

Toledo, Ohio, xxix, 46

Trail of Tears, 20n49

Truth, Sojourner, xxiii

Tubman, Harriet, xxxi

Turner, Abraham (father), 4

Turner, Catharine (mother), 4, 5, 6, 9

Turner, Elijah (birth name of Goings). *See* Goings, Henry

Turner, John, 4n4

Turner, Maria (sister), xix, xxvi, 5, 6, 8–9, 10, 55

Turner, Mary, 4n4

Turner, Nat, xxvii, 85–86

Tuscaloosa County, Alabama, 70

Underground Railroad, xvi, xxvii, xxx, xxxi, 37, 47n31, 50n6, 54n14, 100n30

Vallandigham, Clement L., 93n20
Van Buren, Martin, 28n70
Vanleer, Anthony Wayne, 40, 40n10
Vicksburg, Mississippi, xiv, 32–33,
 33n83, 87
Vicksburg, Siege of (1862), 64–65n19
Virginia, Goings's advice on emigrating
 to, 68–69
Voice of the Fugitive, xvi, xxiv, xxx–xxxi,
 xxxii

Walker, David: *Appeal . . . to the
 Coloured Citizens of the World*,
 xxvi–xxvii, 86n10
Walker, James N., 3–4, 7n13, 8n14
Walker County, Alabama, 70n6
Ward, Samuel Ringgold, xxxi
Washington, George, 97, 98n28
Washington, George Augustine, 36n93
Webb, John, 44–45, 45n24

Weldon, Daniel, 13n33
Wessyngton Plantation, Tennessee,
 36n93
Whately, Judge, 47
White, Maria (first wife), xiv, xviii, xxx,
 34–37, 35n90, 49–50, 55
Wilcox County, Alabama, 70n6
Williams, Elizabeth, 24n63
Williams, Rebecca J. (née Smith),
 10n24, 11n27, 11–12, 12n29
Williams, Robert, 10n24, 12, 12n29
Williams, Thomas, 24, 24n63
Wilson, George, 49, 54
Wilson, Hiram, xxx
Window Shades Plantation, Virginia,
 3, 3n2
Windsor, Canada, 54
Windsor Castle Plantation, 8n14
Wise, Henry A., 76–77, 77n19
Wright, Lydia, 21n55

Carter G. Woodson Institute Series

Michael Plunkett
Afro-American Sources in Virginia: A Guide to Manuscripts

Sally Belfrage
Freedom Summer

Armstead L. Robinson and Patricia Sullivan, eds.
New Directions in Civil Rights Studies

Leroy Vail and Landeg White
Power and the Praise Poem: Southern African Voices in History

Robert A. Pratt
*The Color of Their Skin: Education and Race
in Richmond, Virginia, 1954–89*

Ira Berlin and Philip D. Morgan, eds.
*Cultivation and Culture: Labor and the
Shaping of Slave Life in the Americas*

Gerald Horne
Fire This Time: The Watts Uprising and the 1960s

Sam C. Nolutshungu
Limits of Anarchy: Intervention and State Formation in Chad

Jeannie M. Whayne
*A New Plantation South: Land, Labor, and Federal
Favor in Twentieth-Century Arkansas*

Patience Essah
A House Divided: Slavery and Emancipation in Delaware, 1638–1865

Tommy L. Bogger
Free Blacks in Norfolk, Virginia, 1790–1860: The Darker Side of Freedom

Robert C. Kenzer
*Enterprising Southerners: Black Economic
Success in North Carolina, 1865–1915*

Midori Takagi
"Rearing Wolves to Our Own Destruction":
Slavery in Richmond, Virginia, 1782–1865

Alessandra Lorini
Rituals of Race: American Public Culture
and the Search for Racial Democracy

Mary Ellen Curtin
Black Prisoners and Their World, Alabama, 1865–1900

Philip J. Schwarz
Migrants against Slavery: Virginians and the Nation

Armstead L. Robinson
Bitter Fruits of Bondage: The Demise of
Slavery and the Collapse of the Confederacy, 1861–1865

Francille Rusan Wilson
The Segregated Scholars: Black Social Scientists
and the Creation of Black Labor Studies, 1890–1950

Gregory Michael Dorr
Segregation's Science: Eugenics and Society in Virginia

Glenn McNair
Criminal Injustice: Slaves and Free
Blacks in Georgia's Criminal Justice System

William Dusinberre
Strategies for Survival: Recollections
of Bondage in Antebellum Virginia

Valerie C. Cooper, *Word, Like Fire: Maria Stewart,*
the Bible, and the Rights of African Americans

Michael L. Nicholls
Whispers of Rebellion: Narrating Gabriel's Conspiracy

Henry Goings
Rambles of a Runaway from Southern Slavery
Edited by Calvin Schermerhorn, Michael Plunkett, and Edward Gaynor